the orange line™

A WOMAN'S GUIDE TO INTEGRATING CAREER, FAMILY & LIFE

the orange line™

A WOMAN'S GUIDE TO
INTEGRATING CAREER, FAMILY & LIFE

By Jodi Ecker Detjen, Michelle A. Waters, and Kelly Watson

JMK Publishing Inc.
Newton, MA

The Orange Line™
A Woman's Guide to Integrating Career, Family and Life

By Jodi Ecker Detjen, Michelle A. Waters, Kelly Watson

Copyright © 2013

by Jodi Ecker Detjen, Michelle A. Waters, Kelly Watson

Published by JMK Publishing Inc.

www.orangelinecareer.com

Editing and Production Management by Janet Spencer King
janet.sp.king@verizon.net

Cover design by Colleen Cody
www.colleencody.com

Interior design by LMW Design Inc.
www.lmwdesign.com

To contact the author or to order additional copies of this book, e-mail: info@orangelinecareer.com

Printed in the United States of America

For worldwide distribution

ISBN 978-0-9892077-0-6

CONTENTS

Prologue 1

About this Book: Methodology 9

PART ONE:
THE ORANGE LINE PHILOSOPHY 10

Chapter One: Introducing The Orange Line™ 10

Chapter Two: The Feminine Filter™................................ 18

Chapter Three: The Feminine Filter Problem 28

PART TWO:
HOW TO LIVE THE ORANGE LINE IN YOUR LIFE STAGE.... 36

Chapter Four: The Green Start 36

    Skills for Living the Orange Line 44

Chapter Five: Approaching Burnout 81

    Skills for Living the Orange Line 88

Chapter Six: Family Matters...115

    Skills for Living The Orange Line 124

Chapter Seven: The Sabbatical....................................159

    Skills for Living on The Orange Line 166

Chapter Eight: Re-entry 183

    Skills for Living The Orange Line 190

Chapter Nine: The Mid-Career Transition 215

    Skills for Living The Orange Line 221

PART THREE:
CONTINUING TO LIVE AN ORANGE LINE LIFE.................**248**

Chapter Ten: Living The Orange Line..........................248

Notes...265

Index 279

About the Authors...288

ACKNOWLEDGEMENTS

It is with deep gratitude that we would like to publicly thank the many people who helped us move this book from idea to actuality. It began with Jessica DeGroot, founder and president of Thirdpath Institute, with its motto, "Creating time for life." The bi-monthly leadership calls surfaced our initial ideas and introduced the three of us to one another. Then, our 118 interviewees who agreed to open their hearts and share their stories with us. Some even referred us to their friends and colleagues as well. We are so proud to share their insights.

Once we had the skeleton of a book, our peer editors and student helpers poked and prodded it to life with their doubts, challenges, and validations. They strengthened our arguments and clarified our reasoning. We are humble and grateful for their feedback. Thanks to: Susan Amster, Jessica Danluck Baker, Eve Berne, Pamela Blaise, Andrea Daverio, Charlotte Dietz, Bryan Donohue, Susan Ginsberg, Chanté Griffin, Andrea Keir, Anisa Kosta, Timlin Loxterkamp, Maya Meirav, Jeanine Moret, Rebecca Murray, Louise Pennell, Zeba Race, Christine Sarver, Dayna Scandone, Yixiao Shao, Chetan Sharma, Annie Singh, and Mary Smith.

Going from manuscript to book took some incredibly talented professionals: Colleen Cody (our designer), Janet Spencer King (our editor), and Matt Marinovich (who assisted in editing). Their patience and expertise was extremely valuable and the end result made us proud.

And our deepest thanks go to our families and friends — the people who have listened to us talk about this book for the past two and a half years without abandoning their support (or losing their marbles!). We owe all of you our gratitude and undying love: Sam, Eric, Mike, Peter, Shamah, Shonnie, Jairus, Martin, Patrick, Fiona, Deirdre, and so many more.

PRAISE FOR THE ORANGE LINE

"I am confident that when people look back a decade from now they will view publication of *The Orange Line* as a watershed event. In the book, authors Jodi Detjen, Michelle Waters, and Kelly Watson challenge women to confront assumptions they have that surround and limit their professional *and* their personal lives. While the authors issue this challenge with empathy and caring, they never lose sight of its underlying message: The power of change lies within. The authors' advice is not easy, and their book offers no place for self-pity or excuses for blaming 'the system.' Indeed, it may create discomfort for some women as they internalize its messages. But *The Orange Line* gives hope to all of us who believe that women's integration of work and family is the key to a successful society."

— Paul F. Levy, author of *Goal Play! Leadership Lessons from the Soccer Field* and former President and CEO of Beth Israel Deaconess Medical Center in Boston.

"Simple in their approach, yet complex in their thinking and analysis, Detjen, Waters and Watson outline an ideal new approach for women to balance career, family and life. Their wise advice makes 'Having it all' truly attainable."

— Marshall Goldsmith, author of 34 books, including the *New York Times* bestsellers, *MOJO* and *What Got You Here Won't Get You There,* has been named America's preeminent executive coach by Fast Company magazine.

PRAISE FOR THE ORANGE LINE, continued

"There is no reason women should be choosing work or life in the 21st century. Detjen, Waters, and Watson successfully explain how Orange Line workers choose both...and succeed. For women who want to live life to the fullest every single day, this is a must-read."

— Cali Ressler and Jody Thompson, co-authors, *Why Managing Sucks and How to Fix It*

"This is a valuable book in continuing an important debate around the issues of women in the workplace."

— Heather McGregor, PhD, author of *Mrs. Moneypenny's Career Advice for Ambitious Women*

PROLOGUE

As women, we constantly hear the same messages: "Women can't have it all." "We must choose between work and life." "Everything has tradeoffs." The pace of change is slow, and although women have made great strides, it will take until well into this century to achieve representation in leadership positions commensurate with their population and qualifications. Women are still struggling to manage their lives, juggling competing responsibilities, and shouldering stress. Why is it, in a country where there are more resources, freedom, and creativity than almost anywhere else on earth, women still feel the only way to have a robust career is by sacrificing having a family? Before we decided to write this book, we, too, found this dichotomy frustrating as we navigated our lives and early careers.

Kelly's story

My career was on the fast track at a large, public company. I worked hard and was promoted quickly through the ranks. I thrived on the adrenaline and competition, showcasing my level of commitment by working long hours and taking on a large number of projects. Sometimes, I took risks, like a lateral move after being promised a quick promotion for good results. I fully expected I would be successful, and was, until I decided to have a family. All of sudden, I felt a palpable shift in how people perceived my commitment level. When I became pregnant, my boss delayed my previously approved promotion, saying she would see how things went after my maternity leave. When I returned, my boss delayed it again, saying, "We'll see what happens after you have a few months of motherhood under your belt." In the meantime, my husband joined the company. When we both received a promotion, it was to the same level, but my husband's came with a much larger raise. My boss told me, "It's a family deal and we spoke to him first." I took it in stride because I wanted to make both of us integral to the company.

Then the company started to spiral downwards and we each joined new companies. I took a senior executive role for an international company that required heavy traveling. Struggling to retain my self-respect, I developed an aggressive persona to fit into the intensely competitive atmosphere of the new company. After my second baby was born, I felt exhausted and was tired of keeping up appearances. I asked for flexibility to occasionally telecommute, but this company was run by men with stay-at-home wives. They didn't understand or support the concept of flexibility. Part-time work was out of the question: I felt I would lose all the respect I had worked so hard to build from my male colleagues by asking for a break. So I quit to be with my children full time. At that moment, it felt like a choice that would give me space and time to think.

Once out of the workforce, I quickly absorbed most of the family responsibilities, which freed up my husband to focus more intensely on his work. His career took off, and I dropped off the radar screen. I dove in to perfecting motherhood, philanthropy, and community involvement and made myself as busy as ever, this time without pay or savings for retirement. I recognized this was a dangerous path for me, but it seemed like the right choice for my family. But secretly, I was miserable, finding the work exhausting and unfulfilling.

I ultimately decided to use my "career downtime" to get an MBA and to do some consulting work. With my degree in hand, I transitioned to full-time consulting. Although I am happier and able to care for my kids, I have never lost the feeling that I haven't achieved the career I originally wanted.

Jodi's story

My story mirrors Kelly's in the early days. I took the fast-career track, working sixteen-hour days for a large consulting firm. As I consulted with large, public companies, I would work hard, act like I knew it all, and then go home and play hard. On the surface, I looked like I felt cool and powerful, but inwardly I really doubted myself and felt I might not be good enough. I got burned out with this life and went to work for the government for a while. I was so bored that after two years, I had to go back into consulting. I went straight back to working long days under intense pressure. Finally, the stress got to me and I decided to go back to graduate school full time.

After graduate school and with my first child, I felt the doubts and responsibilities were completely manageable: I worked three days a week, my husband traveled, but he was still highly involved with the family, and we were both learning how to parent. Life was good.

Then we had our second child. Every night my new baby had colic for a few hours. I was completely overwhelmed. I would hand my baby to a respected babysitter, relieved to go to work. My husband started traveling five days a week, coming home exhausted. To compensate, I absorbed full responsibility for the house and the children except for the weekends. All childcare decisions fell upon me. We had moved to a new town where I knew no one. I really loved going to work, but felt guilty about it, even stopping myself from buying new work clothes. I felt demoralized by my low salary compared to his. Meanwhile my husband's career was taking off. I was angry and bitter that I had to own full responsibility for the children and housework. I still wanted to be the "perfect mother" with the "perfect job" just as I had before. But it was no longer possible. I felt like a failure on all fronts. Ultimately, I found a university teaching and consulting role that fed my career passions and allowed space for life and family. Looking back, I still don't understand why it had to be so painful during my children's early years.

Michelle's story

I finished college and married young in Australia. We started a family soon after and I fully enjoyed being a mom and then later working part time. Meanwhile, I was also ambitious and enjoyed learning, completing a post graduate degree at night while establishing and managing childcare centers so I could be close to my three young children. I was doing it all running a successful business, even going back for my master's degree. Eventually, though, the expectations of perfection and my fear of setting boundaries impacted my marriage and health. As my children grew, I sold my business and transitioned into a job overseeing multiple child and family services for a national university. Because of the divorce, I saw my children less often so work became more important. I established the university as the national employer of choice. It was a great opportunity and I was successful. But I remember thinking, *How am I ever going to get time to sleep?* I wanted to prove my worth as an employee and didn't think I could push back on the workload or was entitled to hire help for my household responsibilities. I didn't listen to my body. I should have paced myself earlier and hired home help like a housekeeper or an assistant, but I didn't.

Then, I developed breast cancer. In retrospect, my body was screaming at me to slow down. I continued to work throughout the treatments because for me, work was meaningful and psychologically important. It enabled me to remain optimistic and have purpose. My organization was supportive: They let me work from home and gave me a laptop so I spread my forty hours of work over seven days. I recovered from the cancer and resumed my career, helping my organization to win awards that put them on the map.

After this crisis, I took a senior position in the finance sector, and two years later, I accepted a VP position and moved to the U.S. I quickly adapted to the new culture and work. I even remarried. But my aging mother now needed assistance back in Australia. I struggled to integrate relocation, late-night phone calls, and decisions about elder care accommodations with my work and new life here. Further, I became a grandmother. I felt constantly torn between the conviction toward my purpose and being a loving daughter, mother, and grandmother. I also had a second cancer scare. This time, I listened and began to build the necessary practices to restore my health on a daily basis. I ultimately found a way to integrate relocation, work and focus on loved ones, but I wish I could have found this answer sooner.

Finding Kindred Spirits

The common denominator across our stories is the often unexpected challenges that we faced simply because we had families and few role models. Confronted with these unexpected challenges, we sought solutions. We looked for ways to change the system so that it wouldn't be biased against women with families. We saw that companies were paying only lip service to flexibility, but underneath the hyperbole, women with families were maligned in the workplace and saw their careers derailed. Reward systems were still tied to outdated performance measures such as "face time," which affects women, especially those with children, negatively. We felt strongly that we wanted to change the system.

We met when we joined a working group of management professionals for both women and men, convened by ThirdPath. The group focused on rethinking how organizations and policy makers could help women and men more fully integrate their lives and careers. As part of this group, we shared our stories. We heard what we each went through—the struggles and frustrations as well as where new thinking was emerging. We realized that, despite our diverse backgrounds and professions, we had all experienced the same challenges. We each knew younger women who were still going through similar experiences, and we wanted to help them. We also recognized the benefit of sharing stories and anecdotes. We could take a lesson or an example from someone else's life and really learn from it, giving ourselves permission to try new things without fear of judgment. We were kindred spirits.

Although we agreed with so many others that the system was flawed, we were unique in our belief that government, outside forces, or even the internal human resources departments of companies could not successfully impose change. Instead, we felt strongly that only individuals could change the system by changing their attitude and response—people with sufficient credibility and power within organizations who could balance the needs of the organizations with those of the individuals. We decided we needed to mobilize working women to change the system from within.

We determined the best way to help other women was to learn how they were figuring out work and life, to identify the skills needed, to expand our library of career stories, and to share them. For this project, we interviewed 118 college-educated women. Almost all these women were committed to their careers with potential to succeed. These weren't corner-office superstars, but hard-working women who wanted to integrate work and family. We asked these women about their career plans, dreams, and challenges.

What we discovered surprised us. First, the women were energized by the opportunity to tell their stories. Many had never thought that thoroughly about their passions or been encouraged to talk about their work. Some even felt a little guilty talking about themselves instead of their children. Second, we found a similar level of angst and frustration with the failure of the system to address the structural barriers, flawed reward systems, and shortsighted policies that affect women. So, we weren't the only ones lamenting the inability of corporations to tap the wealth of talent and experience these women offer. Third, we found that women without children had some of the same problems, whether because of other family issues, illness, or just wanting an equally engaging life outside of the workplace.

Finally, we noticed that, while organizations may have offered a hostile environment, it was actually the women who held themselves and each other back. While some were able to get past it, many of the women had adopted a limiting belief system about the world and were reinforcing it with language and behaviors that positioned themselves and their dreams behind everyone else's. We called this belief system, "The Feminine Filter," which we will describe in-depth in Chapters Two and Three. We theorized that, by illuminating this flawed belief system and sharing ways to operate outside of it, career women can, in fact, overcome the structural barriers and maintain a more integrated career.

Are You Ready to Change Your Life?

This book is a resource to help women integrate their careers, families, and lives across their life/career stages, regardless of whether they are just starting out or are embarking on a mid-career transition to something new. The first three chapters of the book lay out the ideal of living an Orange Line career. Chapter One defines the three long-term career trajectory options, including the impacts and choices made along the path. Chapters Two and Three define the Feminine Filter and how women's beliefs, assumptions, behaviors, and language can limit them. The remainder of the book helps women figure out how to live The Orange Line from whatever career stage they are currently in or are about to enter.

First, use this book to understand what's happening in your career, to help you discover if the beliefs you hold are limiting you. Then use this book to help you learn different habits and skills that will enable you to live the full life you want and customize them to your particular career stage.

HOW TO READ THIS BOOK

Instead of reading this book through from start to finish, we suggest you read the first part to understand The Orange Line philosophy. Then read the chapter from the second part that corresponds with the stage you are currently in. Finally, read the third part to understand how you can continue to live an Orange Line life.

The process is not easy, but by taking small steps every day, as each of us has done over the last few years, it is achievable and ultimately, highly freeing. By creating awareness and implementing the ideas and skills we outline, women can learn how to integrate their work, families, and lives. And as women live their lives to the fullest on The Orange Line, we believe that they can make the greatest positive impact, not only in the professional world, but also in their own families.

About this Book: Methodology

We implemented a qualitative research approach using semi-structured interviews of 118 college-educated, U.S. - or Canada-resident women. The interview duration was between thirty and sixty minutes, yielding extensive, verbatim transcripts for analysis. The sample was created using a snowball sampling method using the authors' college networks, Linked-In, online networking groups, and professional referrals. The median age was forty-three. Four of the women were not currently working. All names, some job titles, and some ages were changed for privacy. The study was approved by Suffolk University's Institutional Review Board.

Industries Represented	Marketing/PR Accounting Technology Small Business Entrepreneur	Architecture Engineering Healthcare Government or Law Education (all levels)
Sample Interviewee Roles	19% Vice President/ Director 28% Owner	10% Manager 42% Other
Number of States covered	27 plus Washington, DC, Canada (5) and Australia (1)	
Racial Composition	90.7% Caucasian 4.2% African American or of African birth 1.6% Asian-American or of Asian birth 1.6% Hispanic 1.7% Race Unknown	
Marital Status	59% Married 12% Remarried 11% Currently Divorced	3% Widowed 15% Single
Children	23% Zero 21% One 37% Two	14% Three 6% Four +

CHAPTER ONE:
Introducing The Orange Line™

*First say to yourself what you would be; then
do what you have to do. —Epictetus*

Rarely do you hear a man asked, "How do you do it all—you have a career *and* a family?" Yet people ask women this all the time, as if it is special to do it all, to live a robust whole life—something unheard of. Why is this? Why don't men need "work-life balance?" Is it because women are still not expected to have a career that they are passionate about, more than just a job that is easily shed when the first child comes along or when their extended family responsibilities increase? It all keeps reinforcing the same story, that men can supposedly have their self-actualization, but that if women want it, they either need to marry a stay-at-home husband, or they need to give up having a family.

To illustrate the lifetime career trajectory choices for women, we modeled: A Green Line to represent a career-focused track; A Red Line to represent a career trajectory curtailed when a woman "opts out" at some point; and The Orange Line to represent the possibility of a new approach, an integrated life path. (See Figure 1.)

Stages of Career Progress

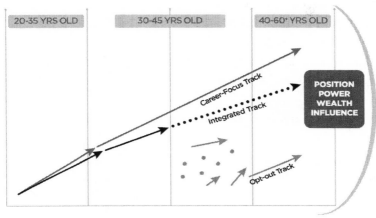

Figure 1

The Green Line: Career Focus Track

Plotted on a graph over time, the Green Line represents a traditional, career-centric life, where education, intelligence, skills, plus a singular focus on career can lead to significant success. In this model, success is defined as a steady, good paying job, power, influence, and, for some, substantial wealth. While this is a simplistic model, many hardworking, college-educated women could achieve this with enough devotion, networking, and leadership skills. It is the career track most men have followed for generations. The path follows a steep career progression through the twenties and early thirties and a slightly flatter climb over time, but it is always moving forward and upwards.

Some may ask, "What's so wrong with the Green Line?" If you love to work, then why not pour your whole life into it? Isn't that how people like Jack Welch, Steve Jobs, and Wall Street traders got where they are? As Keith Hammonds, former Executive Editor at Fast Company notes in his article, "Balance is Bunk," isn't this the whole problem with balance, that real change really takes imbalance? In a time when workers need to be more competitive on a global scale, when fewer U.S. workers are supporting an aging population, is it really smart to encourage people to be anything less than 110 percent committed to their work? And on a personal level, why would anyone hold herself back when a singular focus on work can reap such fantastic rewards?

There is often a tremendous sacrifice to achieve the Green Line. Green liners rarely have time to explore other aspects of themselves. Many of them give up family or close personal relationships. Some work so hard they become ill. The myopic focus on career can crowd out pursuit of other interests and limit perspective. Some would argue that Green Liners reinforce work-obsessed, inflexible workplaces. Life, including family, on the Green Line, is de-prioritized. (See Figure 2.)

Career-Life Paradigm with Career Orientation

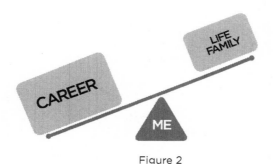

Figure 2

Further, the Green Line approach usually requires someone else to pick up the slack at home, especially when it comes to family. This means that if one partner is committed to the Green Line, the other must give up his or her career for the benefit of the family team. As a result, the sacrificing team member, historically the woman, earns less in her lifetime, saves less for retirement, and may even sacrifice her vocation.

There is another big drawback for Green Liners. When another person has given up a career in order to be the support person, it puts enormous pressure on the Green Liner to stay on track. This pressure can make the Green Liners feel they must stay on the Green Line, unable to explore alternative career possibilities, take a step back, or take risks at work for fear of jeopardizing the whole family. It becomes even more difficult for them to enjoy family and life outside of work. The Green Line career then, despite the external rewards, can lead to a self-perpetuating and unfulfilling life story.

The Red Line: Opting Out

The Red Line represents a career track where someone once on the Green Line, usually a woman, abandons her career at some point to shift focus another aspect of her life. She may have wrestled with the decision to "opt out" when she became a parent to spend more time with her children, or she may have left work due to burnout or illness. She might have quit or been laid off. Some of these women might have tried to re-group and re-enter several times, switching jobs or retraining for a new career. The key defining description for this path is that career takes a secondary role or disappears as the focus moves fully to life and/or family. (See Figure 3.)

Career-Life Paradigm with Life/Family Orientation

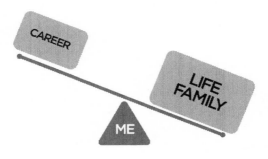

Figure 3

While women on the Red Line may indeed ultimately re-join their career, in most cases, they end up paying a huge penalty for their time off. Our interviewees described lost self-esteem after abandoning their career. Many felt unfulfilled without their vocation to pursue. Some felt underutilized and undervalued due to the lack of rewards and recognition outside of the workplace. For some, there was also constant financial pressure. Although a number of women embark on their careers planning to eventually be part of the Red Line, many others do not have this in mind. This change in course can leave them feeling off-track and out of control. So just like the Green Line, the Red Line career track is not ideal.

The Red Line versus Green Line view of work can block alternate ways to manage a career. Many of the women interviewed spoke of tradeoffs. They felt trapped by these traditional options and felt the only way to have a life was to give up optimizing their career. A common refrain we heard in our interviews was, "If I can't be 100 percent, I won't do it at all." For example, daily decisions such as, "I either have to miss an important meeting or miss my son's soccer game," or, "I can't leave early for my doctor's appointment because that's when our business gets busy," reinforce the idea that alternatives are limited. The tradeoff between work and life can seem black and white for women on the Red Line, and this is a narrow view.

The Orange Line: Integrated Life Track

There is a new career track opportunity. We call it The Orange Line. Instead of a singular focus on work from the beginning, The Orange Line is a launching pad for a robust, whole life integrating work, family, and self. The key difference with this path is that people place themselves, not their work or family, at the center of their life choices. Orange Liners take a more conscious approach, learning to pace themselves early on, taking breaks and enhancing their life with activities and interactions with people outside of work. They design their work environment around their needs and ensure sufficient support in their home lives to preserve their creative energy for what matters to them. The Orange Line worker does not need to choose between work and life; she chooses *both and lives both fully*. Instead of the seesaw, envision a rectangle with "me" as the foundational base. No matter what other elements with which a woman chooses to enrich her life, whether career, family, or otherwise, she is in control, not at the fulcrum, trying to balance. (See Figure 4.)

Proposed Whole Life

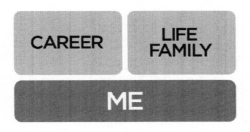

Figure 4

By internalizing this illustration, women can learn who they are and make the most of their talents. They can think of their life and their life's work in a broader context. Life is long; it's not about short-term decisions. Life is dynamic; most women go through different phases and change over time. When women no longer have to choose between career and family, they are free to develop long-term plans where career, family, and other passions throttle up and down in terms of the creative energy they apply along the way.

Living on The Orange Line is not about dividing life into a fixed pie of time slices—so much for work, so much for family, so much for self. Much of the current work/life balance dialogue focuses on time management. While time management is always going to be an important ability, life does not need to be limited by the fixed pie of time. Instead, it's about figuring out where to put effort and creative energy for a bigger return on investment. When women are focused on where to put their energy, decisions about time are easier to make. Women end up with more energy because they are including themselves and investing where they want to invest, rather than doing what they "should" do.

While The Orange Line executive may not end up as powerful or wealthy as the Green Line executive, she will feel more fulfilled and still lead, set policy, and influence others. A helpful analogy to consider is the Jeff Galloway method of training and running marathons. Galloway, a member of the 1972 Olympic team, has written eighteen books on running and pioneered the "Run/Walk" method. He explains that, "Alternating running and walking, from the beginning of a run . . . extends our endurance limits dramatically." This is because taking walk breaks early and often recovers the primary muscles enough to extend their capacity. Applied to careers, this analogy helps demonstrate the big picture: Taking breaks over the long term, shifting from a singular focus to a more holistic one, actually improves the likelihood of making it to the finish, injury free and with a solidly successful result.

The Orange Line, like walking for a minute each mile during a marathon, is hard to follow early on. When a woman is young, passionate about work, and invigorated by the adrenaline rush, it is hard and even counter-intuitive to set clear boundaries, force herself to delegate, take breaks, and to invest time outside of work. However, practicing the skills from the outset and learning how to set a healthier pace will pay off in huge dividends over time.

Stages of Career Progress

While The Orange Line model works optimally if followed as early as possible in a career, it is never too late to embrace it and to make a significant life change. In our research and our own lives, we have seen repeatedly how women seem to go through similar career stages, fall into the same traps, and learn the same lessons. Too many women throw themselves into their careers too hard in the beginning, setting themselves up for burnout. They struggle when family matters arise. They opt out. They struggle to re-enter and re-invent themselves in middle age. All of this wastes their creative energy, time, and emotional fortitude. While many resilient women have overcome the challenges of working through these stages, it often feels as if they are reinventing the wheel, over and over again. Worse, during each phase, discouragement and loneliness can seem unbearable, as if no one else is struggling with these issues.

The names we gave these stages are: the Green Start, Approaching Burnout, Family Matters, Sabbatical, Re-entry, and Mid-Career Transition. We loosely assigned them into the age ranges where they commonly take place. We have dedicated a chapter for each of these stages so women can identify where they may be on their own career track today and learn the skills to move quickly, consciously, and purposefully from that place toward The Orange Line without succumbing to the temptation to slide back onto the Green or Red Career Tracks. (See Figure 5.)

Stages of Career Progress

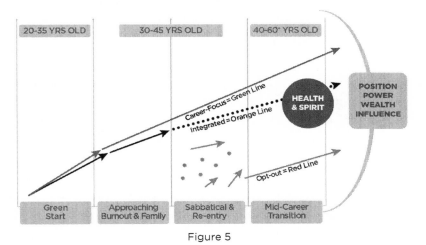

Figure 5

CHAPTER TWO:
The Feminine Filter™

To fully live on The Orange Line, women need to recognize what is blocking them. From our interviews, we determined that the crucial problem is what we call the Feminine Filter. This is a system of adopted beliefs and made-up rules that distract or prevent women from reaching their *métier*. We are using the French word *métier* because it more broadly incorporates purpose and career. Our guess is that if you are reading this book, you care about your career and also other aspects of your life. Once you become aware of these beliefs and recognize how they affect your life, it enables you to then decide whether to release them . . . or not . . . and pursue your career unencumbered by them.

What Is the Feminine Filter?

We created the name, "the Feminine Filter" to describe a commonly adopted belief system for what makes an ideal woman in our culture. Why "filter?" A filter is a "device or substance that passes electric currents of certain frequencies or frequency ranges while preventing the passage of others." On a camera, a polarizing filter "partially or completely absorbs certain light rays." In the context of decision-making, a filter is a polarizing lens through which people see the world; it filters reality so the data they see supports their belief system.

People use filters like this unconsciously to make decisions more quickly. They can filter data efficiently because aggregate experiences allow people to form underlying assumptions about how things work. For example, when people walk into a room for the first time, they take note of most everything: how the chairs are placed, the amount of light, the color of the walls and carpet, and so on. When they walk in for the fifteenth time, they no longer look at these things. They assume they are the same as always because experience has influenced their expectations. In fact, when something is slightly different, people often don't notice because they are now looking at the room through their filter. People also use filters to understand how the world works. Although filters are necessary to help the human mind discern what is important and what can be ignored, filters can also block a wider perspective or a non-habitual response. For example, people may assume a certain behavior based on the way someone looks or because that person reminds them of someone else, rather than open their mind to an unprejudiced new relationship.

The specific set of ideals and rules that make up the Feminine Filter have been built over the course of lifetimes to define the idealized woman. Models, such as Martha Stewart, HP's Meg Whitman, Yahoo's Marissa Mayer, Disney's Amy Duncan, and even Barbie, idealize what it looks like to be the perfect woman. These narrow ideals bombard women from an early age: at home, in the media, and at work. While some women may have had role models who steered them away from such demanding ideals, women tend to be influenced by these perceptions in some respect. It is hard to see only perfect role models and harder still not to see themselves in that context. Women then feel they either measure up or they don't. Sometimes, they even feel relieved when women around them don't measure up; it makes them feel less deficient to believe that someone else is more inadequate than they are. Because the Feminine Filter blocks women's view of their own whole life, they may end up believing the ideal is the *only* way to be a woman. As a result, women try to implement this distorted view of who they should be and what their lives should look like.

While women may have all internalized it slightly differently, Kathy Oneto, Vice President of Brand Strategy, Anthem Worldwide, found in her research that most women have internalized the ideal woman to be someone who follows three rules: "Do it all," "Look good," and "Be nice." Think about the compliments women give each other: "You are so amazing." "How do you do it?" Or "You look so great today." When women don't measure up to the pre-formed ideal, it can cause a flutter of a broad-stroked criticism. For example, walking into a messy house may have other women making unfair conclusions about the woman who lives there. The clothes female leaders wear can get more attention than the ideas they present. And, of course, women often judge assertiveness in other women as "bitchy," or "not nice." Interestingly, most women embrace this Feminine Filter subconsciously, accept it for themselves, and enforce it on each other. And if a woman can't live up to the ideal—if her personality doesn't fit with "nice," for example, she may enact behaviors that are the exact opposite. She might turn into a "bitch" or deliberately dress frumpily to avoid the pressure of living up to the "rule."

Notice "Be smart" is not on this list. In fact, being smart can alienate or threaten others so women may downplay their intelligence. In a Duke University survey, undergraduate women felt that "being 'cute' trumps being smart for women in the social environment." At Princeton, the undergraduate women are choosing not to run for "visible campus posts because they get the message from peers that such posts are more appropriately sought by men." These are examples of women purposely choosing to limit themselves in order to maintain the Feminine Filter.

Filters operate on assumptions. As we saw in the previous room example, people entering a familiar room don't need to expend energy determining whether anything has changed. The Feminine Filter works similarly, using assumptions, whether stated or unconscious, to dictate behavior. In our interviews, we found that women consistently and unconsciously made choices and based their actions on six basic assumptions. (See Figure 6.)

Assumptions

DO IT ALL	LOOK GOOD	BE NICE
1. I am primarily responsible for home and family and taking care of everyone. 2. My commitment to something is measured by how much time I devote to it.	3. I need to be perfect in behavior and appearance at all times. 4. I am not good enough.	5. Tangible, material rewards are not supposed to be important. 6. If I follow the rules, good things will happen.

Figure 6

These assumptions are so fundamental, that on some level, many women get angry or defensive when the assumptions are even mentioned or challenged. For example, here is some language from the interviewees concerning the first assumption with respect to family responsibilities:

- "He works a physical job and he needs his sleep so I get up in the middle of the night when the children cry."
- "He doesn't have flexibility so I need to stay home."
- "I am the mother; the children are my responsibility."
- "Surgery is not a good field for women because there isn't enough flexibility."

All of these feelings reinforce women's acceptance that the assumption is valid. Worse, women sometimes evoke noble labels, such as "selflessness" and "altruism," to help rationalize their decision and feel comfortable with this belief. Think of the power around judgments, such as "perfect" or "commitment." These are loaded words that help reinforce the assumptions and make it harder to argue with them.

WE'RE DOING ALL THE WORK!

Although many more women are working outside the home than in the past, they have not given up most of the domestic duties. Housework, parenting, gift-buying, and social-event coordination mostly still fall on women. Even in households where some of these domestic tasks are outsourced, usually women primarily hire and manage the domestic help. In essence, women do most of the "home" work:

- Married women do 70% of all housework in the U.S.
- When children arrive, women do three times the housework of men.
- A British study suggests that it will take another 50-70 years for Western culture to change so that housework is equally distributed.

As a result, most women fail to question these assumptions. Women never test whether the assumption is valid for them. And worse, buying into them has led many women to adopt self-limiting behaviors—bad habits—that prevent them from living The Orange Line whole life of career, family, and self.

For each assumption, there are also associated bad habits. (See Figure 7.)

Assumptions → Bad Habits

DO IT ALL	1. I am primarily responsible for home and family and taking care of everyone.	**ACQUIESCENCE & SELF-SACRIFICE**
	2. My commitment to something is measured by how much time I devote to it.	**WORKING HARDER, NOT SMARTER**
LOOK GOOD	3. I need to be perfect in behavior and appearance at all times.	**RISK AVOIDANCE & OVER-COMPENSATING** **CATASTROPHIZING** **CREATING A DIVERSION**
	4. I am not good enough.	**SEEKING EXTERNAL VALIDATION**
BE NICE	5. Tangible, material rewards are not supposed to be important.	**LOWER CAREER EXPECTATIONS**
	6. If I follow the rules, good things will happen.	**AVOID ASKING FOR WHAT I NEED OR CHALLENGING**

Figure 7

What do these habits look like? What are their consequences? Let's look at them in more detail.

Assumption #1

Because women assume: **Women are primarily responsible for home and family and taking care of everyone,** they tend to: **Acquiesce to the needs of everyone else and sacrifice their career ambitions and personal goals.**

Whenever a woman cleans the kitchen at work, organizes the office party, skips workouts, or just stays late to finish a project for her boss, she is reinforcing this assumption. A woman might sacrifice her career to stay home with her children because she thinks it's her duty. Or she might leave a job she loves to follow her spouse on an overseas assignment, putting him first. Another example is a woman who postpones exciting projects or even promotions to stay close to an aging parent. In some of the interviews, women said that while others may help, it was up to them to delegate tasks to their spouse and children. Felicity, a forty-two-year-old Business Consultant, for example, said, "If all I had to do was go to work, I could be just about anything. It's all of this other stuff I am responsible for that sucks my energy and holds me back." Many women conflate a desire to be with their families with owning most of the home and family responsibilities.

Assumption #2

Because women assume: **My commitment to something is measured by how much time I devote to it,** they tend to **work harder, not smarter**, focusing on the quantity of work over quality.

This assumption is reinforced when a woman takes on too many tasks and then beats herself up when she doesn't get everything done. Or when a woman refuses to delegate, rationalizing that she's the only one who can get it done right. It shows up when a woman eats lunch at her desk, instead of socializing with the team, so she can check boxes on the to-do list. Some women tend to over-engineer simple tasks like writing out Christmas cards, instead of using an automated contact list. Others volunteer for everything, even working below their capability, for example, stuffing envelopes, which can suggest that their time is less important than others'.

Assumption #3

Because women assume: **I need to be perfect in behavior and appearance at all times,** they tend to **avoid risk and overcompensate** to ensure they make no mistakes. When things don't go perfectly, they may panic about it, making ill-formed decisions.

We see this in women obsessed about their weight and/or appearance or helicopter moms who believe that overachieving motherhood will result in good outcomes for their children. Because of these habits, some women feel they must protect their children from everything: pain, bad feelings, unsuitable friends, illness, and even processed foods. This also shows up when women take an easier job than their capabilities because they fear failure. Women may limit their expectations or keep themselves in their comfort zone to ensure success. Then there are those who get into a rough patch with a spouse and suddenly it is the end of the world, with the only solution a nasty divorce. When a woman thinks, "I just can't do this anymore," it signals perfectionism and panic bordering on catastrophizing.

Assumption #4

Because women assume **I am not good enough,** they tend to **create a diversion** to distract others like "drama" or **seek external validation** to avoid addressing an internal belief that they don't look good.

This is illustrated by women who become overly sensitive to the judgments of others. A woman making this assumption might react defensively to a personnel review or assume the wry face in response to an innocuous comment has something to do with her. Some women take on too much with inadequate support, making themselves victims so they can play martyr to others. We also see this when women compete with other women to have the best home, the most gorgeous wardrobe, or the most polite children. Or they put each other down to make themselves feel better: "I don't like working for female managers." It is also displayed whenever women rely on external measures to define success, such as how many hours they've put in or how many positions they can volunteer for.

Assumption #5

Because women assume **tangible, material rewards are not supposed to be important,** they tend to **lower their career expectations**.

This is illustrated whenever women back away from the big role with the big paycheck to follow a supposedly nobler calling: "I don't want to work for companies, making those guys rich. I want to do something more meaningful," said one interviewee. Or "I'm not all about money. I would rather work for a place that respects people," said another. This assumption also manifests itself whenever a woman forgoes a big title because she is working part time and feels she doesn't deserve it, even though she is doing the associated tasks. This can also show up when women start their own businesses. Instead of getting investor money and launching a large company, which is her secret ambition, she may start a small business and hope to grow it organically. It is not uncommon for women, when they see a successful, wealthy woman, to make excuses for why she is that way and why they cannot achieve it as well. It's as if all of those rewards belong to others, and they shouldn't want them anyway.

Assumption #6

Because women assume **if I follow the rules, good things will happen,** they tend to **avoid asking for what they need or challenging the status quo.**

Early on, women are taught that if they study, do their homework, and respect the teacher, they will be rewarded with good grades. Since it worked in school, it is not surprising that women sometimes continue to think that's how it works at work. You can see this in action when a woman settles for the first compensation offer without negotiating for more, or when a woman automatically agrees to a 6 p.m. meeting without questioning its necessity. We see it in the persistent wage disparity between men and women and in the way wealth gets redistributed during divorce. Women start businesses more often than men, but get a far smaller proportion of venture capital funds. Medical conditions affecting women receive less research than those affecting men. Women may understand this disparity, but fail to ask for what they need or challenge the way things are. Some even justify yet another assumption, that if they just keep working and doing what they're told, it will change in time.

The problem is, nothing is changing. When we succumb to these bad habits, we reinforce the assumptions and the Feminine Filter ideals.

CHAPTER THREE:
The Feminine Filter™ Problem

When women continue to accept the assumptions and rules of the past, they support and reinforce existing rewards systems. People continue to get paid a bonus to work seventy-plus-hour workweeks, rather than for the results they create. Mothers continue to be ostracized or labeled in the workplace for taking time off. From a systemic perspective, this self-limitation has resulted in too few female voices in power positions arguing for change. Although virtually half of the workforce is women, the percentage with influence has barely changed in decades.

Part of the problem is that when a woman subsumes her career goals and interests, she enables more Green Line behavior. The reality is most people at the top have a stay-at-home spouse. The only way senior managers can continue to work the hours and pace required is if they do not have home responsibilities or extensive personal interests outside of work. If women give up their wider goals to support the Green Liners, either by taking care of their home responsibilities or simply by limiting themselves and getting out of their way as they rise to power, they disable others from figuring out how to live a whole life. They perpetuate a flawed system.

If *everyone* assumed it was acceptable to pursue her *métier* because *everyone* is responsible for managing the family and household, if nobody sacrificed his or her innate talent and contribution—then the work environment would likely change in response and might not be so hostile and Green Line-focused. Work could be redefined.

Everything women do models to the next generation what society views as the right way to operate. Actions speak louder than words. Women can tell their daughters that they can be anything they want, but it's a mixed message when they are the only parent limiting work goals and controlling the household tasks, such as making the family dinner or shuttling kids around. Girls may conclude it looks like too much work and give up on the career part. Boys learn they can have exciting careers and spouses who will keep a beautiful home. The more intensely women buy into this system, the longer it will take to change. It perpetuates the idea that The Orange Line is unattainable.

Removing the Feminine Filter

In the following chapters, we will show how these rules, assumptions, and bad habits crop up consistently and how they can limit or even derail women from achieving their *métier*. Women can make more enlightened career and life choices based on their true purpose, instead of blind and habitual acceptance, but the Feminine Filter must be removed first.

Guilt is very effective at keeping behavior in line because its constancy saps energy. Then, when a woman wants to push the boundaries, the guilt fogs her thinking, making her feel too drained to take action: She may think, *I really want to take that job downtown, but the extra commute time will mean I can't make dinner for my family until 7 p.m.* It may get reinforced by the latest study that shows how critical it is for children to have dinner with their family at a reasonable time every night. Think about this energy expenditure. Guilt erodes self-esteem and lowers her ability to spend that energy on something productive or the creativity to think of different options. As long as most women still believe deep down in the ideal woman, guilt will work to keep the assumptions real.

Instead, women can learn to recognize guilt and use it as an indicator that the Feminine Filter is at work. Women can use guilt as a trigger to increase their consciousness of when someone else's assumptions are at work.

A NOTE ABOUT GUILT: THE SWEATER ANALOGY

Joy Chudacoff, Speaker and Life Coach, provided this analogy about guilt: Women often take ownership of others' emotions by taking responsibility for them—putting on their emotional "sweater." They see it, pick it up, put it on, and wear it to help the other person feel better. For example:

A woman works for a bank. The line is long, a customer forgot her bankcard at home and had to drive back to get it, and there were kids in the line who were fighting. A frustrated customer started to yell at the bank clerk, who took the yelling personally. She attempted to soothe over the situation so that customer would calm down. But the customer was just looking for someone to vent her frustration on. However, once the clerk let the customer's emotional energy rattle her, she had picked up and put on the customer's "emotional sweater."

When a woman puts on someone else's emotional "sweater," she focuses on the wrong things. She relieves others from responsibility for managing their own emotions and instead drains her energy. But here's the crucial factor—*she* decides whether to pick up and wear that sweater or just leave it for the other person to deal with. *She* has to agree it is her issue and accept the premise for allowing this guilt to work on her. But when she doesn't pick up the sweater, when she leaves it lying right there on the ground, she defeats guilt and its ability to influence her.

For true, long-term change, most women need to address their underlying assumptions and core belief system. So how do women make this change? By adopting a new belief system. Women need to believe they are important and have the right to pursue their vocation. If women consciously acknowledge these new beliefs, they can start to internalize them, thereby repelling the "do it all, look good, be nice" rules.

Figure 8

Once a woman starts to accept this belief system, she can define what womanhood means to her personally. What are her operating principles? How will she focus her energy, creativity, and love to achieve her goals? By adopting this more personal belief system, with its internal definition and measurements, women will feel they have more power. A woman can determine what she needs to do and how to accomplish it. She can replace rules with principles and reframe the assumptions.

INSTEAD OF EXTERNAL RULES:	WE CAN APPLY INTERNAL PRINCIPLES:	INSTEAD OF ASSUMPTIONS:	WE CAN REFRAME THEM:
Do it all.	**Do what's required, including for me.**	Women are responsible for home and family and taking care of everyone.	**We are all responsible for home and family and taking care of ourselves.**
		Time matters most.	**Outcomes and personal fulfillment are what matter.**
Look good.	**Do what's right, regardless of how it looks.**	Perfection is the goal.	**Doing my best and being good enough is perfectly acceptable.**
		We are not good enough.	**I am a good person, and I am working on my own development.**
Be nice.	**Be authentic, honest, and direct.**	Material rewards are not important.	**I am paid what I am worth.**
		If we follow the rules, good things will happen.	**I take responsibility for myself and ask for what I need.**

Once a woman has changed her core beliefs, the whole way she approaches her life can shift. She no longer has to follow rules or blindly accept external assumptions. She can free herself of the Feminine Filter and seek an Orange Line Career.

The Orange Line Skills

We believe women can replace the common bad habits by developing Orange Line Skills. In this book, we focus on six important skills you can develop throughout your lifetime that will keep you on The Orange Line. These skills are applied across every chapter. Just as with healthy eating and exercise, real success requires regular maintenance. Think of these skills as behavioral muscles that you develop slowly over time. This is how they will provide you with sustained strength and endurance. You will need to practice them every single day—this is a life-long process that requires regular honing. And as you master them, you can learn more of the subtle aspects related to each skill. You can start to build them at any career stage and re-start them any time you feel they need to be refreshed. And, as with maintaining healthy eating and exercise, the difference they will make to your life is substantial.

The **six skills** for living on The Orange Line:

1. Recognize when the Feminine Filter is at work. By developing this skill, you notice when the Feminine Filter shows up and affects your judgment of others or yourself. Once recognized, you decide how to replace or drop the assumption. You can become conscious of language or guilt that hides an underlying assumption and ask if that assumption is true for you. You learn to recognize behavioral patterns that reinforce that assumption. Finally, you can decide consciously how to respond versus reacting habitually.

2. Bring yourself into the equation. You can stop adapting yourself to the system and instead set clear boundaries and expectations. You can take responsibility for what you need and ask for it. You can take notice when you are sacrificing your viewpoint, interests, identity, and well-being for others unnecessarily. You can include both individual goals as well as the group goals. You can decide consciously to push back and include "you" in more decisions by promoting and taking care of yourself.

3. Develop self-awareness. You can begin to ask for feedback to determine your strengths and challenges. You self-assess to discover what is important and who you want to be. You reflect and understand what these new insights mean and decide where you want to improve. You develop an objective sense of who you are and where you fit in the universe. As you learn this, you can practice the previous skills with even more confidence.

4. Build a support system. You learn to acknowledge that you can't do it alone. You determine what help you need and ask for it, deciding what you are willing to give up and what you need to delegate to your family or colleagues at work. Then you spend your time and creative energy doing the things you enjoy most and that make the biggest long-term impact.

5. Get comfortable operating in imperfection. Now you can start to accept that imperfection is a normal part of life and develop a muscle for ambiguity, flexibility, and creativity. You can embrace messiness and learn to have fun with it, maybe even start to look forward to problems, because you can see the embedded opportunities. You can look at what you want to do, see where you are, and brainstorm ways of achieving your goals.

6. Expand your universe. You can open yourself to opportunities by including others who challenge and push you forward. You seek out diverse views to help you create ideas and learn to think bigger about life's possibilities, stretching your capacity and opportunities. You experiment and take risks outside of your comfort zone, purposely exposing yourself to newness so that you can learn more.

When you discover who you are and operate from a place of authenticity, from your whole self, you can more easily take what others say at face value. The dishonesty goes away. Instead of "doing it all," "looking good," and "being nice," you will be free to focus on areas where you want to spend your energy.

You can learn how to live an Orange Line life. Every woman carves her Orange Line differently. Everyone is a work in progress. Some apply Orange Line thinking very well; others struggle every day. Remember, big changes start with small steps. Doing one thing differently—drawing a boundary, pushing back on someone else's "should," walking a minute every mile—will increase confidence and encourage another change step. The end result is that women can live lives that are full and free.

Are you ready to try?

CHAPTER FOUR:
The Green Start

MY DREAM JOB

"When I was young I dreamed of becoming an art director for an advertising agency. I received my Fine Arts degree. After graduating and shopping around various advertising agencies, I realized I loved the business side of things. I worked for six weeks at one of the largest advertising agencies. Then they downsized and I was kept on as a Junior Art Director. I got lucky that downsizing pushed me to sink or swim, fail or succeed. Young, creative, running promotions, I had to manage instantly. The agency empowered me with big clients and gave me confidence. I got the opportunity to be thrown in deep and had no choice but to learn to swim! I worked there for five years, and then moved to a global agency and met my husband. An opportunity arose for him to relocate to New York. The company wanted me to stay on so I went with him and worked in the New York office. After three years of bitter winters, my husband applied for a job on the West Coast and got it. Rather than lose me, the company I was with offered me a remote position working three weeks a month from home and the fourth week in New York. I have been doing this for three years. I'm now a VP, Creative Director. I work with writers and clients on projects, films, and advertisements using digital media. It's a fun job. I love the work—I'm a bit of a junkie. I especially enjoy problem-solving everything. I get up at 6 a.m. and have breakfast and

then work from 7 a.m. to 5:30 p.m. Dinner at 7 p.m. Then my husband comes home and I work a couple more hours, sometimes until midnight. I'm also a big exerciser: I go for a run, I do Pilates, I train, strap kids on, and go hiking in the canyon."
— *Faith, VP Creative Director, thirty-nine*

Many women we interviewed described a positive and energetic start to their careers. We developed this description to sum it up: In the Green Start stage, you have launched your career and the sky is the limit. Like many women, you feel you can do anything. You love work and are learning a great deal. You like getting recognized for your talents and efforts and likely believe the meritocracy exists: If you simply work hard, of course you can have it all. Women have come so far, after all, and most of them have been raised to believe they can do anything.

When forty-six-year-old Business Owner Lori was in the Green Start stage, she found early fast-track success: "I started working for a multinational organization and learned the ropes quickly. I decided cold turkey to start my own company. I recruited one company, and two years later, had a stable of large clients. I was approached by someone to buy my business and I decided to sell. The office I built still exists today."

When women are young, it seems normal to devote total attention to careers. Young, energetic, cash poor from student loans, and eager to move up, they love doing something meaningful. Some companies recognize the increasing mobility of the workforce and offer flexibility or moderation; others are still "old school" and seem to take advantage of this early career period, getting as much hard work and hours out of employees as possible. Most women are willing to work this hard because they know they can always move on at some point. They simply enjoy the rewards of exercising their talents. Others fear pushing back will limit their career trajectory at this point.

Green Start women may be thinking ahead to what the rest of their career path will look like. At this stage, the opportunities seem infinite. We found women usually feel one of three ways about their career future:

- **Green Starters are clear on what they want to do.** Some women just seem to click with their careers right away. These women thrived in the action and reaped the accolades early, reinforcing the focus on career. Teresa, now fifty-eight, started her own business when she was young. "I always knew I wanted to be in marketing. I started in a small, local agency and worked my way up. But I worked hard, and when I figured out I couldn't get far in a little agency, I moved to a big one. I progressed and accumulated a great portfolio of clients. I grew the business, made a lot of money, had great clients, and had a great time."

- **Green Starters experiment.** Some women took a job that wasn't precisely a match because they needed the work and became interested even if it wasn't in their sweet spot. They experimented asking themselves, "Do I like this? How about that?" They switched positions to get a higher salary or a bigger job. They figured out what they were good at and tested whether they could actually do this over time. Hania, now forty and a Business Owner, started in finance, and then went to work as an Administrative Assistant for a small startup company where she got to wear a lot of hats. When the company folded, she worked for the president of a mid-size company. In time, she was given greater responsibilities and eventually coordinated an operational audit. This led to a project manager role that clicked with her. She went back to school for a master's degree and ended up, through hard work and a series of promotions, in a senior management role in a large firm.

- **Green Starters tailor their career to suit their future family.** Some women had concerns about hitting a "maternal wall" which influenced their behaviors and determined whether they chose a job that would accommodate family. For these women, the consideration of a future family started from day one. They lowered their career expectations in anticipation of some future date when they would step out of the rat race. As Sheryl Sandberg of Facebook famously said, once a woman decides she is going to have children—whether she even has a boyfriend or not— "literally from that moment, she doesn't raise her hand anymore, she doesn't look for a promotion, she doesn't take on the new project, she doesn't say, 'Me. I want to do that.' She starts leaning back." For example, one unmarried woman without children planned early on to shift from a higher paying medical role to one linked to public school so she could work school hours once she eventually had children.

Regardless of which of the three are true for them, we found Green Starters wanted to like where they work. Sure, they wanted money, but it was much less important than the right career, something they were willing to trade off. A large number of our interviewees started off with low-paying first jobs they were able to parlay into a higher paying career later. Just because money wasn't these women's highest priority doesn't mean women in this stage are not ambitious. Patten, et al found in the *Pew Social and Demographic Trends* research: "Two thirds (66%) of young women ages 18 to 34 rate career high on their list of life priorities, compared with 59 percent of young men." It's just that women are willing to start lower, move more slowly, and delay gratification longer.

Many women find it relatively easy to be on The Green Line in this phase because they typically are healthy, responsible only for themselves, and friends and peers are in the same situation. It can be a lot of fun to see the direct results of their hard work in recognition, promotions, and money. They may feel pretty proud of themselves (we all did). It can also be exciting to pay off school debt, purchase their first big assets, and start saving for retirement or grad school. After all of the hard work and discipline of school, it can feel like you have arrived—that you are finally an adult.

Green Start Challenges: A Closer Look

Underneath all of the pride, ambition, and excitement of this stage, there may be some problems that threaten to undermine women's early success. Let's go into these Green Start challenges in detail:

- **Green Starters' values may be out of sync with their organization.** In the expediency of launching a career, some women may not have been as discerning as they may have liked about choosing their organization. Or they may see things happening at work that they don't like, but choose to overlook because they either lack the confidence to speak up or don't want to risk getting fired. Many women are not necessarily aware of the ramifications this type of path brings; all they know is they are learning the skills that will help them do other jobs in the future. Heidi, an Insurance Specialist, now thirty-nine, said her first job was, "very lucrative, I was single and making a lot of money. It allowed me to buy my first house. It paid most of the MBA and bought my car. It gave me a great lifestyle, but what did it do to me as a person? I don't know emotionally if I was where I could've been. I sacrificed my value system to work there for so long."

I COULDN'T SAY NO

"I was very uncomfortable about doing a particular assignment. I couldn't say 'No.' I tried to speak to my boss, but he assured me all would be well. I ended up ill. The feeling is when you are a 'type A' you always have to be the best. The harder I work, the more I will be rewarded. If I say 'No,' they'll review me negatively. I want to make myself invaluable so that when I have to negotiate a salary increase, I'll be rewarded. I also don't want to let anyone down."
— *Yvonne, Research Consultant, twenty-five*

- **Work and working hard can become addictive.** Some Green Starters love the responsibility and everything they are learning. They are willing and able to work hard. Most resist stepping out of their organization's cultural norms, particularly if they see others lose their career traction or become victimized for doing so. Some women can get too caught up in the work. Because of their age, it's easier to ignore their body and push through any messages it sends. They can be creative late into the night because of the adrenaline rush. There may be a niggle in their mind that this may not be tenable long-term, but they ignore it. They may start to move into a management position and find it frustrating that others are asking for time to do other things, such as taking courses or going home at a set time for childcare, especially because they want to but are too afraid to ask.

- **Anxiety may be present.** Some women may feel anxious and nervous, wondering if they really do have what it takes to be successful. They hide this well because they see that showing their vulnerability is not well accepted in most organizations. They assume that they must do it perfectly or they will lose ground. They hide their insecurities by being overly aggressive, trying to convince themselves and others that they are perfect. Any imperfection that appears can throw them over the edge, igniting their anger or causing more anxiety. They may feel out of their depth, but they don't feel they are allowed to show it. Yvonne said, "I never feel I look good enough. It demonizes me."

- **Some women may experience sexual stereotyping, behaviors, and/or harassment in the workplace.** While outright workplace discrimination may be a thing of the distant past, many women still describe subtle events and messages that can block their career progress. Many women still seem to have to "prove again" that they are effective at their jobs and deserve to be where they are. Even today, especially in male-dominated industries, the environment can feel unfriendly to women. Pamela, a Programmer, got pushback from male colleagues because they were unaccustomed to women working in technology. They blamed her lack of an engineering degree, but she felt this was just an excuse to keep her off balance. After some years of progressive promotion and experience, she finds it easier. Now, "men are comfortable with me and treat me like I'm a guy."

BUT HE'S THE BREADWINNER

"I had just been promoted to manager and was helping backfill my old sales representative position on the team. I recruited and made an offer to a man, and the offer was accepted. After it was accepted, my regional manager, who was also a man, informed me he had decided to upgrade my subordinate's salary to equal mine, saying, 'I know you were willing to work at that salary when you were in the role, but your new employee is the breadwinner of his family and therefore needs to be paid more.'" — *Kelly*

I BLEW THE WHISTLE

"I reported my immediate manager to Human Resources for his sexual and emotional harassment. All the while the manager was treated with the utmost respect. HR told me I was no longer reporting to that manager, but then didn't assign me to someone new for months while they investigated. When I was reassigned to a different manager and received my first review, he rated me lower than what I had consistently received before and less than the one he had given to my peer who reported to him. I know my work was the same high caliber." — *Nadine, IT Manager, forty-three*

- **Some women may undermine each other.** We heard many interviewees describe women versus women conflict in the workplace. In addition to the usual workplace competitiveness and jealousy, there is also often conflict between two groups of women: those who are career-focused and those more family-focused. Each looks down on the other. Each assumes that the other group doesn't understand how the world works or how they feel. The first group believes that women are invincible to these wider forces and that they can have it all now. The second group believes that women need to start being realistic about the career limitations they will face if and when they want a family. Both groups start to conform to The Feminine Filter standards.

- **Women may be working well below their capabilities and earning potential.** Currently, there is a trend for both men and women in this stage to take jobs beneath their capability. In fact, 53 percent of recent college graduates are un- or under-employed. This may be because the economy has been so poor that many Green Starters are more willing to take anything that is available, such as an administrative role, just so they can get a foot in the door. Women may also do it because they tend to feel more confident when they are overqualified for the job or they may not know their worth. Thirty-year-old Director of Sales, Isabel recalls how "One day my manager told me, 'We're really impressed with your work. We think you deserve more so give us a number.' I had no idea and gave my boss a number. He said, 'Let's say double.'" Though this was a rare response, the manager's feedback illustrates how much frequently gets left on the table by women's under-expectations. Too often, women get stuck and end up with a career much smaller than what they're capable of.

These Green Start challenges may lead you to make thousands of decisions along your career path that impact your long-term potential. You may start with lower expectations or limit yourself because you worry about the family impact. You may work yourself too hard and set yourself up for burnout. You may fail to speak up when something contradicts your values or ask for the compensation and promotions you need and deserve. You may also have internalized a belief system that will set you up for work-life conflict down the road. To achieve a robust and full life on the Orange Line and avoid both the Green and Red Line trajectories, we recommend you focus on the development of the six Orange Line Skills.

Skills for Living The Orange Line

Practicing these six skills at this early stage in your career means you won't have to unlearn as many bad habits or shed years of more entrenched beliefs. This is also the stage where it is most tempting to follow previously established ways of doing things. Many women may not yet have developed the confidence to create their own path. There is less resistance both internally and externally if you just learn the "rules" of the Feminine Filter and follow them. You may have endless energy at this stage so throwing yourself into your career, without regard for health, wellness, and spirit, might be very tempting. We feel if women can learn from our interviewees' lessons as early as possible in their careers, they can reap the benefits earlier and inoculate themselves from the Filter's affects across their careers.

1. Recognize when the Feminine Filter is at work

When Feminine Filter inspired decision-making is happening, it appears in your language, behaviors, choices, and automated responses. You can **listen for and recognize Filter language** in common phrases and messages. For example, when a woman hears, "Your agendas and minutes are so detailed, they're perfect," she can recognize the underlying assumption that her work needs to be perfect. Or when she hears, "You are a valuable employee who works late every night and most weekends," it suggests if she follows the rules and works late, good things will happen. When you develop this skill, you will recognize it in action.

Language is powerful: It can pressure you to accept and adopt the underlying assumption that then influences your actions. Note how this pressure is external and, in many ways, out of your control. Your initial response may be anger. But because the pressure is external, you can't change the fact that it will be directed into your path. Power comes from recognizing it when you hear it and noticing how you react to it: Do you accept it and buy-in to the underlying assumptions? Do you disagree with the assumption? Can you reframe the assumption? When you recognize language for what it conveys, you then have the power to accept or reject it.

The chart below illustrates some of the common language we found in our research and from our interviewees. We use it to highlight the Feminine Filter assumptions. We debunk the assumption to reveal the underlying messages women receive and perpetuate with this language. We then reframe the language, recognizing Orange Line Principles so women can open up new possibilities for themselves.

THE GREEN START LANGUAGE	DEBUNKING THE ASSUMPTION: WHAT'S REALLY GOING ON	REFRAME
The glass ceiling is a myth. I can do anything. **Feminine Filter underlying assumption:** If I follow the rules, good things will happen.	Sadly, the glass ceiling still exists. While Green Starters may look around and see plenty of other female peers, they often don't notice that up in the executive ranks, the picture changes. The fact is, sexism still exists all the way to the top. Denying it only makes it more difficult to deal with and knocks you off-balance when you face it. Worse, you may not challenge it, thinking it an anomaly. Many of the women we interviewed faced some kind of systemic bias, even the young ones.	*There are still plenty of barriers to the top, but I can overcome them. Noticing them enables me to take responsibility for my career and ask for what I need.*

THE GREEN START LANGUAGE	DEBUNKING THE ASSUMPTION: WHAT'S REALLY GOING ON	REFRAME
I am committed to the company because I give my all and work very hard. **Feminine Filter underlying assumption:** Commitment to something is measured by how much time I devote to it.	Success can't be measured in time alone. Time spent goofing around or "zoned out" does not result in positive results for the organization even if you get kudos for working late. Creative time spent working on something you care about is far more likely to produce results. The ultimate success measure is the outcome, not the time invested. Locking yourself into a time-centric success measurement can prevent you from freely claiming and allocating your time to non-work activities in the future.	*I am committed to determining what outcomes are needed by the organization and how that will be measured. I will devote my time and creative energy as needed for successful outcomes, not to show commitment.*

THE GREEN START LANGUAGE	DEBUNKING THE ASSUMPTION: WHAT'S REALLY GOING ON	REFRAME
I don't have time to "schmooze," there's work to be done and I will be rewarded for it. **Feminine Filter underlying assumption:** If I follow the rules, good things will happen.	This implies a very narrow definition of "work." Work is not just the deliverables created. Personal relationships are a major intangible influencing your work results and are sometimes more important than more tangible tasks. Unfortunately, school teaches many women that a heads-down focus on work will get them the A, whereas chatting at the water cooler will get them expelled. At work, it is more nuanced than that: Sometimes, less than perfect deliverables and stellar relationships are more highly desired.	*I am here to provide value for the organization. I can choose to spend my time and energy on whatever will maximize my value, including building relationships. I can also choose to avoid wasting time with activities that do not support my company or personal objectives.*
I will be noticed for my hard work. I will get the promotions/rewards because I deserve them not because I toot my own horn. I do not make less than my male peers. There is a meritocracy. **Feminine Filter underlying assumption:** If I follow the rules, good things will happen.	Men are self-promoters who ask for raises and negotiate salary at every step while women wait to be recognized. By waiting for someone else to recognize your work, you are letting others control your life.	*I can be paid what I am worth. I can take responsibility, find out what I'm worth and ask for it on a regular basis.*

THE GREEN START LANGUAGE	DEBUNKING THE ASSUMPTION: WHAT'S REALLY GOING ON	REFRAME
I don't want to copy those before me. I don't want to be a female executive, politician or CEO and live that life. **Feminine Filter underlying assumption:** Tangible, material rewards are not supposed to be important. And, our commitment to something is measured by how much time we devote to it.	This assumption implies the *only* way to achieve those roles is to behave the same way as the current executives. But the reason women don't know another way is because there are insufficient alternative examples. The system won't change until you take a risk, expand your creativity, deliver results using an alternate model for success, and gain power.	*I trust in my own ability to figure out how to achieve my ambitions and carve out the role so I can live as I want to live.*
I want children and I don't think I can do it effectively if I keep working like this or in this field. **Feminine Filter underlying assumption:** Women are primarily responsible for home and family and taking care of everyone.	So many women submerge their career ambitions for children they don't even have yet. The assumption is that motherhood is their primary role. Many people, including most of our interviewees, manage family and meaningful work just fine, especially those for whom there is no supposed "choice."	*I am creative and smart enough to figure out how to have a family and do the work I like. My future spouse has responsibility for the family as well and together we can decide what our lives can look like.*

THE GREEN START LANGUAGE	DEBUNKING THE ASSUMPTION: WHAT'S REALLY GOING ON	REFRAME
Those women who leave at 5 p.m. to take care of their children are not committed. **Feminine Filter underlying assumption:** Commitment to something is measured by how much time I devote to it.	It is irrelevant how other people schedule their work and manage their lives. Instead of exhibiting jealousy or expecting all employees to work a particular way, it would be more innovative to support creative, alternative work models and focus on expected results. You can also reflect on why you believe this; do you wish you could leave at 5 p.m.?	*Other women have figured out how to manage their time to maximize their careers and lives. I can, too.*
I always place another marker; once I do "such and such" then I'll stop working so hard. **Feminine Filter underlying assumption:** I am never good enough.	For people who seek external validation, especially perfectionists, nothing is ever finished or "good enough." Achievements leave you feeling empty so you seek the next one. Often this is a sign you haven't been clear with your objectives or thought thoroughly about what the achievement really means. You will never get "there."	*I know I am a good person. I can take the space I need to think about what I want out of life and then take time to learn and grow. I can also figure out objective ways to measure my success that are internal, not external.*

THE GREEN START LANGUAGE	DEBUNKING THE ASSUMPTION: WHAT'S REALLY GOING ON	REFRAME
I am a type A personality. My personality enables me to accomplish a lot. **Feminine Filter underlying assumption:** I need to be perfect in behavior and appearance at all times.	Being Type A and trying to be perfect at everything can actually show others you are unable to prioritize. If you work for perfection across the board, you fail to build an ability to determine what needs to be perfect and what can just be good enough. It also sets you up for burnout because you waste energy approaching everything with equal, and sometimes unnecessary, fervor.	*I will decide which tasks require excellence (not perfection). I am willing to allow some tasks to meet, versus exceed, expectations so I can prioritize my energy and time appropriately. I can also decide what tasks are not necessary for me to do and actively delegate or eliminate them.*

The next step in recognizing when the Feminine Filter is at work is to become **aware of guilt**. Guilt is the internal pressure you put on yourself to act, based upon unquestioning acceptance of Feminine Filter assumptions. For example, a woman feels guilt and tells herself, "I need to create the agenda for the meetings and take the notes because I'm the best at it." Or "I should work late while the rest of the team goes golfing with that client just in case someone calls." The words "should" or "need to" verbalize the guilt. She is not doing these things because she necessarily wants to when she uses this language. She is doing it because she feels obligated. Whenever guilt appears, recognize it for what it is: A sign that an assumption has been made that's out of sync with your goals.

The next step is to **observe your behavioral response**. What action did you take? Did you buy-in to the underlying assumption or just react out of habit? How do you feel? For example, did you just acquiesce to a Monday morning deadline for the latest deliverable due date when your manager handed it to you Friday night at four? Or did you renegotiate a fair deadline? Regardless of their internal resistance, if women believe *they are responsible for taking care of everyone*, then most would likely stay all weekend to get it done. The manager might use language for additional pressure, "I really need this done by Monday or the client will be breathing down my neck." Or "You are really saving our team. Thank you." Self-review of your behavioral response, however, may help you notice the Feminine Filter assumptions. You can analyze your response and then reframe the underlying assumption: "I'm feeling uncomfortable because I am being pressured to submerge my own interests to take care of others."

Here are some more examples we saw of women behaving in ways that enacted the Feminine Filter's assumptions. In this chart, we describe what happens when women enact these behaviors and how the underlying assumption could be reframed.

GREEN START BEHAVIOR	CONSEQUENCES	FILTER ASSUMPTION
Absorbing traditional female administrative roles like ordering lunch or taking meeting notes. Women may clean the kitchen, organize the holiday party, or volunteer to type up the changes agreed at the meeting. **Bad habit:** Acquiescence and self-sacrifice.	People assume that because you will do the work for free they don't have to pay someone else to do it. It may also reinforce the stereotype that women want to do these jobs or are better at them somehow. Choosing to do these jobs can rob you of energy for more important and fulfilling work, and prevent the organization from figuring out how to delegate the work fairly.	Women are primarily responsible for home and family and taking care of everyone **Reframe:** *I have important work to do, and if cleaning or organizing is important enough, everyone can share in the work.*
Saying yes to everything to show commitment. Women may work late and go the extra mile to check every box to make sure everyone knows how committed they are. They may also be afraid to "reject" someone by saying "no." **Bad habit:** Working harder, not smarter.	Doing it all enables others to do less than their share, drains energy, and takes up all your time. It prevents meaningful conversations about prioritization for both you and the person asking for the work.	Commitment to something is measured by how much time I devote to it. **Reframe:** *I can say "no" to work that is not contributing to my personal goals. I can also ask for something in return when someone adds to my workload.*

GREEN START BEHAVIOR	CONSEQUENCES	FILTER ASSUMPTION
Comparing themselves to and emulating male colleagues who are more aggressive and appear "hard ass." Women observe aggressiveness in men and believe all managers act this way. **Bad habit:** Risk avoidance and over compensation.	You may submerge more connecting/relational behaviors because it is viewed as too "feminine." You may then start to dislike the job as you suppress who you are to meet standards set by others. But being "hard ass" is costly to organizations as well. "Faking" can get you labeled as inauthentic which can be worse than a "soft" reputation.	I need to be perfect in behavior and appearance at all times. **Reframe:** *I can be myself and be worthwhile.*
Reacting aggressively to hide their insecurities or over-reacting when something imperfect happens. Women who do this may internalize mistakes as their fault and lose confidence. **Bad habit:** Risk avoidance and over compensation.	People start to doubt the emotional intelligence of women who behave in this way. They doubt whether you can handle the current work role or even higher-level positions where there is even more nuance and imperfection. Or others start to avoid you when there is a problem because they fear your response.	I need to be perfect in behavior and appearance at all times. **Reframe:** *I can accept imperfection and am capable of working through it.*

GREEN START BEHAVIOR	CONSEQUENCES	FILTER ASSUMPTION
Letting others judge their performance by seeking out regular praise to feel "good." Instead of asking questions about what is required, women may wait for the external judgment. Visible measures of value such as hours worked, number of reports created, or the number of projects juggled may not correlate with qualitative results. **Bad habit:** Seeking external validation.	You become reliant on others to define what good performance means, thereby limiting your ability to set goals and control results. Also, when you seek external validation, you fail to develop that ability internally. You've now set yourself up for failure. It also suggests to others that you lack confidence.	I am never good enough. **Reframe:** *I know where I need to be, and I can measure my results objectively.*
Avoiding negotiating for promotions and raises and justifying their avoidance by telling themselves that they care more about liking their work, peers, and working normal hours. **Bad habit:** Lower career and reward expectations.	You begin to make less than your male colleagues and watch as they get promoted ahead of you. You start to wonder whether it's because you lack capability, which may affect your self-confidence and hinder your long-term potential.	Tangible, material rewards are not supposed to be important. **Reframe:** *I am entitled to get paid what I am worth and I am capable of asking for it.*

GREEN START BEHAVIOR	CONSEQUENCES	FILTER ASSUMPTION
Failing to promote their work successes and waiting for opportunities to find them instead of the other way around. Women do their work and expect that promotions will just come. They keep their head down, go above and beyond what is expected and assume they will be noticed. **Bad habit:** Lower career and reward expectations.	Waiting for recognition fosters inertia and de-motivation because you may work hard and no one notices. Others get promoted before you, even though you feel you are more competent. Plus, it can take twice as long to move forward than it needs to.	Tangible, material rewards are not supposed to be important. **Reframe:** *I am entitled to the level of work and responsibility I can manage. I am capable of asking for it.*
Ignoring or overreacting to sexual stereotyping, behaviors, or harassment in the workplace. On the one hand, women may be tempted to suppress their feelings of discomfort and ignore comments, suggestions, or outright harassment. Or, women may get so angry they escalate the issue to top management. **Bad habit:** Avoid asking for what they need or challenging authority.	Ignoring the behavior or internalizing it ensures the aggressor wins and will continue the behavior. However, over-reacting may weaken you to a position of victimhood, which can isolate you and identify you as a troublemaker. In a male-dominated power structure, women don't usually get positive results from over-reaction.	If I follow the rules, good things will happen. **Reframe:** *I can verbally draw limits on behaviors that make me uncomfortable and create a healthy work environment for myself.*

Once you understand the pressures and reasons for your behaviors, you can start to **challenge your assumptions** and change the behaviors. One way to do this is to internally reframe the assumption as above: "I am not asking for more money because I am greedy and material things are important. I am asking for a raise to reflect the value I am adding to this organization and my worth in the marketplace." Then, when ready, you can share and use this language explicitly with others so that your needs become visible by verbalizing: "I am willing to complete this assignment this weekend. However, I've noticed we seem to be depending upon evening and weekend time more and more to get our work done. I would like to discuss how we can address the labor shortage or set more reasonable expectations of how much our team can accomplish."

Finally, you can **be more conscious in your choices** and realize that you have an infinite number of options available to you. Instead of saying: "I can't be a surgeon because the hours are too demanding for someone who wants kids," you can say, "I'm going to study to be a surgeon and while I'm at school I'm going to investigate all sorts of ways to practice a surgical career on my terms." Instead of saying, "I can't take that overseas assignment because I don't want to ask my husband," you can say, "I'm going overseas and will find a way to include my spouse in this exciting experience." You can practice saying, "Yes," and trust that you are smart and creative enough to overcome challenges and accomplish your goals.

The goal is to remove the blocks that the Feminine Filter puts in the way of making conscious choices aligned with your goals and needs. By recognizing and challenging the assumptions, you can clear the Feminine Filter out of the way.

2. Bring yourself into the equation

It is tempting to follow someone else's external vision for what you should want out of your career and your life. People, such as your parents, peers, managers, and even spouses, may all have a view, which, while informative, is influenced by their outside perspective. It is important early on to develop your own vision and put yourself at the center of your own life plan.

A major part of this is the ability to **set boundaries and expectations**. You need to get comfortable saying, "No," especially when not doing so causes you harm, even on a small scale, such as cleaning up after a meeting or consistently agreeing to take on a peer's task. As Olive, a forty-eight-year-old IT Director, noted when she was asked by a roomful of male colleagues to order lunch for a meeting, "The uterus is not a food-finding device." Learning this early, even when you are new on the job and feel intimidated, will significantly and positively impact your career-long success. It will help you maintain authenticity and later on, integrate work and life.

When Jodi worked for a large consulting firm, her manager asked her to rummage through the client's files. The idea was to see if there was any useful information that her manager could use to sell more services. It felt horrible. Jodi knew it wasn't right, but she agreed to do it. The next day, the client asked her if she had done it. She readily admitted it and was so relieved to have been caught. Had she instead stepped back and thought about the worst-case scenario, she might have realized she would be caught. The reality was that Jodi had built such a strong relationship with this client that all she needed to do was ask him questions. There was no need at all to rummage for secret information that frankly didn't even exist. As a result, Jodi started to learn to say "No" when pressed to do something inauthentic.

Courtney, a thirty-five-year-old Leadership Coach, learned this because she was clear on what she didn't want. She didn't want to work in Human Resources. She preferred a role in leadership development. When she was offered a job that didn't look like this, she moved on.

Another time, she asked for a part-time position and was told she would need to work twenty hours onsite and still answer emails and phone calls on her own time. She called them on it and said she would not work unpaid hours, so they made a better arrangement.

It's by pushing back, not aggressively, but by clearly knowing what you want and speaking directly and plainly that enables you to articulate your needs to others. Sometimes, it's just a matter of naming it, instead of letting things go unsaid. For example: "So, you are asking us to schedule our cross-country flights on Sunday so our team will look more committed. Is that because someone suspects we have a commitment problem? Can we address that issue instead of perpetuating the myth that giving up a day off will make us better workers?" Sharing and confirming expectations enables both parties to understand what is necessary to achieve a given goal.

As another example, a woman might be willing to help a peer complete a task, training the person so that next time, the peer is capable of completing the task independently. Then when asked again, she can clearly set her boundaries so she doesn't become the peer's permanent help. She can state respectfully and clearly: "I cannot help you with that task today because it's affecting my ability to meet my deadlines." If this is the first time she's held her boundaries, she may get pushback: An audible sigh, talking behind her back, or even stating out loud that she isn't a team player. However, this can be managed by calling out the pushback, again by speaking directly and plainly. By doing this, women actually assertively and fairly bring *all* parties, including themselves, to the negotiating table.

Collaboration is an aptitude increasingly required in today's workplaces. However, collaboration is not possible if women are unclear about what they need or are unwilling to ask for it. Without including their interests, as well as those of the other parties, negotiations become win-lose. To make them win-win, women need to **ask for what they**

need. Our interviewees said that they had to learn through experience that men ask for what they need and consequently get what they ask for more often. According to Babcock and Laschever, in *Women Don't Ask: Negotiation and the Gender Divide*, this starts from the very first negotiation for salary out of college. Men ask for and get, on average, 7.4 percent more than women. Over a lifetime, with identical 3 percent annual increases, and not even considering promotions, this can cost a woman who started her first job at $25,000 per year approximately $568,834 of lifetime earnings. This is a huge cost for failing to negotiate once. When promotions are layered in, this problem compounds and the amount of earnings left on the table can be in the millions.

Many of the women we interviewed expected that their hard work would be seen and recognized and they would be rewarded fairly without having to ask for it. Why don't women like to ask for what women need? Babcock and Laschever think it is because women learn early that, "Nice girls don't ask," and that doing so will generate a negative reaction from people. Not only will they not get what they want, but also they may no longer be liked. Our interviewees found countless times that by not asking, they didn't get what they wanted. They were not spontaneously recognized: They were surpassed by their male peers who asked. In our model, when the Feminine Filter ideals are removed, women can change this mindset for themselves. When being liked is replaced with being authentic, women can be more confident in expressing their needs.

At first, asking for compensation can feel very scary. Here's another way to think about it that might help. In the case of compensation, it doesn't do the company any good in the long term to underpay employees because it sets up a weak and unsustainable business model. Further, it exposes the organization to risk when the employee inevitably leaves and it needs to go to the open market for a replacement.

Finance Manager Aileen, thirty-four, took a risk and asked for what she wanted in a job interview so she could achieve a better work/family balance. "I have never been a seller in interviews. In this job interview, I wanted to be sold. I was asking the hiring manager to prove himself to me. I asked a lot of questions so I could negotiate a work/life balance. It turns out the hiring manager is a family man. He feels the job is important, but his family is not replaceable. I interviewed while pregnant and I told him. He responded 'Okay, we can work around that.'"

Think about it this way: What's the worst that can happen? That the request is denied? A denial is not a personal rejection or the end of the world, but just an opportunity to practice bringing yourself into the equation. A denial is not failure. Quite the opposite—you have succeeded in letting them know you have the capacity and self-esteem to ask for what you need. Moreover, you have put them on notice that you are an "asker," so they will have a hard time overlooking you in the future.

Another element of this skill is **self-promotion**. While it is tempting to wait for others to recognize your work and help you identify career opportunities, this is the slower, less effective route to getting what you need. At the end of the day, it's your responsibility to lead the discussion about your own career path and to let others know what you can contribute. What results do you deliver that contribute to the benefit of the organization? It also is less mature to expect others to notice your performance, rather than taking responsibility for letting others know how you view it. Hospital Administrator Jamie, fifty-six, notes, "I don't have people knocking down my door to make them a director, and I would never have knocked on my manager's door and said I would want to be a director." But what could Jamie or her employees have done if they had promoted themselves? How far could they have gone? Work is not a beauty contest where women showcase their wares in front of everyone and the judges choose the winner. Generally, most managers want promotion decisions to be easy and obvious. Women need to drop their desire to be picked and instead pick themselves.

HOW I PROMOTED MYSELF

"When I look back on my career, I realize I should have been promoted sooner based on the work I was accomplishing and based on others in the organization with similar jobs who were men. I remember being devastated when yet again I wasn't promoted. I remember someone asking me, 'Why don't you talk to your boss?' I replied that I shouldn't have to ask him. They should just recognize it. And I believed it to my core. You should appreciate me so much, you should recognize it. So later on, when it came time, my boss asked me, 'Do you want to work over here in the subsidiary?' I went back and thought about it and acted more like a guy: I did some research, got the data, and decided, 'Yes, I want to work there. I'd be invaluable and you need me, and here is the job I suggest you give to me.' I made myself an Associate VP. He agreed."
— *Glenda, VP Product Management, forty-three*

It's important to understand the difference between self-promotion and bragging. Many women have witnessed others bragging about their accomplishments and therefore disparage the process completely. Instead, you can find the line that is comfortable for you. There are many ways to approach it:

- Send quarterly emails or schedule in-person meetings with your boss to discuss goals you have met.
- Hold regular calls to go over milestones on projects.
- Schedule regular meetings with key people across the organization to update them on what you and your group are working on so they understand how it impacts them.

Make sure you put the self-promotion in terms of the company's interest. Talk about how much value you have added, not what tasks you have completed. Think about what is in it for them.

Another step to bringing yourself into the equation is putting your **self-care** needs on an equal footing as taking care of others, your job, and your other tasks. This is probably most difficult to do early in your career because often women then have good health, lots of energy, and work can be really fun. But the consequences of suppressing self-care are cumulative and can derail you in later career stages, particularly as aspects of life and work change. Training yourself to eat at evenly measured times during the day, taking time for exercise, attending that annual physical, and developing meditative routines to boost your spirit are all extremely important.

MAKE AN APPOINTMENT WITH YOURSELF

"I schedule my workouts like any other meeting. If a client needs me urgently or I have to change, I will, but then I try to reschedule the workout just as I would a meeting. That way, I still get three workouts per week, but the day might switch around. When things are really stressful, these workouts are what save me. I'm always tempted to cut them short, but having the space carved out on my schedule really helps me stick to it."
— *Felicity, Business Consultant, forty-two*

Ironically, another way to stay healthy is to make friends at work. A twenty-year study by Sparks *et al* on the effects of long work hours on health found having strong peer social support was positively related to lower morbidity and disease risks. Another study by Karline *et al* on workplace support found making friends in the workplace is linked to lower blood pressure and a decreased risk of cardiovascular disease.

Bringing yourself into the equation is not selfish; it's responsible. Having a strong sense of self will allow you to live a full life of your own, defying instead of succumbing to external Feminine Filter ideals.

3. Develop self-awareness

The power of this stage is that most women are still comfortable and open to learning new things. You can harness this to turn the microscope inward. By developing insights into yourself early in your career, you can more easily see and resist the Feminine Filter, enabling yourself to live The Orange Line across your career.

First, you can learn to comfortably **solicit feedback.** Feedback enables you to learn more about yourself because you see how others perceive you. For example, when Elaine, Corporate Lawyer, thirty-five, was first deciding what kind of law to specialize in, a supervisor gave her good feedback about her strengths that directed the rest of her career. He was able to guide her based on his observations of her abilities and challenges. Just to clarify, asking for feedback is not soliciting external judgment ("You are so . . ."). Rather it is gathering useful self-knowledge ("I have noticed that when you . . .").

You need to ensure you are asking people who have a real stake in your success and are also willing to be honest with you. Effective feedback is not valuable if it just reinforces your assumptions. Identify people who will give you specific, substantive feedback, such as, "When you are in meetings, I would like to hear more from you. When you say something, it changes the course of the decision." Moreover, if you are hearing similar feedback from multiple sources, it is likely true and something to consider.

Another element is to **conduct a self-assessment** to help understand your strengths and identify your assets. According to Meg Jay, author of *The Defining Decade: Why Your Twenties Matter—and How to Make the Most of Them Now*, we do this so we can develop our, "identity capital and our collection of personal assets." Jay talks about how "identity capital" is built over time by developing a currency of adult life—the value of how you make a difference to your organization and the people around you. Jill, fifty, a Non-Profit Consultant, started out in teaching but didn't like the constraints of the public school environment. She started with a nonprofit and each stage of the way, she built identity capital—as a Fundraiser, as a Program Manager, as a leader, and as a Career Counselor. Later in her career, she was able to parlay this into consulting work for nonprofits in a variety of disciplines. Figure out what you're good at by noticing others' responses and the outcomes you have created.

You need to find objective ways to measure your performance so you can establish for yourself an honest and accurate assessment of how you are doing, helping you to manage how you are being judged by others.

Reflection and analysis is a lifelong, regular process. Paying attention to what you learn as you change roles and jobs helps you figure out what's important to you and how to have an impact. Business Owner Deanna, twenty-four, had a degree in finance and found her dream job working on Wall Street—"the kind of job that undergrads drool over. The money, the prestige, and the mega hours." What she hadn't counted on were "the drugs, the 'greasiness' and grit, and the shallow decision making." She walked in on her first day on the floor. There were one hundred people each with three computers in front of them. One trader shouts to another, "What are you going to do?" and the first trader sells $1 million in shares for no reason. To her, it felt like a soul- less game. "This is not a world I want to be in." Once she reflected on her goals and analyzed her results to date, she realized she had taken the wrong path. She quit and decided instead to start a business.

This check-in can also happen in minutes. Let's say you are making a presentation to a senior leadership team. Before, during, and after the task, you can check in with yourself. How did you feel? Of course you were nervous, but how much of it was because it was a new task? How much because you weren't confident or well prepared? Which aspects did you enjoy? You can review these mini-questions without a lot of work or fanfare. Based on the check-in, you can adapt your next step. You may learn you need to practice more or spend more time research-ing data in anticipation of questions. You may want to hire a speaking coach to increase your confidence. Or you may have found it easier than you thought. You may also decide that you don't have enough information from this first-time event so you may want to do it again before fully assessing it. Almost everyone learns through experimenta-tion. Each time you push your boundaries—face your fear and do it anyway—you learn something more about yourself and it gets easier. It's only fear, remember, not reality.

Reflection allows you to focus on areas you need to improve, or move yourself out of situations that drain your energy and spirit. You can also recognize when something is of your own making and decide to change yourself. You can delay decisions that could have a long-term impact when you are self-aware enough to recognize your own inter-nal anxiety. For example, Madison, IT Manager, forty-two, had signifi-cant performance anxiety in her twenties. She lived most of her days in a high-stress environment. Eventually, she couldn't take it anymore and chose to go to grad school. Had she dealt with it earlier, life and ca-reer would have been much easier. She may not have chosen the same path. Billie, Business Owner, forty-three, was, "deeply in denial about my anxiety earlier in my career." She suffered a lot and it took her years to figure out how to deal with her emotions and anxiety. But eventu-ally, because she learned how to deal with her feelings, she's been able to achieve, "infinitely more than I thought was possible." What these women experienced is very normal during the Green Start.

Reflection can also help you determine whether you are taking things personally that aren't about you. When Kelly was in the Green Start, she was especially sensitive to what others thought and would inter-nalize everything. But as she got older, she realized that most of the time, people are pushing outwards to cover their own insecurities. It's like the child who thinks that when she walks into a room, everyone is looking at her and criticizing what she is wearing when all they really are doing is hoping nobody is noticing what they are wearing. Managers bully when they are insecure about their own status. Peers bully when they think they are falling behind you. Subordinates bully when they are covering up failures. Reflection can help you see which aspects of someone's behavior toward you have nothing to do with you.

As you understand more deeply who you are, you can **create your own unique self-development plan**. You can be conscious about taking your career or life to another level. For example, Director of Operations, Irene, twenty-five, would, "sometimes work fifty to seventy hours per week." She realized, "I was starting to lose energy because I hadn't spent enough of my time doing what I liked." So she decided to implement what she calls "burn-out prevention." First, she negotiated an eight week sabbatical. Next, she created a plan where every weekend, she does something active: traveling or hiking in the mountains.

Your plan sets out clear self-development goals: Maybe it's getting a post-graduate degree, earning a promotion, getting into shape, learning to speak up more, moving to another state, or spending more time with friends. Regardless of the goal, the idea is to concretely set out a plan, including tasks, timelines, and importantly, an objective measurement of success.

4. Build a support system

The most successful Orange Line women realize they cannot operate in a vacuum or do everything themselves. Building a support system enables you to focus your time and energy on the areas that are critical for your success and let go of those areas that don't serve you. Senior leaders and business owners have to learn this skill because their time is too tight to possibly finish all tasks. The earlier you learn this, the sooner you will become a senior leader yourself. Whether it's administrative tasks such as figuring out how to enter expense reports into the system, ordering lunch, or organizing events, women often accept responsibility instead of delegating to others. Women may even let guilt decide that they "should" do these tasks when others "feign" incompetence. It's at this stage that women learn the benefit of support.

The first element in developing a support system for yourself is to **acknowledge you need help.** You may get a certain satisfaction in doing things for yourself and feel you control quality better by owning the task fully. However, this approach only teaches you to keep holding on, even as your responsibilities and workload broaden. Eventually, most women find they don't actually have the time or creative energy anymore to get it all done. This is where they unravel. Further, it teaches others that they can freely keep adding to your pile. Doing everything yourself limits the creative input and experience others bring to the table. It's not a sign of weakness to admit you need help; instead, it's a sign of wisdom and leadership. All of our interviewees who are senior leaders spoke about needing help to accomplish their work and home tasks.

Next, you need to **figure out exactly what help you need**. As soon as you rise above a certain administrative level where you are paid to do menial tasks, you should consider shedding most time-consuming activities that waste your time and creative energy without contributing positively to your results—both at home and at work. This will help you preserve those things that make you valuable—like your knowledge, experience, and higher-level capabilities. Sure, you might be able to organize the office party or clean your home better than anyone else, but when you do these things, you divert your resources from more valuable and important activities. Brenda, forty, an overworked and often overwhelmed Senior Account Executive with a major technology company, recently found herself organizing side trips for her clients to take during the upcoming industry conference. She was on the phone and Internet for many hours in advance setting up golf trips, fishing excursions, and securing restaurant reservations. When asked why she didn't give these tasks to someone else, Brenda claimed she wanted to make sure these things were done correctly for her customers.

Whether the resource exists in the organization or not, there is likely someone better positioned for the task, Brenda was not aware it might be sub-optimal to spend time doing this and had no intention of asking anyone for help. Instead, she will likely stay late to finish her work, cutting into her own personal time, to do these tasks. What could Brenda have done? She could have hired someone part time to help her, she could have outsourced the work to a concierge service that many companies offer as an employee benefit, or she could have talked to her company about creating a new role, so that someone else could do this task. She could even have worked with other teams to see if they needed similar tasks done. Forty-four-year-old, Sales Engineer Lela didn't learn this lesson until she became a mother, but realizes she could have learned it much earlier: "There came a point I realized I didn't have to be the smartest person to get my job done. I just needed to know the right people." Once she figured out she could leverage other people to get more done, she tapped this resource quite successfully.

It then becomes a matter of **figuring out to whom you can delegate**. Cross-organizational relationships enable you to delegate and get support even if you have no direct employees. You can trade tasks or pool resources to share hired help. You can be creative here. Even if you don't have any employees, you can delegate work tasks to peers, interns, and even your boss. Twenty-three-year-old Accountant Adelaide's recent job change meant, "I'm more stressed because I don't have the support. At my old job, there were a lot of staff I could delegate to, but I work with so many managers for such short periods of time, I haven't built rapport and am in between. I am isolated for now."

HOW TO PICK THE RIGHT TEAM

"The hardest part is finding the right person to delegate to. For example, we have our Facebook page and I had to find the right people to help me with that. I needed people who were compassionate, could communicate and knew if something was 'hot' and had that warm personality that you need in social media. So I have people in two other departments to help me. I had to find people who could think like me—whom I could trust with this delicate work. It's identifying the right person. You have to pick your team. I have staff who take care of the website. They're not writers so I had to reach out to find people outside of the group, but that's part of the culture. If someone calls you and asks for help, you do it because we're all short staffed. Give and take. There are dozens of people who can call me or I call them and get help." — *Priscilla, Marketing Director, forty-nine*

Finally, to delegate effectively, you need to **manage the work**. It is not enough to get the task off your plate or pay someone to do things for you; you need to manage them. This is where a woman often gets frustrated. She hires a housekeeper who scratches the floor so she insists it is impossible to get help to her standards. She asks someone to copy a bunch of presentations for her and then gets called out in a meeting for having the slides out of order; so she decides the only way to get it right is to do it herself. Like most things, it takes years of practice before anyone becomes a really good manager, and even then, things will not be perfect.

Managing help requires communicating clear expectations up front. You also need to invest in a training period, where demonstration and close supervision can lead to higher quality outcomes, and monitor results, providing clear and honest feedback. This process can feel awkward and uncomfortable. Women may feel they don't have any time to train someone else. They may be afraid they won't be liked if they provide clear and direct communication. Many women do not enjoy telling others what to do, especially when they first become managers. By looking at this process as a short-term investment for your long-term benefit, you can work to overcome your hesitancy.

One idea is to let people know that this is the first time you've had to manage others and you don't exactly feel comfortable telling them what to do. Respectfully, ask them how they think you should word things, how they think you should give them negative feedback, and how they think you should reward them when things go well. Humility can go a long way here: Everyone probably knows you're not an experienced manager so pretending to be one will come across as inauthentic and arrogant. By sharing your apprenticeship with the people you manage, you allow yourself to practice in a safer, more supportive environment. With practice you will get better. It may also help to think of good management and clear, honest communication as a gift of fairness given to the people who support you.

Figuring out that you need help, what specific support you require, who can support you, and how to manage them is critical to finding career success. In essence, you need to practice not "doing it all" yourself.

5. Get comfortable operating in imperfection

Let's face it: Life is full of mistakes, omissions, confusion, and sub-ideal events. Nothing is perfect. But when the Feminine Filter screams to women to look good and follow the rules to get their rewards, they somehow internalize this as a need to be perfect. Early in a woman's career, she may think there is a perfect job out there for her and she needs to strive to find it. She may think there are perfect career paths as well. She probably worked hard to be perfect in high school so she could get to the right schools to be set up for the right job to launch the right career. This may have caused her to avoid interesting or challenging courses where she might not have scored top grades. It may have prevented her from traveling or experimenting with different jobs because she didn't want to mess up her résumé. Or, it could have affected her confidence as she failed to live up to these impossible standards. Her life may have already been less whole because of the quest for perfection. By needing to be perfect at her job in the workplace, she is limiting her long-term career similarly.

So your first step in developing this skill is **acceptance**. Life usually doesn't work in a straight line. Many of the women interviewed for this book aren't following the career path they started out in. The point is not to have *the* answer as if there is only one, or to think you are abnormal if you don't follow a pre-set path. The point is to persevere and experiment so you can figure out how to find work that adds value to your life. This means allowing yourself to make mistakes and do some things imperfectly. The key is knowing what really matters. Some women were great students because they figured out early on that to be successful in school, they need to follow the rules: "Be good—sit still, raise your hand, write neatly, and stay well organized, do your homework, and regurgitate back what the teacher said." And then real life and navigating a career required a whole new set of abilities to be successful, instead of problems to be solved in ninety minutes. Some women did better in the school environment because at work they may still be waiting for someone to tell them the rules. In place of rules, many women need to recognize that they need to figure it out and accept that perfection is not attainable. But a full, rich life is.

Once you have accepted the reality of imperfection, you can **embrace imperfection** and take advantage of it. What does that mean? When the impossible standard of perfection is removed and you accept that the outcome will be less than perfect, you can feel more comfortable experimenting and taking risks. You can push the envelope a bit more. Kelly was told by her boss, "If all I see is you doing things perfectly, then I can't trust you because I assume you are not pushing hard, taking risks, or optimizing your business. By avoiding mistakes, you are telling me that you are leaving opportunities untested and untapped. That's not what good leaders are made of." By embracing imperfection, you learn and grow.

Before changing careers, Researcher Meagan, fifty-six, was a Sports Reporter covering typically all-male athletes. Most Sports Reporters at the time got their best interviews in the locker room after a game. She wasn't allowed in the locker room. But instead of fretting and letting it stop her, she waited until the players and coaches left the locker room before making her interview request. They respected her for that and started giving her private interviews. So instead of fighting the other reporters for the mass story, she got the intimate story, one on one.

How can a woman embrace imperfection? She can get perspective and figure out what is good enough. This may seem counter-intuitive to A-type personalities who are used to overachieving everything. You may feel you would rather fall short of a goal of perfection than a goal of less-than-perfect because the end result is further ahead. But in reality, "great" results are most often not "perfect" results. 3M developed sticky notes when they were trying for a super-sticky adhesive. By perfectionism standards, they failed. In perspective, though, they achieved a fantastic success. Lots of startup companies do business in less than perfect surroundings with less than perfect support systems. The founders of Google annoyed each other when they first met, but their banter led to huge success. In innovative companies, mistakes are not just allowed, but sought after. Jeffrey Pfeffer, in *How Companies Get Smarter: Taking Chances and Making Mistakes*, writes that mistakes suggest that people are experimenting and the creative edge is being pushed.

LAUGH AT YOURSELF

"I was making my first major presentation for a client at my consult-ing firm. I was given the most boring part of the presentation, but I was so nervous, I almost threw up in the bathroom. In the middle of the presentation, I garbled my words trying to say 'master billing sheet' and instead said 'masturbate.' I was mortified, but in reality, I just woke up a few members of the audience who had been sleeping. We all had a good laugh after that one!" — *Jodi*

Once you have accepted that imperfection is the norm and that you can thrive in that environment, next you can **plan for it**. You can put backup systems in place so you can avoid panic and help yourself feel better when the inevitable imperfection occurs. The simple task of anticipating potential reactions can enable you to respond more ra-tionally. Project Director, Gina, fifty-one, recognized that she "can get worked up, so I like to prepare ahead for a difficult meeting. I try to always expect the unexpected because someone is going to do some-thing to throw you. I think, well, here it is. Then I can recover more quickly."

Women hear that the Green Start is supposed to the best time of their life, but as expert Jay notes, "They are the most uncertain and some of the most difficult years of life." If women start their careers expecting imperfection, they are much more likely to enjoy this time of learning and collecting their identity capital. Jay also notes that it's rare that someone realizes her life's work in their twenties; so instead of stress-ing about perfection, why not just jump in and try things out!

6. Expand your universe

Being conscious of how you build your community and expand your universe makes a difference. You can widen the breadth of your potential and realize opportunities you might otherwise have missed.

The first element of this is to **seek out people who will challenge you** and push you forward. In addition to the typical approach of finding a mentor at work, you also need to find people closer to home who are more likely to influence you, such as close friends or a spouse. If you hang around with people who think work is just a paycheck and that organizations will just exploit you until you quit, this will ultimately limit your thinking and your universe of opportunities. Further, if you only associate with people who are just like you, you will miss out on the diversity of ideas you would gain from others.

CHOOSE YOUR SPOUSE WELL

Choosing a spouse may be one of the single most important relation-ships for expanding your universe. Most of the women we interviewed either spoke highly of their spouse, "He's amazing, I couldn't do it without him," or talked about how they had made the wrong choice. It was always in the context of the level of support they provided—not financial, but emotional and logistical support—support that enabled them to grow and take opportunities. Women often make the deci-sion about the person they marry early in life, long before they know who they are. They also unrealistically think they can change people to become something they are not. Researcher Lindsey, fifty-one, said she wished she'd continued graduate school, delayed marriage, and even counsels her daughter not to marry because of her negative marriage experience. Another interviewee found her husband's Femi-nine Filter-inspired views limiting to her career progress because he did nothing to help on the domestic front. If she could go back, Mar-keting Manager, Gabriela, forty-four, said, "I would've not felt pressure to get married and have babies. I wanted to travel, but my parents wanted me to work. When you are young, you need to expand and try out what you want to do. Take risks." Lily, Senior Programs Director, forty-eight, advised, "It's important for your partner to view your career as equal to his. You need to have a conversation about where you want to be in ten to twenty years, and if you are prepared to give each other time away from the kids and household chores. I have been incredibly fortunate to have a partner in the same career field who understands what I do and shares equally in home and child-raising responsibilities. It's important to know how we each see ourselves in ten years and that we both have the same outlook." This decision is viewed by our interviewees as critical. Consulting Principal Marsha, fifty-three, notes, "Pick your husband wisely."

Peer and professional relationships also open up opportunities for career success. Whether coworkers, former college classmates, suppliers, or clients, peer relationships can expose you to new ways of thinking. You can expand this through networking, but many women don't like the idea of traditional networking. Going to an event to gather business cards and ask people for help seems shallow and impersonal to many of them. And it is. But Candy Deemer, in her book *Dancing on the Glass Ceiling*, has reframed networking as sharing our gifts, contacts, and resources with people who need them. As women, this may make it much easier and more authentic-feeling to network because it's about sharing ourselves. When you look at networking as relationship building, now it can become a positive experience. You also can do this outside of "networking events." If you meet people on a plane or in a coffee shop, now you can have a conversation with them, asking questions about their work, and seeing what you can do to help them in some way. It's a chance to give something, rather than ask someone for something. And once you have helped others, they stay in your contact list ready and hopeful that you will need help from them someday.

Further, staying connected to peers over time builds a strong network. Building strong relationships with your peers early on grows these relationships as peers move up the ladder. In ten-plus years, suddenly your peers are in managerial positions and become possible work connections if you need them. Corporate Lawyer Elaine, thirty-five, said, "Now I like and understand networking more, but back then, I found it distasteful." Fortunately, she kept building anyway. You get better at networking just through practice. This means supporting other women, too, instead of cutting them down. You can feel good about investing time in these relationships because they usually pay off down the road. You need these relationships inside and outside of work as well.

The second element of expanding the universe is to **think bigger,** being open to possibilities. Nonprofit Senior Executive Maya, fifty-six, was told by a friend, "There is this organization looking for an Executive Director. You should apply." So she went home and got onto to the company's website. "It was the last day to apply, and it was 10 p.m. I called some of my friends. They told me I had to do it. One of my friends said, 'You hesitate because you think you want to do an A+ job, but just do it. Whatever you do will be good enough.' So, I did it. Later the company called me and said, 'We think you're an ideal candidate. Could you put together your package?' I got through the extensive rounds of interviews. Then, while my husband and I were on vacation, they called back. The phone call dropped all the time. But I got the job."

Technology Salesperson Jessica, forty-five, finds she doesn't "run into a lot of women because I'm in technology. The ones I run into are in marketing or HR, relegated to a 'pink collar' track [women-dominated support roles such as Human Resources and Marketing]. The best way to be successful is to achieve respect and that comes from P&L [profit and loss] responsibility or bringing money into the company. Most jobs women have take money from the company. It helps if you can tell someone, 'I've done sales' or 'closed a deal.'" Jessica makes a great point: You can think beyond traditional female roles in the company that are tucked away in the back office to find jobs such as Sales and Business Development that are more visible and make more of a difference to the company's bottom line.

The third element is to proactively **expose yourself to something new**. Probably the best way to do this is through travel. And while you probably feel at this point in your career that you have the least amount of time or money for travel, this is not necessarily true. The Green Start may actually be the best opportunity for travel because it is often before women have added responsibilities like a family or mortgage. Other ways to experience new things include taking on new projects at work, signing up for courses, joining clubs, reading, and even volunteering.

Many of our interviewees used this time to get their masters degree or explore other professional interests. Many did this within their job. Accountant Kaylee, thirty-four, "wanted to do more things professionally. At work, I had some freedom to come up with projects I wanted to do like run orientation, and the company was very receptive. One of the older guys told me this is the stuff that keeps a job interesting. I also reached out to do training in my field for other companies. I would take days off and teach for them on a contract basis. Eventually I realized that I wanted more time to do some personal travel, which I did. After that, I returned to school to get my MBA. Now I leave my work on time, I take courses, and I do other things that are of interest to me. I am always building different skills even though I don't know what I want to do next. I do know that my original decision to do a wider variety of things allowed me to morph rather than become pigeon-holed."

Senior Marketing Associate Leona, thirty-three, experimented with a variety of roles in her large organization to allow her to find new opportunities and explore her interests. She finally found a role she enjoys. "It's a small group of project managers from a number of countries. I work on conferences, events, and relationship-building both internally and externally. There is a lot of funding in this area, and it's a great opportunity. I'm now going in the direction I want, using my language skills, and I'm willing to stay here for a while." However, she's still stretching. "I'm not going to just sit down. I still want to see what else is out there. I don't want to miss the boat. It's easy to get comfortable. A lot of people who work here have been here since their undergrad years. I'm not going to move just to move, but I'm going to keep moving forward."

As you expose yourself to new ideas and experiences, you can use them in your personal and professional decision-making. Options abound because you have more ideas to tap into. You expand the possibilities naturally because you've seen more. At work, this helps you be someone to whom others come for strategies. In your career, you are less likely to get stuck because you've practiced thinking bigger and it comes naturally to you.

The fourth element is to **take a big risk** so you can face your fears. This doesn't have to be something dramatic or death defying like skydiving, just something that makes your stomach hurt a little bit. For some, it might be public speaking or, more dramatically, moving abroad. For others, it could be practicing Orange Line Skills including living with imperfection or delegating something and letting it go. One interviewee pitched one of her client's businesses to a room full of venture capitalists. She said it was the scariest thing she had ever done, but now she would do it again in a heartbeat. Doing so expanded her universe.

Jill, non-profit Consultant, now fifty, didn't like her first job out of college. She took a big risk and moved out of the country. This enabled her to parlay her initial risk into a career in outdoorsy organizations. Senior VP Tamara, now fifty-nine, took a risk and applied to a top graduate school—and got in—thus launching her career. Our interviewees moved states, countries, took different and new jobs, and just experimented. College Career Counselor Portia, thirty-two, noticed, "As I got more comfortable, I would push myself more to get out and to take more risks and try new things as opposed to just staying where I was."

You can get comfortable taking risks and become adept at identifying which risks will help propel you forward and which are unlikely to yield the outcomes you are seeking. One caveat though: Risks are called risk because there is a probability of failure.

The first time Kelly applied to business school, she didn't get in, but the application process put her in the path of a new mentor and resulted in a lucrative promotion. When she finally attended business school years later, she got much more out of the program because of her executive experience. Failures don't always turn out this well, but no matter what the outcome, you usually learn something from failure. You can expand and grow your Orange Line life by purposefully exposing yourself to new people, ideas, and experiences that challenge you and propel you forward.

Conclusion

This stage is where you can set yourself up well for Orange Line living and tackle the Feminine Filter before you get too entrenched in its bad habits. You can leverage your skills and experience and expand your universe to reach the goals you want to achieve. You can learn to work for yourself, not necessarily in terms of starting your own business, but in realizing that what you want is possible. You can give yourself space, determine your values, and set boundaries at work and in your relationships. You are learning to ask for what you need and recognizing that no manager or company is going to give you a job, promotion, or the ideal salary simply because you want it. You need to decide what you want, make a concrete career plan, work toward achieving it, and let others know when you have delivered results. At this stage in your career, it's your job to make your career and your *métier* important in your life.

CHAPTER FIVE:
Approaching Burnout

WORK IS EVERYTHING

Cindy is building a business to support her family and realize her professional career goals. But, she says, "There is the financial stress and fear of finding customers, insecurities of not reaching my goals. What if I put my work out there and the cash flow is not what I need it to be and I just can't do it? And And And.

"When I get overwhelmed, I keep working—I work all the time. Part of it is I believe my work is the answer for everything. My business is going to build my career and give me the financial resources to support my family. I have to remind myself that, yes, I need to work to reach my goals, but working all the time is also a defense mechanism to help me avoid dealing with the fears and stresses.

"Sometimes, when I realize how close to the edge I am, the instability feels overwhelming. I feel out of control. And the frustration—I'm working and working and nothing's happening. No results. It paralyzes my creativity. I feel fatigued.

"One time there was yet another crisis when I couldn't pay a bill. I was completely overwhelmed. There were not enough customers and I couldn't cover my expenses. I was freaking out, really paralyzed.

However hard I was working it was not enough. I wanted to walk away from everything, but I couldn't. I felt claustrophobic, like I was trapped in hell.

"I ended up calling a friend who told me to sit still. She said, 'Sometimes, it sucks and you have to sit in it. Just stop the cycle, just stop. Let the dust settle.' It was not about taking a vacation, it was about sitting still and stopping. It took thirty-six hours of giving myself the space and quiet to calm down. And I really stopped. It was as if I had been on a hamster wheel and I finally got off. Afterward, I did find a way out of my crisis—I asked a client to give me a down payment on her work and she agreed.

"Now I'm working on reframing the role of work in my life. I'm trying to recognize the success and the achievements of work without tying it to all the other goals I have for my life, like feeling fulfilled and happy. If another problem is making me sad, working twelve-hour days isn't going to fix the problem. I'm trying to build boundaries around the role of work in my life and spend time only with people I want to be with.

"I also prioritize sleep. Rest. If I'm tired, I'm tired. It's just like if I'm hungry, I'm going to eat. I stopped maintaining a certain persona that I didn't feel obligated to anymore.

"Sometimes, when I feel really burdened and that things are unfair, I remind myself that I chose this life. Yes, the circumstances can sometimes be really difficult, but I want it all and I choose it. I accept this life. What would I take out? Nothing. I like it all. It doesn't matter if it's not perfect. This is what I chose." — *Cindy, Consultant, thirty-five*

We found a large number of our interviewees had experienced one or more periods in their careers when they were approaching burnout. Efforts to rise in their careers at the expense of the other parts of their lives had started to take its toll. Stress levels were highly elevated. Their ability to perform at work was compromised. They began to tire. And, in most cases, just as their endurance was stretched to the limit, something broke. It wasn't even something big, just the proverbial straw that broke the camel's back. It's like hitting the big hill at mile twenty of the marathon, when there is still a significant race to run, but you feel like you just can't face another uphill step.

Maybe you have felt this way, too. Change is usually the catalyst for the increased stress. Underlying this is a sense of unfairness and often an inner guilt struggle. Many women can be even more susceptible to the "shoulds" of the Feminine Filter placed upon them by other people. Many women feel as if they are letting everyone down—work, family, friends, themselves—but they feel powerless to improve. Feelings of futility tax instead of feed them just when they need emotional food the most. The temptation to give up work altogether or take a low-stress job, rather than taking a needed day or two off, is probably greatest at this stage.

Burnout usually happens gradually. You don't just wake up one day "burned out." Research suggests there are three phases:

- **Stress arousal**: Your body reacts with stress signals. You are irritable, feel anxious or forgetful and may struggle to concentrate.

- **Energy conservation**: You try to figure out how to conserve your energy doing things that are uncharacteristic. You might be late to work, withdraw from friends, be resentful, or increase caffeine intake.

- **Exhaustion**: Your body starts to show the signs of the prolonged stress. You may get digestive problems, fatigue, insomnia, or even feel you're unable to get up and go to work.

Many of our interviewees described similar phases of exhaustive stress. Business Owner Lori, forty-two, reached a point when she was totally overworked, physically and emotionally taxed, and even uncharacteristically disengaged with people, turning them off so she didn't need to deal with them anymore. Things were no longer exciting; life became a chore. She experienced anxiety, confusion, and an atypical inability to be decisive. She describes a pivotal moment when "I'm walking down the street and I'm clicking along in my heels with an armload of papers—the last version of a brochure for an important client—and I'm barking out orders to a designer on my cell phone. I came into my office, chucked the pile of papers and files into my inbox, and the pile in my inbox suddenly crumbled under the weight of it all and papers were strewn all over the office. I burst into tears—everything seemed to unravel. It was a metaphor for my life at that stage. I just couldn't bring myself to pick it up again." These are people who previously loved their work and were defined by it, but as pressures mounted to unsustainable levels, their passions turned from thrilling to threatening.

What causes burnout? Some of the stressors that pose pressure are external: ubiquitous technology, 24/7 availability, the increased pace of change, bad economic conditions, global competition, constant reorganization, corporate expectations and cultural norms. Interviewees describe getting calls while on maternity leave, regularly being expected to travel on business on evenings and weekends, and being penalized for stopping or taking breaks. Exciting projects and promotions as well as rewards and recognition seem to go to those who work through illness and stay late at the office. Those who pushed back or took medical leave often ended up laid off or sidelined. Career-track employees are expected to avoid "work-life" balance programs if they want to progress. Commitment is still demonstrated by "butts in seats" and "face time," rather than results. A bad economy gives employers just the right amount of "fear power" to get employees to prove over and over again that they really truly want their jobs.

However, women can only blame the world for so long: Much of their stress is actually *internal, self-imposed,* a product of their own making. It stems from precisely the things that have made them successful to date: Their perfectionism standard, their ability to handle a large amount of responsibility, their self-motivation and conscientiousness. Because women in this stage spend a large proportion of their time working and have achieved rewards and recognition for this work, they are highly invested in their jobs and tend to think of work as being disproportionately important in their lives. This can contribute to a loss of perspective so intense that it fosters insecurity. Sometimes, this leads to situations where their values are misaligned or the inappropriate expectations of others are tolerated. The job becomes everything and the fear of losing it becomes pervasive.

Some stressors, like the ones at home, have external and internal components. The sheer time required to maintain relationships with friends and a spouse, as well as be a parent, a care-giver, take care of the home, and perhaps have a meaningful hobby can be enormous. Plus, often women have little control over when and where they will be needed. Children don't get sick at convenient times. Friends call for help just when time is limited. Schools don't plan their in-service days around parents' work calendars. But those stressors exist for everyone, everywhere, including men. In addition to an unbending external environment, some women choose to engage in labor-intensive household activities based on an image of the ideal woman. They may choose to do all the nightly cooking or sew their children's Halloween costumes. Some enroll in an MBA, remodel the house, and take on a promotion simultaneously. Although individually these things may be relaxing, stimulating, or fun, compounded they can drain a woman's energy and drive her to burnout.

Sometimes, it is internalized assumptions that make women's lives difficult. One working woman we spoke to takes on all of the housework plus care of the baby because her husband has a very physical job and "needs to sleep" when he comes home. She is exhausted herself, but feels this is only fair, and she couldn't have it any other way. Carmen, Lawyer, twenty-eight, has rationalized the assumptions differently: "My husband works full time. He doesn't seem to notice if I do work late at night if things are busy. He is an only child so he doesn't always see things that need doing. I need to ask him."

Tense, Anxious, and Overloaded

But doesn't everyone go through this stage? Women may accept that "this is the way things are" and push through, hoping the phase will pass. However, underlying the "busyness" are some potentially career-limiting problems.

- They may fear stopping. Almost everyone has approached burnout at some point in his or her life. What makes it so dangerous for career women is that societal norms and the language inside their heads tell them they have to do all of these things—they can't give anything up. The insecurity about what will happen if work isn't perfect or if we show our human side can fuel self-destructive patterns. A consequence of feeling overwhelmed is wallowing in it and becoming more alarmed by the sensation than is healthy. It's like when a woman lies awake at 2 a.m., going through her interminable to do list, it feels impossible and catastrophic. But at 8 a.m., it feels manageable.

- Long-term health risks. Ironically, while women are in this stage "doing it all," the one area they seem most able to cut back or give up entirely is their own personal well-being. Many women quickly give up workouts, doctor's appointments, and healthy meals, scrambling to complete every task. There are long-term cumulative effects from approaching burnout. A woman becomes the ultimate martyr when she sacrifices her health to look after everybody and everything else. Over time, women in this stage may begin to notice moderate illnesses or signs of bodily wear: infections that linger too long, skeletal or muscular problems, or systemic issues like irritable bowel syndrome. The problem is, it isn't serious until it is serious, and then there is little they can do to turn back the clock. Biologically speaking, cortisol production in women is quite different than in men. Men get a burst of it and then it drops off in a few hours, whereas in women it takes much longer—twelve hours at least to subside.

- They may become work-centric. The problem with approaching burnout is the transition is subtle. It can start out just being a busy period. Incrementally, the "busy periods" get more frequent and closer together, and soon they realize they've played the "it's my busy period" card too often. It is hard, then, to think of a time when things are not busy: "Busy" is the new normal.

- They may make career-limiting decisions. The biggest problem with approaching burnout is the bad decisions women can make when they are wound up. It may be a collection of compounding mistakes that reduces their worth to the organization, or dramatic, shortsighted decisions reached as a result of exacerbation. Examples include ending important relationships, drastic reversals of policy, giving up ground on projects, and quitting altogether.

We suggest if women approach this stage applying Orange Line think-ing and build the six skills we highlighted previously, burnout can be prevented. Here's what those skills look like at this stage:

Skills for Living The Orange Line

1. Recognize when the Feminine Filter is at work

Because under stress, we are more likely to default to old assumptions, this is an important time to recognize when the Feminine Filter is at work, monitor your response, and find your equilibrium.

First **listen for and recognize Filter language** behind widely used and accepted statements. For example, if you hear someone say, "You can't take a vacation now. We can't finish our project if you are gone!" Ini-tially, you may feel flattered that you are needed. But in reality, this assumption suggests you are responsible for taking care of everything. It's also an indicator that you may be enabling others by not giving them the space to learn and grow. Language like this is external pres-sure to adopt these assumptions and live by them. Observing the as-sumptions underneath these statements helps women realize their po-tential negative impact.

The chart below illustrates the common language we heard from wom-en who were approaching burnout. We use it to highlight the Feminine Filter assumptions at play. We then deconstruct and debunk it to reveal the messages that are received and perpetuated with this language. We reframe the language, illustrating Orange Line Principles to open up new possibilities.

APPROACHING BURN-OUT ASSUMPTIONS	DEBUNKING THE ASSUMPTION: WHAT'S REALLY GOING ON	REFRAME
I can't stop now—I have a reputation to uphold and others expect certain things of me. If I stop, people will question whether I can handle all this and am as good as I was made out to be. **Feminine Filter underlying assumption:** I need to be perfect in behavior and appearance at all times, and I'm never good enough.	First, this says you have an unrealistic expectation that you need to be perfect, at everything, all the time. Second, this says you feel insecure about the results you deliver; that you aren't good enough. What people really see is a capable person burning herself out on tasks that don't really matter.	*I am a good person and great at many things. As long as I am doing my best, I don't need to prove myself to anyone. It's okay for some things to be done "well enough" right now. That shows I am mature and capable of prioritizing what really matters.*
I will manage—it is only temporary; I just need to get through this short time. I can rest when I get through this crunch. **Feminine Filter underlying assumption:** I need to be perfect in behavior and appearance at all times.	Crunch periods should be definable project periods of, say two-three weeks at most. Anything longer is more likely a sign that you have taken on too much. Working beyond capacity for too long leads to reduced productivity and burnout. Anxiety can set in when your body and mind are stressed, which adds further pressure and impairs clear thinking.	*I will recognize when I'm asking too much of myself. I accept that I need time to rejuvenate. I can actively take things off my plate and manage my workload.*

APPROACHING BURN-OUT ASSUMPTIONS	DEBUNKING THE ASSUMPTION: WHAT'S REALLY GOING ON	REFRAME
I'm only worthwhile if I'm over-achieving my responsibilities, doing it all, and keeping all the balls in the air, perfectly. **Feminine Filter underlying assumption:** I need to be perfect in behavior and appearance at all times.	You may be overly focused on external measures of your success by doing a lot of things so that you can get recognition. Doing it all indicates you may not be ready yet for leadership because you don't understand how to prioritize, delegate or share work.	*I understand that doing it all doesn't give space for others to learn and grow. I am willing to ask for help and allow for others to learn. I will remember that the only person I can control is me.*
If I just keep everything all together, I'll be taken seriously and get where I want to go. **Feminine Filter underlying assumption:** If I follow the rules, good things will happen.	Often people hide things to either hold onto knowledge and power or avoid scrutiny in the hope they can solve the problem themselves. Ironically, those who show a little vulnerability get respect and support. Doing everything is a really good indicator of someone who is afraid to take risks, unable to draw boundaries, delegate, or prioritize effectively.	*If I recognize that I need help, I can be more open. That will make me more effective as a leader.*

APPROACHING BURN-OUT ASSUMPTIONS	DEBUNKING THE AS-SUMPTION: WHAT'S REALLY GOING ON	REFRAME
All of this is controllable; I just need to work harder to get it under control. **Feminine Filter underlying assumption:** I need to be perfect in behavior and appearance at all times.	The reality is, no one can control everything. Customers will have emergencies, bosses will make mistakes, subordinates will drop balls, and peers will try to take the best projects. Why expend so much effort and emotional energy trying to keep everything and everybody under control?	*I will start to learn how to discern which balls are okay to drop. I will ask myself, so what if this happens?*
If I am indispensable, then they can't possibly get rid of me. **Feminine Filter underlying assumption:** If I follow the rules, good things will happen.	Setting yourself up as a gatekeeper does not necessarily result in job security. Gatekeepers tend to implode when the company realizes that unnecessary blockage or work is being required. Further, it traps you at a lower level because you keep yourself involved in tactical instead of strategic decisions.	*I do not need to be the person who checks a box or has to be indispensable. I will trust that what I am doing is right for the company. I can take responsibility to do my work well and empower others to do theirs.*
If I keep doing more, I will keep getting better results. **Feminine Filter underlying assumption:** My commitment to something is measured by how much time I devote to it.	Up until now, doing more has yielded a good result. But doing more is an inverted U curve. At some point on that curve, doing more results in lower returns. Your job in this stage is figuring out that point.	*If I keep doing more, eventually my productivity will be lower. I can determine where that point exists for me, and how to be confident about stopping when I reach it.*

APPROACHING BURN-OUT ASSUMPTIONS	DEBUNKING THE ASSUMPTION: WHAT'S REALLY GOING ON	REFRAME
If I do everything myself, it will get done right and I can ensure it will be the best possible quality. **Feminine Filter underlying assumption:** I need to be perfect in behavior and appearance at all times.	When you take on all the tasks, you fail to develop others or yourself. You end up doing tasks you might be good at, but do not challenge you or build new skills. Nor do you learn how to delegate and manage others.	*I need to help others deliver high quality work. I need to challenge myself to learn to manage people, which requires making mistakes and letting go.*

Be aware of guilt. Guilt is internal pressure to buy-in to Filter assumptions. When a woman decides to go against the expectations of the assumption, she often feels guilt. For instance, if she goes on vacation she may feel guilt and spend much of the vacation being available by phone, rather than relaxing. This guilt tells her she is pushing against the Feminine Filter's rules. Its effect is to cause her to behave in a way that minimizes the guilt, at her own expense.

By becoming aware of this guilt, you can then start to realize its underlying message. You may be especially vulnerable to guilt when you are overwhelmed, because being tired and stressed depletes energy that could otherwise be used for guilt-management. Notice words like "I just can't," "I should," or "I need/have to." These are indicators that can help you learn to recognize any assumptions guilt is pressuring you to accept.

Next, **observe your behavioral response.** What action did you take? Did you buy-in to the underlying assumption, react out of habit, and take on all the work? Did you spend all week telling your family that you have to get this done, instead of going to the beach? If you are in a busy period at work and a friend suddenly pressures you to give her some attention, do you acquiesce to the request? Did you succumb to guilt? Do you feel resentful, but do it anyway? By becoming aware of the underlying assumption and how you responded, you can start to notice the impact it is having on your life.

In our interviews and research, we saw women behave in ways that enacted the Filter's assumptions. Below we highlight these, describe what happens, and reframe the underlying assumption:

APPROACHING BURN-OUT BEHAVIOR	CONSEQUENCES	FEMININE FILTER ASSUMPTION
Straining relationships. Often when things get busy, women have a tendency to cut back on the amount of time and energy they spend with people. They might email instead of picking up the phone, thinking it faster, more precise, and more expedient. They might also skip informal face-time, or forget to ask people how they are doing before plunging into business. **Bad habit:** Working harder, not smarter.	Underutilizing relationships under-optimizes productivity, even in the short term. Worse, it tends to damage relationships because people don't see you as someone they can learn from or who trusts them. They become less invested in you and your success.	My commitment to something is measured by how much time I devote to it. **Reframe:** *I can build and leverage relationships to meet my goals.*

APPROACHING BURN-OUT BEHAVIOR	CONSEQUENCES	FEMININE FILTER ASSUMPTION
Hiding or denying the problem. Women may think if they don't tell anyone what is going on and keep all of the balls in the air, nobody will know and the problem will go away **Bad habit:** Risk avoidance and over-compensation.	Here, you hurt yourself more because you may be seen as a dishonest, ineffective leader. You also repel prospectively valuable help and resources with this behavior, further harming your effectiveness and efficiency.	I need to be perfect in behavior and appearance at all times. **Reframe:** *I can admit when I am in trouble and ask for help.*
Making something bigger than it is, attributing long-term, negative implications to a small event. Women may "make a mountain out of a molehill" or blame the external environment. They may feel like the grass is greener at a different company, at a different job, at a different career, or with a different spouse. They may reinforce it with language: "I can't do this anymore," or "Something has got to give here." **Bad habit:** Catastrophizing.	You may make bad decisions when in a panic. Divorce, job change, career change, and relocating all may be the "right" decision, but when made during this stage, the decision has a high chance of being the wrong one. In this heightened emotional state, you may struggle to identify options or solutions to the challenge.	I need to be perfect in behavior and appearance at all times. **Reframe:** *I can take a deep breath, step back, and put things into perspective before making decisions.*

APPROACHING BURN-OUT BEHAVIOR	CONSEQUENCES	FEMININE FILTER ASSUMPTION
Maintaining the perfectionism standard while doing it all. We heard women describe it as "spinning plates" or "too many balls in the air and afraid to drop any of them." **Bad habit:** Catastrophizing.	While "doing it all" is a bad habit at any career stage, when approaching burnout it is especially dangerous because the anxiety, frustration, and feelings of failure can exacerbate stress levels and further diminish productivity at a time when you are most vulnerable.	I need to be perfect in behavior and appearance at all times. **Reframe:** *I can prioritize what needs to be done well.*
Prioritizing the tasks that are visible to others to get credit for the hard work. **Bad habit:** Seeking external validation	While you may get many short-term tasks done and appear to others to be working hard, you may fail to complete the items that enable you to achieve desired results. Your burnout could increase and your relationships may suffer.	I am not good enough. **Reframe:** *I am confident in doing what I know is right, regardless of how it looks.*

The next step is to **challenge the assumption**. When someone says, "I need you to be available every day," or, "You can't be a manager if you are here only part time," you can notice the underlying assumption: Commitment to something is measured by how much time you devote to it, not the results you deliver. This reflects an outdated view of management, where employees are treated like children and managers like babysitters. These statements put you on the defensive or drain your energy because they demand the one thing you may not have at that moment—time. Instead, identify and then challenge the assumption internally and then externally: "Actually, they don't *need* me to be available; they *want* me to be available. I can work with them to help them feel more comfortable." Or "I can think of several ways I can be successful managing while working part time." The reframe opens up space for you to discuss what type of management results are expected and what traits are important for the role.

Finally, by recognizing the work of the Feminine Filter and its underlying assumptions, you can **be conscious in your choices**. Being conscious helps you decide whether to accept or reject these messages and how you choose to respond. It also opens up many more creative possibilities. During approaching burnout, instead of trying to do everything perfectly to the point of running yourself down, you could choose one thing, something really important to excel at and over-achieve—something where the outcome is important and will make you confident about your skills. By consciously choosing, you give yourself permission to do less well at everything else, or to delay other things until the really important task has been completed.

You can see how your choices may have boxed you in with rules that aren't working for you. Then you can begin to get yourself back on track.

2. Bring yourself into the equation

How you position yourself, your goals, and your needs when you make decisions is key to living an Orange Line life. When you are approaching burnout, bringing yourself into the equation seems like the last thing you have time to do. It's not about being selfish, it's about having a strong sense of self. This confidence is precisely what can help you move out of this stage and prevent it in the future.

You've heard it so many times before: Women need to do a better job at **setting boundaries and expectations**. It feels so hard to do, especially in this stage, because of women's natural tendency to avoid letting anyone down. This can easily become the excuse for not saying, "No" when they should.

For example, Business Consultant Felicity, forty-two, was completely overwhelmed with work projects when a friend asked for a favor. Normally, she would be very willing to help and really wanted to in this case, but she knew it was truly going to break her. She felt she *should* prioritize her friend over everything else, because that was the *right* thing to do. But at the end of the day, she already had a full workload and was only going to be frustrated helping her friend. And despite the fact that she could even possibly get paid, it was going to derail other paying projects. What did she do? She invested five minutes in finding someone else who could help her friend equally well and made a referral. Her friend protested a little, but realized Felicity wouldn't have handed the project off unless she really needed to. In the end, Felicity ignored the pushback and did what she needed to do despite the guilt.

Sometimes, setting boundaries is about valuing your time and setting realistic expectations. One interviewee found she lets clients take too much of her time at work because she is always available for their calls. When she is out, even for a few hours, she sets up her email and voicemail to apologize for being out and explain how they will get a response within twenty-four hours, instead of the usual four. She has set the expectation with them that she is almost always available to answer them when they call, regardless of the importance of their request. This may have self-limited her ability to control her work time. She can't later blame the "crazy work hours and culture" of the business for placing so many demands on her because she has set this up herself by not setting limitations on her availability. Instead, she could leave a more generic message on her phone and do her best to respond to messages as appropriate. Sometimes, this could mean an immediate response, and sometimes, it could mean never calling back, depending upon the situation. This frees her up to decide.

Another step in this process is to **ask for what you need**. You are not doing the organization or anyone any favors by hiding problems or martyring yourself for short-term results. In fact, you are harming the company and your own career long-term. VP of Operations Shawna, fifty-one, said, "You have to ask for what you need. You can't be afraid of it. I have to balance feeling guilty. I have worked with challenging people. I've always asked for time off when I needed it. If I needed to take my son to an appointment at 3 p.m., I would say, 'Here's my schedule, and then I'll be back online working to make up the time later.' I did this so I wouldn't feel there's anything lost. I worked my ass off. I felt like I earned the credibility to do things like this. They know I am true to my word. If they need to reach me, they can."

Because of the Feminine Filter, women often dislike negotiating on their own behalf, especially when they feel vulnerable as in this stage. However, this is probably the time when they come at negotiation with the most ammunition. They can use the fact that they are doing too much to set better expectations.

You can practice this by getting something in return every time someone asks you for something. If you are asked to take on a new project, you can ask for more resources or to remove other items from your plate. If you are asked to stay late, you can ask for time next week during the day to get your oil changed. And when you are planning the year/quarter/month, you can build in any expected anomalies or workload impacts, both professional and personal, that you know about, instead of just trying to squeeze them in with the regular work. Call it out so everyone knows what you have been asked and that it is extra. When you know there is a two-day trade show coming up, you can set your own and others' expectations that two days of your normal duties are not going to happen. Too often, women forget this and try to find that extra two days by squeezing their personal selves out of the equation.

Sometimes, to accomplish this, it's wise to share a bit of your personal pain, despite feeling uncomfortable. Shawna said, "I started this job, and then I had an issue with my daughter. Her dad had remarried and puberty hit, and she was very angry. I was really concerned and wanted to send her to a new school. But I needed to check it out, and I had to tell my new manager that I had to go to visit this school in another location. I had to be vulnerable to share this. I told my boss I needed his support and he was supportive. He had to trust me, that I wasn't going to be really distracted by this, and it paid off for him. Some employees are mysterious. It's hard to feel empathy about their situation if we don't know about it." Shawna recommends not being overly personal and dumping problems on your employer, but being up front about what is going on, giving them enough details that they can understand what you need to do and why. It lets the manager know the employee will be able to get the work done and honor her commitments despite the distraction.

Most women also need to practice getting comfortable with **self-promotion**. This may be counter-intuitive at a time when you feel most like hiding or escaping scrutiny. But just like any other time in your career, you need to be out front, setting the pace for your career and letting others know how much value you bring to the table. Others need to see how you manage yourself through crunch periods and maintain composure even when stress levels rise. You also need to be acknowledged and rewarded for going above and beyond the call of duty; otherwise it can easily become an everyday expectation.

Instead of hiding from pressure, Sales Manager Cecilia, forty, uses her manager to help her identify the priorities so she can spend her time productively on the work that really needs to get done. When she gets overwhelmed, she does, "a sanity check-in with my boss to make sure I'm meeting his expectations. I realign my workload and priorities to his, so I'm sure I'm working on the right thing. Where should I be focused? I figure, that is why supervisors are there—for help—so I ask for it. Sometimes, I just need reassurance that I am focused on the right things." By doing this, she also lets him know just how much she is working—which lets him know what she is doing because otherwise he may forget. She also asks for compensative time off when she has been burning the midnight oil and needs to regroup. Self-promotion in this stage may not be about driving hard for a promotion to the next level. It is about making others aware of what's on your plate and your value to the organization.

A final step to bringing yourself into the equation is to ensure that you are exercising **self-care**—taking care of your physical and spiritual needs with the same amount of energy you are devoting to taking care of everyone else. Creative Director Faith, thirty-nine, knows she can't function well in her executive career and as a parent without exercise. She takes time every day to go for a run and to eat healthy food. Despite her commute and obligations, she takes time for herself. By identifying what is important to her, Faith is able to carve out time for what she needs and just does it. This practice enables her to manage her work and home life without burning out.

It's hard to do this, especially when women are in a crunch because of guilt. They are afraid to be caught eating, exercising, or even stepping outside for a break. They think people will judge them, so they keep going. But you need to ask yourself, "How will those people judge me when I break down mentally or physically because I didn't take care of myself? Will I be seen as a better manager then?"

In the sport of running, trainees are cautioned to deliberately plan recovery breaks before they are necessary. These recovery cycles can improve long-term training results and help avoid injury or burnout. Whether or not you know you are currently overwhelmed, have a busy crunch period coming up, or have been through a rocky time and are reflecting back on it, consider planning regular breaks in your work in the future to make yourself a stronger performer.

Bringing yourself into the equation enables you to remember that you are important, too. It is a critical skill for living The Orange Line. Rather than viewing this as selfish, see it as taking responsibility for yourself and your career.

3. Develop self-awareness

First, you need to recognize that you are approaching burnout. Most women struggle to see this in themselves because it creeps up so slowly. It's hard to be perfectly objective, so you may need to **solicit feedback**. Are people telling you, in their actions or words, that you might be losing perspective or approaching the edge? Have you heard, "Wow, you look tired" or "I haven't seen you in ages, what's going on?" You might need to notice whenever you become defensive. This is usually a sign that people have touched a nerve, and while you know they're right, you haven't wanted to admit it to yourself. It can be helpful to ask a friend or colleague to give you an honest assessment, or remind you whenever they notice dark circles under your eyes.

Another step is to **conduct your own self-assessment**. Sometimes, you need to admit when the problem is you. The reality is most people invest their time where they are most comfortable. So if you are at the office all the time, that's probably where you really want to be. You may complain and say you wish the job weren't so taxing, but the reality is, if you really needed to leave, you could leave. If you like to work, admit it, and then get help so your home life doesn't spiral you to the edge of burnout. Admit what you want and then build your life around it.

Some people create a constant state of "overwhelmedness" because they like the sensation of being crazy all of the time. Although this is dangerous for health and performance, the addiction is hard to kick. There is something about feeling busy, needed, important, and liked that fuels adrenalin. Ask yourself if the sensation is worth the downside and check yourself every time you say you are "busy." Is it real?

Thirty-five-year-old Manager Ada was a single mom struggling to make her job work in a toxic environment. The stress was very high and the pressure increased as the company was bought. However, Ada believed she had no choice—she had to stay in the toxic environment because she needed employment. Eventually, the toxicity became unbearable. With the insight gained through her master's program, she realized the organization did not match her values and, "I found the courage to leave." Once she moved to a more positive environment, her stress level lowered and her passion for her work returned. Sometimes, self-assessment can uncover a values-disconnect with your work environment.

Armed with feedback and your self-assessment, you can now create time and space for **reflection and analysis**. Almost all of our respondents said the first thing they did when things got overwhelming was to stop. Some took a break and got some exercise. When Business Owner Sophia, fifty-eight, gets "overwhelmed, I meditate and do yoga and breathing. This gives me perspective so I don't get overwhelmed." She says stress comes from, "always thinking about what hasn't been done yet. You need to think about what has been done. Pray, sing, and go for long walks. All of these things help me breathe again." Services Manager Maribel, thirty-one, said, "I go to the gym. It's a huge stress reliever. Last night I ran around the neighborhood for twenty minutes. It's a terrific benefit because I come back a new person."

PLAY FIRST!

"Internally I had learned there is always something to do. I had learned to deal with the feeling of urgency. I was raised with the principle that you do your chores first and then play. The problem as an adult is that the chores never get done. If you've decided this, then you burn out. Making that realization and adjustment has helped a lot."
— *Olive, IT Director, forty-eight*

Simply pausing can help overcome the feelings of vulnerability women often have at this stage that can block their ability to self-assess and hear feedback. You can start by taking just one hour a week where you do nothing but reflect. Schedule it if you have to. Some interviewees found journaling helped; others talked to friends. The key is not to obsess about what has to be done, but instead, step away to reflect on your approach, looking at life from a different perspective.

In this stage, women need to delay making long-term decisions. What we found in our interviews is that many used the excuse of approaching burnout to avoid doing the personal work of solving their problems and changing those behaviors that lead to burnout. Years after burnout, our interviewees reflected back and realized that even though they quit jobs, initiated divorce, or moved across the country in response to burnout, they found themselves right back in the approaching burnout phase again a few months or years later.

Before deciding specifically what to do, you can reflect to determine what the real issue is so that you change the core problem. For example, forty-two-year-old, IT Manager Madison seriously considered leaving her husband when her children were toddlers. The pressure of parenting was immense and her husband's workload was so high that he wasn't around much. However, the underlying issue was that she was blaming him, instead of taking responsibility for her pain. Eventually, she took responsibility, increased her domestic help, and went back to work. She was happier and her marriage improved.

Once you have regained perspective and recognized that you are approaching burnout, you can **create your own unique self-development plan** for getting back to "you." When there is too much to do, the only way out is to prioritize and make choices. It is usually more respectful to others and less stressful in the long run if you consciously choose what not to do, and proactively communicate that fact up front. Usually when women get to the approaching burnout stage, as time seems to speed up and they desperately juggle a larger and larger number of balls in the air, they lose track of just how many balls really are up there.

EVERYTHING HAS A PLACE

"We organize using a master to-do list in MS Excel where work, family, school, medical stuff, and fun are all combined into one. My husband keeps a master calendar in the kitchen. It's a huge five-foot white board with a rolling daily calendar for five weeks out, seven days a week. We do meal planning on Sundays so we can go shopping and be organized for the whole week. We keep a dedicated place in the garage for the kids' sports equipment and take photos of complete uniforms so the housekeeper knows where to put the pieces. Library books have a central place, too, so they don't get lost in the house. We have dedicated places in the house to throw junk when a quick cleanup happens—and we know where to look when we lose something." — *Vivian, Nonprofit Coordinator, forty-seven*

Deciding what to do by applying a conscious set of principles allows you to be more efficient with limited time. Figure out: What is essential? What takes up a lot of time? What gives me energy and what depletes me? Decide what not to do either through delegation, delay, or eliminating the task from the list. Aisha, VP Corporate Counsel, fifty-eight, offered the following advice: "I have a personal coach who reminds me of what she calls, 'The Toothbrush Syndrome.' If you're concerned about cleaning the corner with a toothbrush, you're missing what's going on in the center of the room. If you think that last detail has to get done, you're missing the big picture—like doing the dishes while the guests are sitting together talking. It's not always the most urgent that is most important. In fact, most of the time, it is not the most urgent thing at all."

One system found to be highly effective is described in the book, *Get-*

ting Things Done, by David Allen. He describes a system of combining all of the personal, work, and family lists into a single list and applying prioritization standards to it. This is supposed to take the stress out of worrying about all of the little things hanging out there because they have all been consolidated and filed away until there is time to work on them. Whatever system you choose, remember, don't think about carving up your pie of time and allocating it to get as much done as possible. Think about investing your creative energy the most wisely to maximize the return for things that matter to you. Once you are back on somewhat solid ground, looking back enables you to determine which areas you need to develop.

By developing self-awareness, you can create your own conscious plan to take you away from the burnout precipice and back to Orange Line living.

4. Build a support system

In this stage, getting support may feel impossible. It seems as if everything you bring in goes right back out again. You may feel you don't have time to bring in help because you are too far behind already. Some women also may fear asking other people for help. They don't want to burden them with their problems when they are already burdened themselves, and they also can be uncomfortable with owing people. Many women would rather help than be helped. But building a support system will enable you to work through your burnout.

First, you need to **acknowledge that you need help**. Acknowledging that you are not able to do it all may be the hardest step. When you have taken on too much work, letting go of it can feel as if you have failed. Thirty-four-year-old Project Manager Alexa said what limits her from being her personal best is, "My inability to delegate responsibility well. I have trouble letting things go and trusting others to get them done just as well. And by not letting things go, I'm not getting as much down time to do other things I might enjoy. And by not 'sharing the wealth of work' with others, I'm not giving them an opportunity to succeed or fail."

As women age, the ability to delegate becomes even more important. You will likely want to leverage your skills, experience, and wisdom to accomplish more with less. So many interviewees described positive experiences with delegation and they noticed that the more they delegated the happier and better grounded they felt both at home and at work.

The next step is to **figure out exactly what help you need**. One hard part of delegating is the process of deciding what and how to delegate. On the home front, most interviewees hired house-cleaning help, delegated cooking, driving/shuttling, and appointment scheduling. Leadership Coach Courtney, thirty-five, even delegates parts of projects. She has someone write the first draft, and then does the last 20 percent of her workshops and content design herself, enabling her to delegate the time-consuming layout and then tailor it to her style. With this approach, you can break down projects into component pieces and then decide which are essential to own and which can be given to someone else.

Next, **figure out to whom you can delegate**. This is where having a strong network can come in handy. Knowing people who know people—one interviewee's Mom's Club has a referral board for reliable local trades people—can take the time and risk out of getting help. As we've mentioned previously, not everything has to be outsourced to paid help. Many interviewees were successful at asking friends, co-workers, and family for help to get them through a crunch. Most people love to help and generally respond really well to being asked. Billie, Business Owner, forty-three, has "built a lot of resources into my life personally and professionally. When things get crazy, I figure desperate times call for desperate measures, and I call in the reinforcements."

You can also delegate up. When you are stretched at work, talking to your manager about what his/her priorities are can help you discern what to let go of. Giving tasks back to your manager enables him or her to find someone else to whom to give the work.

Finally, **manage the work.** Most of our interviewees said delegation required time and energy to manage, which is why they avoided it. Moreover, many of them described experiences when they delegated something away entirely, only checking in occasionally and then secretly complaining about the results. A better approach is to ensure that the person understands your expectations and gets regular feedback about their results. It takes the guesswork out of helping you. Quality control can be difficult, but managing it is about setting goals and reviewing progress. Remember that everyone is human and you will all get more done if you communicate and work together.

Forty-two-year-old, Business Consultant Felicity said, "When my daughter was born, we were in the hospital for almost a week, so I was dying to come home to sleep. When we arrived home, a friend of mine was there and spent several hours talking while I fought to stay awake. I should have handed her the baby and closed my bedroom door, but instead, I felt the need to entertain. I was angry with her for not doing what I needed, but that was unfair because I never told her what it was." Asking for help, making sure it's exactly the help you need, and managing that help gets you through these intense periods.

5. Get comfortable operating in imperfection

Especially when you are approaching burnout, your need for perfection adds to your workload and threatens to overwhelm you. Let's face it, no one can control the external environment and every once in a while, the best-laid plans are going to get messed up. Life is imperfect.

Work doesn't come in neat, even packages; it comes in a cascade of opportunities, crises, and unpredictable demands. Most women described feeling palpable relief when they finally internalized this skill.

When you are in this stage, **accepting imperfection** and letting go of the need for error-free results can feel daunting, if not impossible. Yet that's precisely what you need to do. You need to get comfortable operating in this messy, ambiguous world so you can remove the unnecessary pressure this creates, especially during crunch times. When you strive for perfection, you waste a lot of energy focused on your deficiencies and stressing about it.

Start by looking at the bigger picture and getting some perspective. Can you let go of your expectation that every task you work on has to be done perfectly? Is that really the expectation others have of you or your own interpretation? Would others be happier dealing with a more relaxed colleague who maybe dropped a ball occasionally or didn't produce the perfect, error-free document? Maybe wait an extra day to respond to emails. Maybe format the presentation the night before it is due and accept whatever it looks like, rather than editing it a hundred times in the weeks leading up. This means you need to accept the "good enough" work of others as well. When someone has a misspelled word in an email that doesn't change the point of the message, does it really need to be pointed out and corrected?

As you experiment with acceptance, you can eventually move to the step of **embracing imperfection** and leveraging the opportunity it provides. One woman mentioned hearing a turnaround expert at her company say that in times of stress, it is easy to see what people are really made of. Imperfection always exists, but how leaders manage imperfection in stressful times is really telling of how well they lead. Their first inclination may be to think, "Oh no, now I have to be perfect at managing imperfection!" Instead, another way to look at this is by embracing the idea that the goal is not perfection, but doing your best. This isn't to add pressure to an already stressful time, but rather to shake apart the notion that the goal is perfection at any time.

THE ORGASM CHART

By embracing imperfection, you can find humor in any situation. "I generally earned the respect of my male colleagues. With one or two guys, there was a bias, but it was very rare. I kept a positive sense of humor. Once I was the only woman in a large meeting with many senior executives, sitting at the very back of the room when, on the last slide of a presentation, there was a chart that was briefed as the 'Orgasm Chart' because the data was so fantastic. As if in slow motion, every head in the room seemed to turn back to look at me. Without thinking, I replied, 'Gee, you guys only have one?' The room exploded in laughter, and many of the guys came up afterward to shake my hand. It was one of those 'did I just say that out loud?' moments, but I had been accepted." — *Lily, Senior Programs Director, forty-eight*

Embracing imperfection means trying something even though it might very well fail and being ready to admit the failure. One team at a top company used to run over five hundred different reports every quarter until a massive layoff significantly reduced headcount on the team. Instead of trying to keep up perfectly with all of the reports, they risked pushback by eliminating them one by one until someone noticed. What they found was that most of the reports were redundant.

Instead of bemoaning imperfection, recognize that it is there and **plan for it**. Almost all our interviewees spoke about the value of planning to avoid being overwhelmed. Senior Sales Manager Hannah, fifty-seven, doesn't get overwhelmed "as much anymore if things aren't going well. I've allowed myself to pace my life so I'm not overwhelmed. Now it's more about not choosing perfection. Two years ago, I had an awful year. It was not pleasant. It was very stressful. I had to figure out how to dig out of the problems and keep my spirits up. I needed a lot of encouragement with how things were going. The next year, we turned things around and I had my best year ever."

DON'T LET THE DAY ROLL OVER YOU

"I avoid getting overwhelmed by expecting and planning for crunch times. In the past, I would react and it would show. In all areas, I would wear my heart on my sleeve. I've learned now that time management is huge. It prevents you from getting overwhelmed. If I know I have a big week or month—I eat, sleep, and get ready mentally. I make sure I take time to unwind. Whether it's just meeting a friend, being a couch potato, or reading, I need to make sure I work in that down time. I work hard, am practical and realistic about how I manage my schedule so I don't get as overwhelmed as I did before. I think of it like pain management. I try to set myself up to be successful. Do you want to be in the driver's seat or let the day roll over you? I think you need to be proactive." — *Doreen, Human Resource Specialist, fifty-one*

If you lower your own perfection expectations and tell others up front that a particular result is going to be less than perfect, people can be surprisingly accepting, particularly if it is something where a perfect result is neither expected nor appreciated. There can be nothing more frustrating to a manager than when they see an employee obsessed about getting one thing done perfectly at the expense of completing a lot of more important tasks.

When approaching burnout, it is especially important to get comfortable anticipating, accepting, and embracing imperfection. That way you can plan for it and live with it, instead of it adding to your burden of stress.

6. Expand your universe

It may be scary to make some of these changes. Delegating involves taking the risk that you are no longer in direct control. Drawing boundaries carries the risk that you will be disliked. Operating in imperfection means life will be messier. It may seem easier to just continue busily running the treadmill and hoping things will change on their own for you. This is why it is important that you expand your universe of possibilities and create solutions you may not have seen before.

One way to do this is to **seek out people who challenge and push you forward**. When you are approaching burnout, you can seek out people who agree with your basic philosophies, support you with positive messages, perhaps offer you a shoulder to cry on—and who will safely let you know when you are burned out. When you are overwhelmed, you don't need the people around you reminding you of all of your failings or slamming you with the Feminine Filter's assumptions.

During the approaching burnout phase, it may be difficult to expand your network or community by meeting new people. Instead, you may want to focus on pruning out people who don't move you forward. You can tell who they are because when they walk away, you end up feeling worse about yourself than before you spoke to them. This is a red flag that they are draining you. HR Specialist Doreen, fifty-one, has, "learned along the way to get rid of toxic behaviors or people so I don't have to deal with unnecessary stresses. I am an intuitive person. I give a lot of leeway, but when I figure out people's intentions, I don't waste my time anymore. Maybe it goes with the age thing: We know what brings us happiness. We know the kinds of people we want to be surrounded by. We need to make choices—you either say this person is important to me or you say this person is not coming from a good place. Make those hard choices."

For example, one woman was recently in a six-month-long crunch period where she added a new, struggling business to her portfolio of projects. During this time, there were many existing clients competing for her time and attention. One client was particularly troublesome: Despite having already completed the major thrust of his project, he wanted additional time from her. She drew boundaries, offered to devote future free time blocks, even delegated to equally capable support staff, but he was insistent that only she could meet his needs and it had to be immediately. The client started to insist that her lack of availability would jeopardize all of her previous good reputation. He also made it clear that he expected all of this additional time for free, and that she would just do it for him because he was entitled to it. This woman knew the relationship had become toxic to her energy and creativity; thus it needed to end. She respectfully withdrew from the project. It was a difficult decision to make, but it created space for her, and helped her avoid complete burnout.

Another way to expand the universe during this phase is to **think bigger**. Again, this seems really hard to do when you are already approaching burnout because it seems like it will just give you more work. But often times, you could be doing something twice as big, expending the same amount of energy. For example, one business owner went from running a small, single-store retail business to a chain with three stores and a website. She still works just as hard, but the resulting revenue and return on the effort is four times as large. The same can be said for many professions; the amount of work doesn't change as you move up the ladder, just the amount of money or size of the team you manage. And, if you are going to be working this hard anyway, don't you deserve the bigger paycheck that goes along with it?

Exposing yourself to something new is another way to help you out of your burnout. This may mean being open to new ways of doing things. It's hard, when you're suffering under the crunch of work, not to get defensive about other ideas or outside opinions. Stepping away and doing something completely different helps you gain perspective. You might invite a yoga instructor to speak at your team outing or reach outside your work group to find a completely new work approach.

Finally, you can expand your universe by **taking a big risk** and facing a fear. This might be something as simple as letting go of a toxic relationship or a routine task that is contributing to the pressure right now. Maybe you can push back on the idea that the only time the team can meet is at 6 p.m. on a Thursday night. Perhaps you can ask to be recognized for the work you have done with a salary increase. The point is not so much what the risk is, but how taking the risk stretches you. If the thought of doing it makes you feel anxious, then it's probably a good sign this is a risk worth taking. The more you practice doing it, the less big these risks will seem to you, and the more opportunities it will create.

Making a conscious effort to expand your universe of possibilities is an important skill to practice for living an Orange Line life.

Conclusion

These stories illustrate that all women have rough patches. Instead of panicking or "catastrophizing" when things become messy, ambiguous, and feel out of control, or trying to solve the problem before you understand what's going on, acknowledge to yourself what is happening through your body sense and emotions. By slowing down your thoughts and gaining perspective, you can make small changes to fix things and move forward. Sometimes, you need to understand that this is a difficult, temporary situation and you just need to hang on and survive it. Other times, you need to proactively slow down, stop, and take the time to nurture yourself physically and mentally. You may even need to make really hard decisions about whom you choose to be around during this time. By understanding the problem, to what extent you are making things worse for yourself and adopting Orange Line Skills, you can improve your situation.

CHAPTER SIX:
Family Matters

SO MANY GREAT LITTLE THINGS

"I had my two kids while working at a law firm. I realized pretty quickly that the law firm environment doesn't fit my personality because it's very hierarchical, particularly with patent law. I was struggling with where to go. I had a great maternity leave and they paid me well, but I looked ahead and wondered how I was going to keep all the stuff that's super important to me and keep a career.

"After I came back from maternity leave with my second child, I decided to make the move to a new company a good friend had already joined. I had been on their case constantly: The role was in recruiting, which wasn't what I dreamed about, but it had a creative element and the company looked great. I've found lots of ways to be challenged at work and to feel successful as I'm surrounded by very hard workers and I've even been promoted in my less than two years here. I work more hours, but take the commuter bus. I actually walk out at 4 p.m. and am in my driveway at home pretty much by 5:45 p.m. I can occasionally work from home.

"There are so many great little things about this place—for example, the autonomy in my job, awesome benefits, office being closed for the last week of the year. I'm technically working fifty-five hours a week, but I get on the bus at 6:30 a.m. so it's not time I'm missing with my family. We have a nanny who now lives with us and works Monday through Thursday, and then my mother-in-law comes in on Fridays. My daughter is in pre-school. My husband just got a promotion as well and used to work from home, but now has to commute. So that is another struggle we face, but it isn't different from many people. We sometimes video chat during the day or he brings the kids up to pick me up. They like it when they come to my office—there are toys there, ping pong tables, etc.

"It's a start-up company, only five years old, with a 'San Fran' vibe to it. To that end, a large portion of the work population is young and not necessarily married with kids. In fact, I'm the only person on my entire team with kids, and until recently, the only one even married. There are often events or happy hours that come up at the last minute. I kind of want to play the game, but I have to know my limits as well. Except for rare occasions, getting home to my family is always my priority. My husband is a hands-on dad. Everything that's done is a partnership. He bathes one, and I bathe the other. He does the laundry. We take turns reading stories at night."
— *Trudy, Recruiter, thirty-two*

We found most of our interviewees entered a phase where family matters arose and consumed them so they had to find a way to integrate this with their work. For most, it was marriage or parenthood, but even single women described situations where work took a back seat to an illness in the family or a similar event. For some, the family phase re-occurred multiple times during their career as they raised children and then again when their aging parents required support. And because the Feminine Filter tells women that family is their responsibility, family matters had a meaningful impact on their careers.

Parenthood 101

New mothers typically experience three main phases as they figure out their new role or adjust to an additional child.

- **Early adjusting:** In the first few months, mothers are getting to know their child, adjusting to the rhythm of motherhood and getting back on their feet. In addition to developing confidence and the concentrated learning that happens in this period, mothers are also dealing with intense emotions of confusion, happiness, frustration, and joy. It is a very "hands-on" phase. Director of Sales Isabel, thirty, expressed it this way: "All you do is the baby, no sleep, just feeding." For many, this makes the structure and demands of work seem like a distant world. For some, there is even a sense of panic that things would never be the same.

- **Later adjusting:** In this phase, most women feel more in control. They get their energy back somewhat and can consider their own priorities again. They also tend to become quite attuned to the needs of their child(ren) and how to parent. For some, work has become significantly de-prioritized, while others struggle to find a routine that would keep them working.

- **Feeling adjusted:** Here women settle into a routine and are finally back to normal, feeling like themselves again.

During this transition, many women we interviewed found they were bombarded with external ideas and opinions about successful mothering. There is probably no other time in their lives when they will garner so much unsolicited advice: It seems everyone has an idea about how women should parent.

Once School Starts

Once their children entered any type of school, life for our interviewees usually became easier. At that point, the children were older and more able to help themselves.

IT ONLY SEEMS LIKE FOREVER

The reality is that the physical, time-intensive part of raising children is short term. Leslie Bennetts in *The Feminine Mistake* notes, "The really difficult period [of parenting] amounts to fewer than fifteen years out of the fifty-plus I will spend in the workforce overall—a relatively short period, if you take the long view. In exchange for staying the course, I've been able to enjoy an immensely rewarding career—not to mention an income that has sustained my family during some really difficult times when my husband's employment was interrupted." Most women are moving out of the physically and emotionally hard years as their children enter into school.

For many parents, this school-age group is a lot of fun because the family can do more things together with less required physical work, like carrying diapers, toys, and toddlers around. Parents often remember their own childhood at this age so they can relate to their children's experiences of going to school, struggling with friends, and starting sports. Women often make new friends during this period because they associate with so many parents in a similar life stage.

It's also a time when the after-school activities, such as getting their children from school to their extra-curricular game or practice, became challenging for interviewees and they needed to rethink how to get that done. The work hours hadn't changed, but women often had to use different types of childcare now, whether it was school-based or babysitting. Summer vacation was also a challenge as camps often have set hours that don't align with the working day.

Don't Dread the Teenage Years

Parents often are warned to dread the teenage years, but in terms of managing career and family, many of our interviewees found that these years could be easier because there was much less need for childcare. This made for fewer pressures at home. Many parents of teenagers found that their children were not home much and were quite helpful around the house. This made it easier to focus at work.

Lawyer Marcia, thirty-eight, relies on her teenagers: "I call the house and ask the kids if they have dinner figured out. My daughter is happy to make salad, and my son wings it." Technology Salesperson Jessica, forty-five, found that the career traction she gained by working when her kids were younger is really paying off now that her children are teenagers because she can invest more in her career.

However, for some parents, the emotional aspects of parenting teenagers were challenging. Forty-eight-year-old Marketing Manager Lee found, "As my son became a teenager, he decided to live with me full time so I had to give up a client and I stopped traveling. It was a huge balancing act." Another interviewee had to deal with her son's significant emotional problems after her divorce. It became extremely distracting and almost cost her job.

Caring for Parents

Several of our interviewees experienced career impact when they were called upon to care for their aging parents. For them, it was not as visible or welcoming a transition as was becoming parents. On top of all of their other work and home responsibilities, these women dealt with negative emotions as they watched parents lose their abilities. The process is incremental, so often women didn't have a plan. Unlike parenting, decisions about elder care generally involve many more stakeholders and are rarely easy. There are a myriad possibilities and cost options for available care, which can make decision-making difficult. And the Feminine Filter influence caused many women to believe caring for parents is primarily their job.

WHO'S LOOKING AFTER THEM?

"In the U.S., 36.5 million out of 112.6 million households have at least one unpaid family caregiver," according to a recent survey out of Bard College. And 66 percent of elderly caregivers are women.

The Pressure of Being Mom

Because of the added responsibility of caring for children or parents, there are challenges that threaten to undermine womens' ability to keep their career and life in focus:

- **Increased workload.** When family gets added to a woman's life, it can bring excitement, change, and enjoyment as well as a lot more work. Further, the work is physical and emotional, which can drain energy and creativity. Pregnancy and delivery can tax physical strength and post-partum can leave women exhausted. Women may think it is their responsibility to be the primary parent, caretaker, and homemaker. This essentially doubles their workload. All they see are the number of hours they've put in. Increasing them is not possible because there are not enough hours in the day. They crash into bed exhausted.

- **Childcare challenges.** Women may think it is all their responsibility to figure out the childcare options and manage the logistics. The burden can feel heavy, and they may not have previous management experience to rely upon. They may decide to hire a nanny, only to find it difficult to find someone reliable. Or they may decide on a daycare facility. Some services are good quality, while others leave much to be desired. Plus children get sick more in daycare, which can put extra pressure on mothers to be available. The cost of childcare, especially for infants, can be rather daunting and an enormous chunk of the family budget. Further, many women are in the "sandwich generation," caring for both children and parents simultaneously. What most women find out pretty early on is that time spent with an infant is physically demanding with very little down time. At first, when Corporate Lawyer Elaine, thirty-five, was on maternity leave, she thought, *I don't need daycare.* "I had a one-year-old and a newborn, and a husband who traveled 75 percent of the time. It was all me. It was a laborious, very long summer and very challenging. I came back from maternity leave early . . . and got a nanny."

- **Momism in the workplace.** Women may find people suddenly treat them differently at work now that they are a parent, as if their careers are no longer important to them or their skills suddenly vanished. They may find that people make assumptions about their abilities and pass them over for projects and promotions. Women sometimes find that bosses penalize them for any work absences related to motherhood. When a man leaves early to coach baseball, he gets credit, but if a woman leaves to take a sick child to the doctor, she is ostracized or called out for a lack of commitment to career. While Sales Manager Eva, forty-three, "was on my second maternity leave, they reorganized my team. I ended up with the worst team and all the great results I had for the beginning part of the year went to someone else. They got credit for the top two percent performing team that I had built. My numbers looked terrible. And there was no asterisk by my name, saying they gave me a crap team that year or that I was out on maternity leave for a large part of it."

- **Their marriages may become troubled.** Once children arrive, the time women spend with their spouses is primarily focused on their children. It is similar when they provide elder care. There are growing pressures on the couple to manage the time and emotional commitment of children or elderly parents, which can tax their patience, energy levels, and ability to get along. Moreover, many women may find men less willing to help out with the family as they might have expected, which can cause resentment. As a result, many marriages fall apart under the increased stress of children. In our interviews, most women felt they got divorced, not because of the children *per se,* but because they married the wrong man in the first place. Yet, this often showed up only after the children were born. Marketing Manager, Gabriela, forty-four, did 100 percent of the home tasks during the week because her husband left early and came home late. Professional Facilitator Shirley, thirty-five, got married because she thought she was supposed to and discovered their expectations weren't the same. She wanted to keep growing at twenty-eight, but her husband thought they'd reached their goal.

Don't opt out; take a sabbatical

The question of whether to "opt-out" and take care of the home and family or continue to work has been regarded as the defining question of a woman's life. This choice has hurt women significantly as they make lifetime decisions based on a single life event.

Instead, we recommend finding a way to make career work with family. Don't opt out; take a sabbatical if needed. An Orange Line Sabbatical is a planned, conscious decision to take time off from work for a specific purpose and a limited time—whether that's to be with family, restore your health, care for a sick family member, attend school, or travel—with the full intention of returning to your career. Specifically:

OPTING OUT	INSTEAD, WOMEN CAN TAKE AN ORANGE LINE SABBATICAL
Career is put on the back burner and mostly or completely ignored. Women don't think about whether they will return to work. They assume their working spouse will take care of them financially, so they stop thinking about their careers. Instead, they make themselves entirely available as a support system to the children, the home, and their spouse, giving them false flexibility as parents and spouses, enabling their spouses to freely be Green Liners. They assume that if/when they decide to go back, their careers will be ready and waiting and their spouses will take their turn in supporting their career.	You decide to de-prioritize **career** for a short period of time. You fully expect to return at some point. You determine how long based on your goals, family situation and personal desires. You maintain your credentials, skills, investments and connections. You believe that work and life are important. On Sabbatical, you may consciously choose to put work at a lower priority; but you still understand its importance to your life goals. You do not invest your time and creativity in low value domestic work. Your spouse continues to share responsibility for family and household.
Family becomes everything and women organize their lives around family priorities. "Mom" owns the emotional and domestic responsibilities. She supports the children and spouses: driving, cooking all meals, and ensuring she takes care of all chores and challenges so her family members can concentrate on themselves. Mom is the invisible support system for her family's growth and development, but "she" is missing. Family becomes her full time job. The rest of the family learns that mom has a place and the next generation does the same thing.	**Family** continues to be an element of your whole life along with yourself and your future career. You might decide you want to be with your children during their first years, care for a sick family member or be there when the children are having a challenging time. You recognize that you are important as well. Others in the family contribute and "mom" is not the only one who maintains home life.

OPTING OUT	INSTEAD, WOMEN CAN TAKE AN ORANGE LINE SABBATICAL
Self is something that usually comes last. Children and spouse priorities override their personal objectives. Their self-esteem may lower as they continue to spend money they didn't earn or they aren't seen as the valuable contributors they once were. They become emotionally and financially vulnerable to the risks of divorce or death of a spouse.	**Self** is important and investment in yourself, whether it is time alone, with friends, or a significant hobby, is valued as equally important as the development of children or your spouse's career. You figure out what will help you maintain or strengthen your self-esteem and invest time in those pursuits. You bring your interests as an equal party into family decisions. You ensure your own personal financial condition is maintained, including your retire-ment savings and credit rating. You can re-enter the workforce at any time and take care of yourself in the event of a catastrophe.

Instead of getting bogged down by the extra demands of this phase and feeling you need to make a dramatic change, practice Orange Line Skills to give yourself more options. You may find that you simply need to get more help or cut back on your short-term career expectations. You might even want to take a brief sabbatical so you can focus on your family without the distraction of work. To maintain your career, you will need to be intentional about your next steps. Below is how you can adapt our six Orange Line Skills to this phase.

Skills for Living The Orange Line

1. Recognize when the Feminine Filter is at work

The Feminine Filter often is the loudest when you have family respon-sibilities. Because women have accepted that *women are the ones who need to take care of home and family*, when they attempt to include career as well, the pressure to implement the Feminine Filter increases substantially both internally and externally. As reported in the *Economist*, this has led to thinking that the, "biggest obstacle to women's career advancement is children."

The first step in recognizing the effects of the Feminine Filter is to **listen for and recognize Filter language**. You might hear, "It's best for children when their mother is at home with them." Or at the office, "Why does she leave at 5:30 p.m. every day. She's not committed." You might even repeat the assumptions to yourself as we saw in many interviews such as Marion, VP of Operations, forty-six: "In my career, I'm neither utilized nor rewarded for my skill set and level of education. But if I wanted to be successful in my career, I would need to center on myself and give up taking children to the doctor or being there to care for my mother."

When this is in the common language, women accept the underlying assumptions readily. By being aware and calling them out, you can begin to examine them. You can see the underlying assumption that good mothers spend all their time with their children or take care of their parents or good workers spend all their time at work. Then instead of internalizing these messages as fact, you can recognize them as others' attempt to enforce their beliefs on you.

The chart below illustrates the common language used by our interviewees when they became mothers. We use it to highlight the Feminine Filter assumptions at play. By reframing the language and highlighting The Orange Line Principles, you can open up new possibilities and debunk the myth of the ideal mother.

FAMILY MATTERS ASSUMPTIONS	DEBUNKING THE ASSUMPTION: WHAT'S REALLY GOING ON	REFRAME
Family is incompatible with work at my company. Having a child changes everything. **Feminine Filter underlying assumption:** If I follow the rules, good things will happen.	Having a child changes your life, but that doesn't mean that you can't negotiate or that something bad is going to happen if you let some tasks go. Simply having a child can also open possibilities as you figure out which aspects of work are important and which are extraneous.	*My career is important as well as my family and they are not mutually exclusive. Men do it consistently and it's feasible for me as well.*
Moms aren't as committed to the job. **Feminine Filter underlying assumption:** My commitment to something is measured by how much time I devote to it.	What you are really saying here is that when you become a parent, you get distracted, invest time and energy elsewhere and that it has a negative result on your work. Isn't this also true of your husband? This assumption is untrue and dangerous because then you may waste even more time and energy trying to prove otherwise.	*I will show my commitment by achieving the outcomes that matter for me and my organization, regardless of how much time and energy I may also spend on something else in my life. I will also communicate my desires and interests openly so I may fully participate in exciting projects and work that will further my career interests, regardless of what I am doing in my personal life.*

FAMILY MATTERS ASSUMPTIONS	DEBUNKING THE ASSUMPTION: WHAT'S REALLY GOING ON	REFRAME
The kids are my primary responsibility because I am the mother. Men and women are different; women are better at managing the home. My spouse gets too stressed out around the children. **Feminine Filter underlying assumption:** Women are primarily responsible for home and family and taking care of everyone.	The "men and women are different" generalization is not a valid excuse for forcing people into career roles. That's like saying, "men are bigger and stronger so they should be responsible to stay home and farm our food while women use their social skills to run the world." Both women and men are capable of managing and organizing childcare.	*Both parents are responsible for home and family. My spouse is as capable as I am. Together we can figure it out so we can both pursue our métier and enjoy our family.*
Childcare is not good for the children. **Feminine Filter underlying assumption:** I need to be perfect in behavior and appearance at all times.	Research suggests that high quality day care can have long-term, positive effects on children benefiting them even up to thirty years later. It also positively impacts reading and math scores. This is not a valid excuse for giving up your career and staying at home.	*Quality childcare is fine for my child. If I have a strong desire to be home with my child, I can choose to be at home. If I want or need to work, I can feel good about leaving my child in quality child care.*

FAMILY MATTERS ASSUMPTIONS	DEBUNKING THE ASSUMPTION: WHAT'S REALLY GOING ON	REFRAME
It's going to be like this forever and I just can't keep going like this. **Feminine Filter underlying assumption:** I need to be perfect in behavior and appearance at all times.	This is overly negative because you may be expecting some perfect vision of yourself as a worker and a mother. Young children require a lot and their needs can feel exhausting and never-ending. But this is short lived. Once they start school, they are capable of taking on more responsibility.	*I can do well enough, not be perfect during this period and think more long-term. I can wait until I can be more objective about major career decisions when things are not so crazy.*
Now I have a family; my career doesn't matter anymore. **Feminine Filter Underlying assumption:** Tangible, materialistic rewards are not supposed to be important.	Many people feel this way for a few years after having children. Early on having children can be all consuming and can feel like there is little space for careers. Statistically, women will outlive their spouses and be capable of working for many years after their children are grown. Why give up on one piece of your whole life?	*My career is important as well as my family.*

FAMILY MATTERS ASSUMPTIONS	DEBUNKING THE ASSUMPTION: WHAT'S REALLY GOING ON	REFRAME
I have to quit. It would be better for my family if I stayed home. **Feminine Filter underlying assumption:** I am primarily responsible for home and family and taking care of everyone.	Pamela Stone, in *Opting Out: Why Women Really Quit and Head Home,* found that job conditions are the main reason women leave work, not family pressures. Why is the only solution to quit? Are you saying that you don't have the ability to come up with alternatives or that you are the only one who can manage the family? This is not true.	*I don't have to choose to quit. My family and I can devise many solutions to manage the current situation.*
Good mothers "raise" their children themselves and that means I need to be there 24/7 for my kids. **Feminine Filter underlying assumption:** Commitment to something is measured by how much time I devote to it.	Time is not a proxy for quality. Both parents are "raising" their children; they can be good role models, whether or not they work outside of the home.	*My spouse and I will do our best for our children together. We will consider what our children really need and not what others tell us is "good."*

FAMILY MATTERS ASSUMPTIONS	DEBUNKING THE ASSUMPTION: WHAT'S REALLY GOING ON	REFRAME
If my child goes to school without his or her hair brushed, others will say I'm a bad mom. **Feminine Filter underlying assumption:** I am never good enough.	You have allowed your child's hair to become a proxy for your parenting. Others may say you are a "bad mom" or not conscientious, but does it matter? If you own how neatly or perfectly your children are dressed, then you stifle their individuality and ability to determine for themselves what they want to wear.	*If others judge me based on these external factors, it is their issue not mine. I am content with how I parent and am able to let go of the minutiae if I need to.*
By staying home, I'm investing in the family. **Feminine Filter underlying assumption:** If I follow the rules, good things will happen.	Another way to look at this is that women are investing in their spouse's career by being the main provider of free childcare. Their spouse's career is a riskier asset than they may fully understand at this stage. This may have negative future financial and career implications for them that they also need to consider. Is the only way they can invest in their family to stop investing in their careers?	*There are many ways I can invest in my family and career at the same time including outsourcing childcare and housekeeping, sports, etc. It is a partnership. I must also make decisions with full understanding of risk so I can protect my career and financial future.*

FAMILY MATTERS ASSUMPTIONS	DEBUNKING THE ASSUMPTION: WHAT'S REALLY GOING ON	REFRAME
I need to live up to my mother-in-law's standards. **Feminine Filter underlying assumption:** If I follow the rules, good things will happen.	Some of our interviewees described getting pressure from their mother-in-law. From their mother-in-law's perspective, the mother's career and personal passions are lower on the priority list behind her son's career and her grandchildren's well-being.	*The person most naturally invested in my career and life is me. I can listen to others' opinions with the understanding that their interests may differ slightly from my own. I am my own best advocate.*

As we've said before, another way to uncover assumptions is to **be aware of guilt**. This is the internal pressure women may put on themselves, based on what they assume. Now that you have a family, for example, you might say, "I can always get another job, but I have only one chance to raise my children." While this is true at face value, it also implies that working is irrelevant now that you have children. It is also true for your husband, but he probably won't let that derail his career.

Often women feel guilty when they make a choice that differs from the assumption that mothers should be present. Further, the underlying guilt felt when they work suggests they accept the assumption that tangible, material rewards are not important, putting their own long-term financial security at risk. Guilt tells you that something is out of sync. It suggests that what you are choosing is not in line with what you "should" be doing. However, it also highlights the assumptions that are at the root of the guilty feelings. Once highlighted, you can examine them to see what is true for you.

Of course, **observing your behavioral responses** also highlights your assumptions. In our interviews, we noticed women behaved in ways that enacted the Filter's assumptions. In the next chart we highlight these, describe what happens when women enact these behaviors, and highlight how you might reframe the underlying assumption to help change the behavior.

FAMILY MATTERS BEHAVIOR	CONSEQUENCES	FEMININE FILTER ASSUMPTION
Taking over management of the children and family. **Bad habit:** Acquiescence and self-sacrifice.	By managing all of the doctor appointments and routines, you actually become the only one who can talk intelligently about your children's health or put them to sleep at night making it self-reinforcing. Your spouse may step back and let you do all of the work. He fails to develop an ability to manage at home.	Women are primarily responsible for home and family and taking care of everyone. **Reframe:** *We are both responsible for taking care of the home, family and our children.*
Neglecting themselves and dropping their interests for the interests of the family. Many mothers said that setting aside time for themselves was less important than getting everything done. **Bad Habit:** Acquiescence and self-Sacrifice.	Decision-making becomes lop-sided. By dropping your interests, others start to devalue your interests as well. You may not take care of yourself and have less energy to help others or get your own work done.	Women are primarily responsible for home and family and taking care of everyone. **Reframe:** *I am capable of taking care of myself and my husband is capable of taking care of himself. We need to take the "oxygen mask" first so we can be present to the needs of our children.*

FAMILY MATTERS BEHAVIOR	CONSEQUENCES	FEMININE FILTER ASSUMPTION
Doing it all. This illusion of doing remarkable work while running an efficient household and raising children singlehandedly can be glorified and tempting to embrace. It gets reinforced when people say, "She is so amazing! How does she do it?" **Bad habit:** Working harder, not smarter.	When you do it all, you teach others that they are less capable so they don't need to step up. This can create dependency. It also signals you don't have the ability to prioritize or delegate. If you refuse to take anything off your plate, you are setting yourself up for burnout or worse.	Commitment to something is measured by how much time women devote to it. **Reframe:** *I am good enough as I am and I don't need to prove it to anyone else. I can prioritize my energy on what really matters.*
Becoming the perfect parent and homemaker or competing with other moms at mothering. **Bad habit:** Risk avoidance and over-compensation.	You set yourself up for failure when you eventually can't keep up with these perfectionism standards. Instead of focusing on your goals and what is important to you, you succumb to external definitions of what success looks like and what is important.	I need to be perfect in behavior and appearance at all times. **Reframe:** *Doing my best and being good enough are perfectly acceptable. My measurement of success is deeper and isn't evaluated by the feats or failures of my children.*

FAMILY MATTERS BE-HAVIOR	CONSEQUENCES	FEMININE FILTER AS-SUMPTION
Submerging their career goals because they are caring for their families. They make categorical statements like, "I can't travel at all" or "I can only work if it's part time." They don't take the managerial title even though they are doing the work because they are concerned about the commitment required. **Bad habit:** Lower career and reward expectations.	You box yourself in and limit your opportunities. Your career suffers and you risk financial security over the long term. You also reinforce the current stereotypes about mothers and the workplace.	Tangible, material rewards are not supposed to be important. **Reframe:** *My career is important and I am entitled to pursue it regardless of what is going on at home. I may need to adjust in the short term, but no more than my husband or anyone else should.*
Pretending nothing has changed. Women may keep their heads down and keep going so that they can hide any indication that their family situation is taxing their time and physical energy. They don't ask for help or change how they manage work. **Bad habit:** Avoid asking for what they need or challenging the *status quo*.	You don't request the help you need and have to work twice as hard to keep up the perfectionism standard. You become obsessed with how much time you spend on your family situation rather than your results, which trains others to do the same. You set yourself up for failure, not success.	If I follow the rules, good things will happen. **Reframe:** *I take responsibility for myself and ask for what I need. I can determine what is important right now and what is unnecessary.*

Once women understand the pressures and reasons for their behavior, they can start to **challenge their assumptions.** They can reframe the assumption: Women are primarily responsible for home and family and taking care of everyone instead to parents are both responsible for home, family and taking care of themselves. Author Kristin Maschka explains in *This Is Not How I Thought It Would Be, Remodeling Motherhood to Get the Lives We Want Today*: "I didn't want my husband to miss out on the richness of the relationship I had with our daughter. There was a richness that came from putting a cold washcloth on her feverish forehead, from reading and giggling about stories in her bed at night, and, yes, from the times she drove me crazy and I yelled and then said I was sorry and she hugged me anyway. I didn't want David to find many years later that he didn't know his own child, had missed her childhood, and couldn't have a meaningful conversation with her. I wanted more for him—so badly it brought me to tears. And I was pretty sure he wanted it, too."

As a result, you open up creative options for how you can respond. You can **be more conscious in your choices**. When everyone in the family is responsible, suddenly the cost of daycare is compared to the combined salary, not just Mom's. When it becomes normal for Dad to leave at 5 p.m. to pick up kids at daycare, it may even become the cool thing to do. Together you can brainstorm new, creative ways to take care of the family as well. Maybe one partner drops off so the other can get to work early and the other picks up so the first can work late. Both get to put in plenty of hours on the job and both participate in the childcare process. And you alternate so you aren't always the one who leaves work early. New ideas and new choices emerge. When doing your best is good enough, you can reduce stress and are free to let the kids play in the mud a bit. You may even start to opt-out of externally imposed expectations, such as playdates, potlucks, and elaborate birthday parties. Instead of being guilted into taking a reduction in pay to work part time, you can consider how your focus at work and great life experience compensates for any additional time you may spend out of the office while your children are young.

Recognizing when you have bought into the assumptions and rules of the Feminine Filter and consciously choosing your response is a life-long skill for living on The Orange Line.

2. Bring yourself into the equation

With a growing family and more people to consider, learning how to bring you into the equation is getting harder and even more essential at this stage. It can become very easy to submerge your own interests for everyone else.

The first step is to **set boundaries and expectations**. For Marlene, now fifty, Director at a large company, it was about leaving every day at 5:30 p.m. sharp and avoiding weekend work when her children were young. This was important because her husband worked nights and the daycare closed at 6 p.m. She was a rising star in her career, yet was able to deny requests for routine evening meetings and overflow work. Instead, she came in early to organize herself or finish projects, and she kept extremely focused during the day to maximize productivity. Even her networking, which she prioritized, she conducted efficiently and fastidiously. She avoided hallway gossip and time-waster meetings like the plague. Marlene refused to take on projects that were too adminis-trative or had no concrete purpose. And she developed a great eye for recognizing what activities were going to move the needle and which were going to end up nowhere. When there was a genuine crunch pe-riod or need to travel for an occasional event, she would increase her childcare and devote herself to the job. But she refused to let it become an everyday requirement. By getting solid results for her employer and wasting no time while on the clock, she was able to get off the clock ef-fectively, keep work in the box where she needed it to remain, yet still move her career forward. Today Marlene is an executive and the major breadwinner in her household.

Marlene is a great example of Orange Line living. She illustrates that when women are comfortable setting boundaries and not worrying about being judged, they can accomplish many things. But letting go of the judgment and worry can be really hard. It's part of wanting to be liked, and there is a fear that if they go too far, people will react negatively.

MY BOUNDARY WAS THE DOG

Jackie didn't want to admit this at first in her interview because she still feels guilty about it. "I had a dog before the baby. There was so much to do with an infant, and as she got older, the dog got to be too much. It was such a miniscule thing, but it was too much. A friend of mine adopted it. She's doing great—very happy to be away from the baby. I felt if I had to do one more thing today, I just couldn't do it." This woman's strength came from the fact that she analyzed the situation, realized what she needed to do, and did it. She says: "So I cut back all the things I don't have to do. I still do laundry, etc., but I've limited it to keep myself from becoming overwhelmed. Saying 'No' isn't a problem. I have no trouble saying 'No.'" The decision wasn't a choice between the baby and the dog. It was a choice between her own self-worth and the opinions of others. Jackie won.
— *Jackie, Paralegal, fifty-two*

Technology Sales Specialist Neeta, forty-one, is effective at drawing boundaries at home because she understands her value. "Having two kids, what's hard is being around non-working moms and the immediacy they want and always needing things from you. I have to push back. The school party is not the most important thing I'm going to do today." She has prioritized how she will expend her energy. "I need more important work than this. When I was home on maternity leave, my husband needed me to go back to work because I was stressing about stuff that didn't matter to us. I need to stress, so I need it to be over something important that makes money, not trivial stuff." When asked if she needs to work or loves to work, Neeta said, "I love doing a good job and I like getting recognition. Work gives me an outlet to fulfill that need for recognition. At home, I would be putting that on my kids just to validate me. Work makes me happy." Knowing what she needs for herself has helped her frame what she should be doing and makes her at peace with her decisions. When someone challenges her decisions or tries to guilt her into helping with the school party, she has the confidence to push back.

Next, **ask for what you need**. When women have a family, often their first impulse is to ask for some kind of work flexibility program, such as working part time or leaving at a set time each evening. Usually this results in a cut back in pay or advancement. Instead of focusing everyone on your situation, what you might need is simply to remove some less important projects from your plate or cut out some time-wasting meetings so you can get your work done at a reasonable hour each day. Is it worth your long-term earning potential to have homemade baby food or could you make a store-bought choice work? If you have to have homemade, is your spouse willing to make it, too? Further, is your spouse willing to ask for work flexibility, too? Here again, if you are both responsible for home and family, then you both should be willing to do what that means for your family. If not, then you need to ask yourself why it has to be you.

Be cautious about negotiating for part time. Often, when women negotiate for this, they end up working more than the agreed hours for less money, which undermines their value. If you do decide to negotiate for part time, work the hours negotiated. If more work needs to be done, renegotiate the agreement or make it clear that this is not a regular occurrence. And as Mrs. Moneypenny counsels in her book, *Sharpen Your Heels*: "Don't keep reminding colleagues that you are working part time as they see that as 'lacking commitment.' If someone tries to fix a meeting with you on a day when you are not in the office, say:

'Sorry, that's not convenient for me.' Don't explain that you are 'only' working part time, or they'll switch off. You will be discounted. A man would say that he has a portfolio career."

Find flexibility between the lines. Some companies pay lip service to flexibility to look good, but in practice fall short. Often times, flexibility has more to do with the few people who work around you than the broader organizational policies. Find out how much you can carve out for yourself. Many men quietly leave work during the day to go to the gym, run errands, or coach baseball. No reason is any more valid than another for leaving work so find out what level works for your group. If you are getting the job done and can keep everyone focused on your results, you may find more flexibility than you ever expected can be achieved.

Forty-eight-year-old Lawyer Anita asked a lot of questions during her job interview to make sure the company really did give the flexibility they espoused and to avoid future work-life conflict down the track. She also made sure the result was documented in her contract. Others have found that instead of asking for specific accommodations or workplace flexibility when getting the job, it's better to wait until flexibility is required and then just take it and do what they need to do. Often this requires the confidence of knowing who you are and how much value you contribute to your employer.

"When negotiating my initial position at my company," forty-nine-year-old Marketing Director Kyla says she asked for a consulting gig. "After several meetings and much consideration, the partners decided to offer me a position as an employee. I was pleasantly surprised, but then the real negotiating started. I needed benefits and couldn't accept the position without them. Furthermore, I didn't want to work full time as my daughter was a toddler. So they agreed to give me full benefits and set up my schedule as twenty-four hours a week with the understanding that I'd work full time one day. Oh, and did I mention,

I also wanted to work at home? They agreed to two days in the office, and one day at home to start."

You need to ask for what you need at home as well. This is where things tend to become overwhelming for women because the Feminine Filter assumption about women being primarily in charge of home and family is ubiquitous. You may buy in to the idea that the home must still be kept to the standards of an idealized 1950s housewife. Did you know that even in the 50s, 34 percent of women worked outside the home? Now many women have accepted new standards: Everything must be "Green," home-crafted, "All-Natural," and anti-bacterial.

Keeping up with this standard would take a whole team of people, so even if a woman had "help" from her spouse and children, she would fail to get it all done. So you need to agree on what is the expectation, focus on what is really necessary, and then partner to do the work. If he's not willing to help meet the expectation, then that is a sign you haven't both agreed to the expectation. Sometimes, PB&J for dinner is good enough, especially if it means you can squeeze in a walk together before dusk—or dressing each morning with clean clothes out of the dryer. Some families use paper plates for meals to make cleanup easier. Kelly has a rule that anyone sitting in front of the TV needs to be folding laundry while they watch. At one point, thirty-eight-year-old Lawyer Marcia's husband "evaluated how much we were paying the cleaner and said we could save a lot by reducing the cleaner's hours. I answered, 'We could save a lot by cancelling cable, too.' End of discussion."

Setting expectations up front can prevent you from having to keep asking for help or negotiating more flexibility. One woman, a doctor, said, "I tell my children's teachers at the start of every year that I don't do school projects. I'm not good at building missions out of Popsicle sticks or sewing pioneer costumes. If it can't get done at school, or without parental supervision, my children can't participate." This was such an empowering, liberating thing to hear. First, it sets a boundary that most women can relate to—arresting the ever-creeping expectation on parents to become more and more involved in the formal education of their children regardless of their skill-set or desire. Second, she did it up front, so expectations were set in a fair and professional way with minimal emotion. Think about giving yourself permission to opt out of all kinds of these types of unessential expectations: bake sales, soccer snacks, organizing the office holiday party, etc. You can decide how you want to contribute or not. And as long as you set the expectations up front, you don't need to feel like you are letting anyone down.

As in the other career phases, others need to know about the value you bring to the job when you are engaged in family matters. **Self-promotion** at this stage can be communicating the joy you find in your work. In our interviews, a vast majority of women, when asked, "Do you have to work or want to work," offered a resounding, "Want to work!" Even the few who felt they only "had to work" discussed how much they liked contributing professionally. By telling your peers, colleagues, children, and friends how important work and family are to you, you build their respect around that aspect of your life and engender their support when you need it. This has long-lasting benefits. The women we interviewed whose mothers worked all felt less conflict about combining work and family.

Another element to bringing yourself into the equation is **self-care**. It's putting the oxygen mask on first when the plane is going down so you can be fit to help others, too. When children are young or when you are caring for a parent, this might mean getting time alone to take a shower or go for a run. It may mean ensuring you get enough to eat or sleep. Giving yourself permission to schedule these things on the calendar, like a meeting or an appointment, with the same importance as anyone else's priorities. With all of the Feminine Filter's noise about women's responsibility for the family, it can be hard to think about and include yourself without worrying that you are being "selfish." That word carries with it so many negative connotations and socially unacceptable behaviors. Women, more than anyone, are encouraged to be selfless: at church, at work, in the PTA, and at home. It gets amplified even more when they become mothers. But having a strong sense of self is different from being selfish—it is saying that knowing your own goals and living your *métier* is what you, as a person, are designed to do. This makes you better able to truly give to others because you value your uniqueness.

3. Develop self-awareness

Once women have children or care for a parent, a new layer of who they are appears. This layer is rarely apparent before children arrive, despite anticipating or planning for a family. Women often have to reset and learn a lot of new aspects of who they are and what they find important.

One way to get perspective is to **solicit feedback**. When you first start to parent, there seems to be no shortage of advice you receive—unsolicited—from your parents, friends, even strangers at the grocery store. If you are feeling vulnerable or lack confidence, which many parents experience, you can internalize this unsolicited feedback. Instead, be more proactive and solicit feedback about how parenting has changed you. We are not talking here about feedback concerning your parenting style; rather, this is feedback about who you are as an individual.

Another way to gather information about yourself is to consciously conduct a **self-assessment**. How do you think parenting or caregiving has improved your work? Have you gained insights and wisdom? How has it changed your perspective? Some women described their post-childbirth work selves as more grounded and mature, which allowed them to be better managers and leaders. Others realized that they were not as organized or detail-oriented as they thought. Often at this stage women don't slow down long enough to consider if they are enjoying what they are doing or not. It may help to observe and then compare your relative level of calm or contentment. If you see a woman pick up her children from daycare and be extremely engaged and attentive, you may think about how often you let work concerns spill over into your time with family. Conversely, if you see a woman volunteer to photocopy the class's homework assignments for the teacher when she is already overwhelmed, you may feel comfortable that you did not prioritize this choice.

Once you have gathered internal and external feedback, you can **reflect and analyze** what you found. Having a very strong sense of self enables you to decide your own path in the face of external judgments and pressures. Fifty-six-year-old Hospital Administrator Jamie continued working as a parent of three despite pressures from her family. Then, when her youngest started school, she "knew I wanted more" and shifted roles within her career several times, each time building her capabilities.

Reflection can also take the form of experimentation. For example, you may want to experiment a little with the traditional spoils of motherhood. You may actually be looking forward to baking cupcakes, girl scouts, or soccer, and if anyone tries to make you believe those things were bad, questioning your commitment to The Orange Line if you bake cupcakes, then you can push back. You may enjoy doing many traditionally feminine tasks like cooking or scrapbooking. This is part of the discovery process. The key piece is to make space so you can enjoy these activities and be careful not to fall into "ideal" mother traps. For example, Sales Manager Eva, forty-three, thinks her kids have to have an elaborate birthday party every year. Her husband would rather not. The self-awareness part comes when Eva asks herself who the birthday party is for. Do her children really need one every year? Of course, if you like baking cupcakes and it doesn't interfere with your work, then by all means bake cupcakes. Just ask yourself the right questions: Why do I feel the need to do this? What am I giving up by spending this time and energy right now? Be conscious of your choices.

Carving out this space to reflect can be challenging, especially if it means balancing demanding work and family schedules. Yet, this time to reflect is essential. You may notice as Sales Manager Delia, forty-three, did, "finding time alone has been very difficult." But even though she has "only the drive to and from work and the walk up the stairs to lunch," it is still time she can use to reflect. Maybe it's a simple breath at every step you take, listening to a self-help tape en route to work, taking a walk or enjoying nature at lunch. Regardless, it is space you can use to reflect on yourself and your life.

Use this knowledge about yourself to **form your own unique self-development plan**. For instance, you may realize that these traditional roles are not your cup of tea. Kelly spent years trying to balance being a "perfect mommy" with being the "perfect employee" until she realized that she was better suited and happier at work than at home during the day. Once she understood this about herself, she was able to create a plan, focus on her career, and hire professionals who were better at taking care of young children. She still takes time out of the work day to attend important events with the children, including volunteering her time to teach kids about business at their school and coaching them in soccer. But by becoming more aware of her strengths and passions, she was able to make a career plan that leveraged them. Michelle felt the opposite; she loved being home with the children when they were young, and when they grew, she wanted to be back at work.

Children teach women a lot about who they are. But children can also make it challenging, making women feel as if they are pushed seemingly from all angles. It helps to keep perspective. Realizing that waking up in the middle of the night lasts only a short period of time can help it feel easier. Parenting does get easier. If you plan for it and manage your emotions, you are more likely to enjoy the process.

4. Build a support system

This is probably the most difficult, yet the most necessary skill to develop once the family arrives. The work involved in raising children or caring for parents can consume the hours and drain energy. If you are going to live on The Orange Line, with a rewarding career and strong sense of self, you can't do it alone.

First, acknowledge **that you need help** both at home *and* at work. It can be easy to find excuses to not get the necessary help. You may think it costs too much or that you can do the work more quickly and better yourself. Or you may equate all time spent with your children equally, so that changing diapers or making their dinner is as important as taking them to the park or helping them explore the world. So you keep everything close to the vest and deny yourself help. Nonprofit Senior Executive Maya, fifty-six, "had to learn to ask for help. I was bringing home the bacon. There's a notion we can do everything and we are afraid to show others that we can't."

Instead, you can learn to think differently about help. Help is an investment. The more time and creative energy you free up now to spend on pursuing career interests and/or enjoying your family, the better off you will be in the long term. Remember, no one gets credit for checking off boxes, or for the quantity of time spent on stuff. It's the outcomes and personal fulfillment that matter. The kids don't want to see your back as you scurry around the house cleaning up. They want to engage with you about their day and share stories. One interviewee remembers her mom gave up her career to be at home, but was busy all of the time doing housework while her dad devoted his few non-work hours to playing with them and taking them to the park.

Of course, the cost of help seems high, especially when compared to most women's salaries. But that is not a fair comparison. Both parents need childcare and housekeeping. Also, these items are a career investment – just like college – that will pay off in the future. Creative Director Faith, thirty-nine, said, "We are lucky to have a nanny. We don't save much at the moment, but the investment is in the longevity of my career. I have to have resources to manage it and know we invest every cent to make it." She recognizes that devoting her time and energy to her job increases the potential for promotion and higher earnings in the future. So comparing her salary today to the help she is able to fund is not a complete, fair comparison. It's about comparing her lifetime earning potential, as well as her ability to achieve her *métier*, that is important.

It also gives your family options. One interviewee put her career on the backburner while the children were younger. Now that they are teenagers, they ask for more time with her husband. But her husband travels a lot. She regrets shortchanging her career because if she had not, it would be easier now for her to provide more income and enable her husband to step back.

It's also important to acknowledge what help is needed at work. Perhaps prior to children, a woman had been the go-to-person for all issues and extra work. Or she never really needed to delegate her work. If she fails to acknowledge that she needs help now, she could end up shouldering unnecessary work, causing her to work extra hours or give up less outcome-driven aspects of work, such as socializing with her peers. If women give up these connections, they will have fewer people to rely on to help them.

The next step is to **figure out exactly what help you need and to whom you can delegate**. By looking at your workload and deciding which aspects are crucial to the job, you can decide where to get help. At home, anything that doesn't result in direct, engaged interaction with family members or rejuvenates your energy could be considered for outsourcing or at least, shared with others. The only thing Technology Salesperson Jessica, forty-five, doesn't delegate is "having sex with my husband. Otherwise it can be delegated." How did she learn this? "It just is. I've seen friends divorce. A friend was working four days a week, so that her husband could excel. He worked super long hours at work while she did everything at home. Then he fell in love in with his associate and was gone." So Jessica has "two people come once a week to clean. I pay people to do laundry, meal prep, mow the lawn, or order groceries. If it's free shipping, I ship it." If it doesn't move her toward her goals, she adds it to the delegation list. It's about perspective.

Now, you may be thinking, "I don't have the money to hire help." But outsourcing is not just about hiring people. It's about getting help you need. Joining a local Mom's Club or church group can expose you to other people in your same circumstance who can share meals, pediatrician referrals, and even pick up your kids if you get stuck in traffic. Kelly's husband was out of town recently and she had three kids needing pickup at the same time in three different locations. Because of a long reciprocal relationship with a Mom's Club friend, she was able to get everyone home. In some cases, getting help is about lowering the expectation of what needs to be done. All meals don't need to be hot, three-course affairs served at the table. Sometimes, eating out or having cereal for dinner is good enough and extremely helpful.

Eleanor, forty-five, runs a busy public relations firm with her husband. She is the mother of five children and actively involved in her community. She credits delegation with much of her success. "I have learned the importance of delegating. We have ten to fifteen different, scalable, outsource workers we call on at any time. I keep client management, certain writing projects, strategic planning, and media outreach as items I wouldn't outsource. At home, there used to be lots of things I wouldn't delegate, but then I broke my leg last year and had to give up everything, including driving. Our household kept going. I learned that I am not required for anything at home except loving and supporting my family." You can even practice delegation when you go on vacation and learn that almost anything can be delegated.

We've mentioned this before, but we feel it needs to be reinforced: Women should always make sure they are sharing home responsibilities. Business Consultant Felicity, forty-two, delegated more responsibilities to her husband and found that better solutions emerged. Since he hates doing household chores of any kind, his first impulse was that none of these things were important. Dry cleaning piled up, garbage overflowed the bins, and mail piled up on his office floor. It took a while, but he eventually reached a breaking point when he realized how much work was magically getting done before. And while obviously some household chores are important and need to get done, his pushback also facilitated dialogue about what things really need to get done and why. Were they doing tasks because they were necessary, like dry-cleaning, or out of fear of external disapproval, such as sending the kids to school in perfectly matched outfits?

His next impulse was to delegate everything unpleasant away. He delegated some tasks to the children, installing an allowance system that taught each of them how to contribute and value this contribution financially. This valuable life lesson will pay off long term as the children grow to realize they have responsibilities in the household, but that these responsibilities are not determined by their gender. In addition to the usual housekeeping, babysitting, and gardening support, they have kids' lunches prepaid at the schools, grocery staples delivered monthly, and dry-cleaning picked up and delivered. And for all of the things he couldn't fully outsource, ultimately, he stepped up and learned how to do them, like making the beds, helping with homework, and cooking.

It's important to note that Felicity had to give space for her spouse to learn. If women have been managing everything in the house for years, it will require them to allow their spouse to make mistakes and not rescue them. This same principle holds true for all delegation. Women must accept errors initially because that's how people learn. Felicity had to let go of some things that she used to think she couldn't do without like picking out her own groceries. Her husband taught her how to see the bigger picture.

Women can even delegate to their children. Two-year-olds can put things back in the toy box or on the shelf. Pre-schoolers can learn to dress and fold their clothes and pack a bag for daycare. School-age children can pack for a trip and clear the table after dinner. It may not be perfect, or even good, but it is good enough. Demonstrate the task and then let go. They will love having a sense of independence and gain pleasure by mastering a task. Use age-appropriate direct speak with the children. For example, for young children, you can say, "I'll show you how to fold your blue coat and put it in the bag. Now you do it."

Finally, you must **manage the work**. As we've said before, you can't just expect providers to do things exactly the way you want without sharing information. You need to be clear about the job expectations. You also need to invest some time in showing people how to do things the way you want them done. It's important to supervise closely, particularly in the beginning. Further, you can't expect people to improve if you don't monitor their results and provide clear, honest feedback. Eva, a Sales Manager, forty-three, conducts formal annual reviews for her housekeeper and nanny and ties compensation increases to the results. She is also unafraid of upgrading the talent when things aren't working out. If that is going a little bit far for your comfort zone, at least having a conversation about expectations and results keeps everyone on the same page.

Getting support requires patience and persistence. Support is crucial for living successfully on The Orange Line. Remember, it takes a village.

5. Get comfortable operating in imperfection

Life isn't perfect and children or parents show up as they are. There are no rulebooks in this process so you need to learn to live with the imperfection. Work is messy. Kids are messy. Life is messy. Learning to operate within the "messiness" and problem solve is a skill.

To develop this skill, you first need to **accept imperfection**. By accepting this reality, you can remove any feelings of disappointment or self-doubt you might feel when things don't go perfectly. Knowing life is messy and unbalanced helps you realize you didn't do anything wrong to make it that way.

Often as parents, women assume that they must be perfect so that their children turn out perfectly. But what message are they sending their children with this expectation? By allowing imperfection, they give their children space to be imperfect as well. Do they really want their children to grow up believing that they are somehow "less than" if they are not perfect? Harvard researcher Rosabeth Moss Kanter writes in her blog, "One major hurdle to having it all is artificial images of perfection." Her advice? "Stop seeking perfection and settle for good-enough, or even not-at-all."

THE PERFECT BALANCE

"Probably the biggest step in figuring out how to integrate work was knowing when to let go at home. Because I'm a neat person and I didn't marry a neat person and we didn't have a neat child, I realized if I spent all my time yelling at them to be neat, we were going to get a divorce. Women say I gotta find the perfect man: I say you gotta find the perfect balance." — *Priscilla, Marketing Director, forty-nine*

The corollary to this is that by allowing themselves to be imperfect, women can also learn to accept imperfection in others. At first, when they become mothers, women may look at other mothers and judge them for their inability to do certain things. Or when they do elder-care, they may expect the caregivers to do everything perfectly for their parents. Self-acceptance enables them to be more forgiving of others. Imagine how it feels not to be judged—to be accepted as is, imperfections and all.

You can even **embrace it.** If you can step away from the need for perfection, you can explore the possibilities and proactively find or carve out the environment you need. You can even have some fun with it. Marketing Manager Lee, forty-eight, uses "a good sense of humor. If I laugh and say this is stupid, then I'll just deal with it. Like what my love life was like post-divorce. That's part of the relief. We've gotta see the funny side. We take ourselves too seriously." Once you get comfortable doing some things "well enough," it can be kind of addictive.

MY BADGE OF HONOR

"I wear my messy house like a badge of honor. It means I'm doing something else, something more important, really well. I think it's good if you've accepted it and it's okay—I don't get freaked out any-more. But my kids are well fed and clothed, and I read to them. I'm in survival mode until they go to college. I walk by the litter box, ac-cepting imperfection in those kinds of things. I'm not sure my moth-er-in-law would agree with me. I'd rather be spending time with my kids versus worrying about the house being in tiptop shape. My stay-at-home mom made my lunch until high school. My kids, they have things they are responsible for like recycling, picking up their room. They are learning that I can't do it all for them. They have to be re-sponsible. Other moms I know are getting urgent text messages like 'Where is the jersey?' Is it really that important? Detaching is a really good thing once in a while." — *Ilene, Operations Manager, thirty-eight*

As women develop the muscle to let things go that don't really matter, they can prioritize their energy on things that really matter. This can be freeing and can make others around them more relaxed as well. For example, Jodi had a soccer party at her house after a game. She had come off a day of back-to-back meetings/calls/work and then went straight to the game. She could have stayed home and cleaned the house, earning accolades from the other parents about how such a busy, working mother could have such a clean and perfect house. Instead, she told everyone that it was going to be a mess, setting their expectations low because she wanted to see the game. No one even cared. In fact, everyone offered to help set up for the party and clean up. It turned into a fun, sharing experience. This role modeling also gave all of the other parents permission to have get-togethers when their houses were messy as well.

When a woman lets go and sends her kids to school with mismatched clothing and a brown-bag lunch they made themselves, instead of a matching twinset and eco-friendly lunchbox, hopefully that gives others permission to do the same. Or forgoes a tightly packed activity schedule to put on some music and dance around the house together. Or celebrates a birthday with a quiet family dinner out, rather than a catered and themed party. There will be no visible achievement and no bragging rights, but it will be good enough. Similarly, there is no perfect career path—if women don't get promoted every year, but are still moving forward, isn't that good enough? Plus, their good-enough careers are likely to be only short-term while the children are young or parents are ill. Eventually, it will change.

If women try too hard to avoid imperfection, they may find they never take any risks. So they delay their development. For example, one interviewee is a teacher. She has a well-thought out lesson plan for all of her classes. However, sometimes the students ask questions or raise points that derail the class a bit. Instead of aiming for perfection and pulling the reins too tightly, she may allow the class to go off-plan and finds that is when some of the best learning for the students happens. In perspective, was the point of the class to stay on the lesson plan or was it to learn something? Results are what matter, not perfection.

Once you accept and embrace imperfection, you can **plan for it**. When you come to expect a transition for your school-age children every September and June, it doesn't blindside you that you have more parental distractions during those times. You may even schedule work projects around it. You can anticipate a long wait at the doctor's office by always having extra work or a book tucked in a bag. That way, you don't panic when it happens. And you can anticipate kids getting sick only on the days you absolutely have to be in the office, so you can pre-negotiate emergency backup childcare arrangements. One interviewee's local hospital offers a "mildly-ill childcare" for kids too sick to go to daycare, but not sick enough to require parental supervision. Erica, Professor, forty-three, makes her family leave the house after the housekeeper comes so she can have one dinner per week in a clean house before it inevitably gets dirty again. By expecting imperfection in their lives, women can be better equipped to deal with it when it happens.

HOW CAN WE DO IT?

You can also involve others in the planning. When Francesca decided to go back to graduate school, she had a family meeting: "Here's what I'm planning on doing: getting my degree. It's a family decision and it's going to take a lot of my time. They agreed and took on additional roles within the household. For example, I did oil changes, so I gave that to my husband and we allocated the various jobs across the family. I worked full time and took five classes because I could finish in a year. Every day at lunch I studied. I took the train so I could study to/from work. I lived on five hours of sleep. I promised them one year. They committed to it because I was committed to it." She didn't negotiate her goal. She negotiated and discussed

how the resulting imperfection could be managed more effectively.
— *Francesca, COO, forty-nine*

When you have family responsibilities, life can feel more intense and busier. This is the ideal stage to learn the life lesson of loving and learning from imperfection. By living on The Orange Line, you can get comfortable with, plan for, leverage, and maybe, just maybe, even love the messy world we live in.

6. Expand your universe

Especially when you have children or are caring for a parent, the world can get very small quickly as you become focused on your family and your work. It can feel like you can barely keep together the life you have, let alone expand it. Further, although there are many models out there for motherhood, most of them are traditional and career-limiting, making it hard to see new paradigms. But they do exist. You can expand your universe by broadening the way you look at how you integrate family with career and yourself.

You can start by **seeking out people who challenge and push you forward**. For one thing, you can seek out examples of people who are living the life you want as role models. Physical Therapist Jan, twenty-five, wants a family and a career. She observes her co-workers who are "dedicated to their jobs and families. I'm learning from them how to balance work and family. It's a job that's great for moms. We have a new mom and a single mom with four kids, and it's wonderful to watch them balance everything from doctor appointments to breast feeding. All day it is modeled for you."

Business Owner Hania, forty, established "a support group of women that spanned ten years of my life. We just disbanded last year. My group of women was diverse. I was the youngest, and the oldest was in her sixties. There were six of us in total." They were all in different industries and at different organizational levels. "We got together the first couple of years weekly. It was a major thing, having that support system." This group of women was not family or accidental friends: It was a group of professional mothers designed to challenge and support each other's careers. Many of the women we interviewed were part of similar groups. It was their "bedrock"—a place to come for solutions and ways to minimize the Feminine Filter.

It is also important not to limit yourself with negative people. One woman described a stressful period when she had an infant at home and a huge project at work. Her mom came over to "help" and pointed out how dirty the kitchen floor looked. "Like that was the most important thing. What is strange is how I internalized it. She was right. I was a bad housekeeper. My infant wasn't even crawling yet. There was no reason in the world why my floor needed attention at that moment, but I felt like a complete failure." Instead, imagine how she would have felt if the observation from her mother had been, "Who cares if the floor is dirty, the baby is fine. Focus on that work project right now because it sounds really fun and you can probably learn a great deal from it."

If you surround yourself only with the people who reinforce Feminine Filter messages, especially since the role of women as primary caretakers is such a ubiquitous and charged assumption, you are going to struggle to develop Orange Line Skills. Because Jodi was feeling the pressure of these messages, she built a community of women under the premise of challenging each other to grow. A subset of the original group still meets and talks about challenges. "We call each other on our 'stuff' and don't let anyone get away with not owning their part in whatever issue is being discussed. Sometimes, we don't like to hear the feedback we get. We learned to be open and able to go outside of our comfort zone to push ourselves forward."

You can join other groups like www.thirdpath.org to enable you to think more broadly about your career/life design. You can get training, find a mentor, or hire an executive coach. You can experiment and play as you decide what you want to do. If you expand your thinking, you can use your skills both at work and home to improve your life on both fronts. You learn from all aspects of your life.

Next, you can consciously strive to **think bigger**. When you reach the parenting stage, instead of pigeon-holing yourself into positions that are "mom-friendly" so you can spend less time at work, or giving up responsibilities so you don't let anyone down, you can stretch into positions that leverage your experience and mental energy, rather than your time. You can think of how your career goals can still be realized as you parent your children.

Management roles can be perfect for this. At first glance, this may sound counter-intuitive, but in fact, when they have a family, like it or not, women practice the art of management every day. Why not get paid to develop this skill? Also, this way, you use the same amount of time investment to get a much bigger result. Instead of teaching, consider stretching to Assistant Principal. Instead of Customer Service Representative, consider a training or supervisory role. Even expanding your current role, taking on a new project, or doing something more visible can challenge and help you keep moving forward. We are not talking about the assumption time equals quality here; we are talking about long-term quality outcomes that reflect your aspirations.

When you have a family, you should not be taking on projects that just require more time. Rather, you should shed time-suckers and instead focus on work that requires higher quality strategic thinking, management ability, or mental acumen. It's not about cutting back or diminishing yourself. Hania found: "When I came back from maternity leave, there were changes and things going on in the organization. I said, 'Wow—I'm going to become a project manager and make this my profession.' I was having an amazing time at work. It was a great company with amazing leaders and outlook."

You can think creatively and put yourself in the best position to provide for yourself and your family. Forty-seven-year-old Fundraiser Laura's job is based in a city close to her parents, but she works remotely from home. She negotiated to be in headquarters monthly "so I could be around my parents more. I go down to visit them every couple of weeks or so. I can go there more often, if necessary."

TRAVELING WITHOUT KIDS

"I love to travel. Since having children, I have found it challenging to travel extensively for my job. The first time I traveled after the children were born, I thought, *Wow, I love this so much.* As my children got older, I traveled more. I find these week-long trips are just enough to feed my passion for travel, but not too much of a burden that the family struggles." — *Jodi*

Once you have taken a few steps forward outside of your comfort zone, you can practice **taking a big risk** so you can face your fears. For many, it may be risking social reaction by pushing back on the Feminine Filter's assumption that they are primarily responsible for home and family. Being yourself and living an authentic life can be a big risk when there is so much external pressure and internal guilt telling you to do otherwise. For others, it may be scary to leave their infant with strangers or travel for work without their children, both of which get easier by doing it.

Facing fears sounds scary. Women often run from it. But our interviewees found the opposite. The ones who took a big risk for them, like asking for flexibility, asking their spouses to step up more, or even asking for a promotion, found that in the end, it wasn't as scary as they initially thought. They worked up to it, prepared, and did it. Each one looks back with pride. They found confidence in themselves because they were able to take the risk and learn from it.

Conclusion

No matter how you define family, this stage may be the most disruptive to your *métier*. Practicing Orange Line living can make the single biggest impact on your long-term career success. The key is to know yourself, take risks, and step outside of your comfort zone. Recognizing the opportunities for career and personal growth while maintaining a strong sense of self helps remove the Feminine Filter rules. And by staying flexible and broadening your options, you can get the support you need to embrace family, career, and life on The Orange Line.

CHAPTER SEVEN:
The Sabbatical

FINDING A HIDDEN TALENT

"I was a production manager for eight years. During that time, I met and married my husband, and five years later, we had our son. I was commuting at the time, my husband had his own business, and I realized I wanted to spend more time with my son, instead of working eleven-hour days. My husband and I talked and while I was the one with the security, health insurance, etc., we decided his business was stable enough we could take the risk. So I decided to step off. I wasn't sure I wanted to spend 100 percent of my time at home being a mom, but I figured I would do things like volunteering to fill the time. It turned out to be really hard for me. I felt unsuccessful at motherhood, and I had a hard time with not accomplishing even the simplest tasks on my list of things to do. I often felt like I was in jail when I was stuck in a chair, nursing all day with, by then, my second baby. If I hadn't stopped work, I could have been a producer. But I really wanted to be home with my boys.

"So I decided that with my writing experience, having helped on some publishing projects in the past, and with my connections, I might be able to write a book about production/animation during my time off. There is a passionate niche market for art books, and I knew people who would help me. A woman colleague understood my need for flexibility and was in the right place to help me get my first book deal. I would work late at night at writing and find ways to get the interviews done while the kids were in activities during the day. It was a big success. Since then, I have done six art books and one text-book on producing animation, all while being at home with my boys. I made this happen for myself. I grabbed the bull by the horns on the writing thing, but it was because of my connections that everything else has fallen into place.

"When I take on a project, I get really busy, but I'm still a mom first. I am a type A personality—I can't let a ball drop. There are moments when I'm very stressed. I try to still cook nice meals because I enjoy cooking every day. When the boys were really young, I had a hard time. My time was not mine—the kids took it all. I couldn't get any-thing done, and it made me feel like such a failure. I'm learning to let go more. I am getting less focused on household perfection—on hav-ing to clean every day or having perfect meals. I have never thought I could live without the carpet being vacuumed, but this is changing daily. My husband is a good team player. I wouldn't have married him if he weren't such a partner in everything we do. I feel that I've kept my network strong and with the book projects, I could re-enter the industry in a full-time gig at any time." — *Keimera, Author, forty-two*

In our interviews, we found many women made a conscious decision to take a break from work, a hiatus, for an extended period of time. Many found life on sabbatical was very different from the hectic pace of working life. Perhaps for the first time women could be present to themselves and take time to smell the roses. They had the time to go inward to find their joy and affirm their values and aspirations long-term. They may never have had this opportunity prior to entering the workforce, but now they had the space to discover what was right for them. Now they could embrace the opportunity and make it a positive experience.

Some women took a break early in their career. By taking such a break, Business Owner Sheila, thirty-five, was launched in a new direction. Her mother passed away when she was young. Before she died, she told Sheila to go out and see the world. After graduation, instead of continuing a desk job like her peers, she followed her mother's advice. She had always been tired of cold, northern winters so she went on a trip around the world. One sparkling day on the Great Barrier Reef, she knew she had to figure out how she could travel for a living. She now runs a successful travel company.

For others, the sabbatical was precipitated by an unplanned event such as a lay-off, illness, or the death of a loved one. In some cases, the decision was percolating for quite some time and an event, or series of events, convinced them to stop, such as pregnancy, job dissatisfaction, a bad boss, relationship issues, marriage, relocation, or the desire to pursue a new career or entrepreneurial venture. Sometimes, a break was disguised as working part time in a non-consuming role. In our interviews, virtually all the women who chose what we define as an Orange Line Sabbatical intended to return to work at some juncture. Even the four women we interviewed who battled cancer were keen to resume work, contribute, and retain their professional identity.

There are many reasons that women take a sabbatical:

- **Motherhood.** For the women we interviewed who took a sabbatical, motherhood was the most common reason. All but three intended or had intended to resume work as soon as possible. The motherhood reason is socially acceptable, with women often receiving validation from others when they quit work to care for children. It's easy to comprehend, aligns with gender norms, maintains the *status quo*, and provides a new challenge. Initially, the motherhood identity can be quite strong and women may push their career identity aside.

- **Care of other family members**. Death, illness, or the care of an aging parent is another major reason for taking a career time-out. Similarly, the added pressure of having children with disabilities made some women step out of their careers.

- **Work isn't working.** Other times, unable to push back on busy work, excessive hours, or a less-than-perfect work situation, women simply become exhausted and burn out. To re-charge their batteries and nurture themselves, they may take a break. They may even put their hand up for a lay-off package because the funds provide an excuse to take a break and re-group for a time. Other aspects that may influence the decision to stay in or step out are issues related to their peers, their boss, or a toxic workplace.

THE FINAL STRAW

"People you work with affect your general state of mind. If you have great co-workers, it makes work easier. Every day you face your co-worker, and the last co-partner I dealt with didn't value my opinion: He felt his opinion was more important. He belittled me. He had been there for so long—no one lasts more than two or three years with this guy—but I never equated it to his style. I was in tears most of my commute home. I remember feeling *I don't know how to quit even when I'm miserable.* I'm not sure, but maybe my decision to opt-out would have been different if it hadn't been for him." — *Gerry, Former Banker, forty-nine*

- **Lay-off**. A forced sabbatical can also occur after an untoward event like a downsizing, company merger, or dismissal. Although the decision is out of their control, it can rock women's confidence. They may oscillate between alternatives, like scrambling to get back into the corporate world that demands all of their energy, only to be let go again, or choosing something completely different like a not-for-profit or early retirement. It can be destabilizing, particularly coupled with a recession when they know securing any job is going to be difficult.

I DIDN'T SEE IT COMING

"In hindsight, I was naïve, too focused on understanding the job requirements, never pre-empting a job loss following a reverse acquisition. I lost my job and the dream. The isolation felt overwhelming. It was a forced sabbatical and I had no idea how to re-enter. Yet because ten years prior, I had transitioned into corporate life, I believed I could start again! This situation forced me to go deeper, get perspective about who I am, with or without work. It became evident that it was a process and I couldn't force the outcome. In fact, the harder I tried, the more brick walls I hit. Slowly, I chipped away at re-entering. Past perspectives about 'letting go,' breast cancer, and other life events helped. Humor and gratitude for the simplest grace, a smile from a stranger, phone call home, and support from those closest to me also helped. I got through it." — *Michelle*

- **Spouse's relocation**. Sometimes, women may decide to stay out of the workforce after relocating for their spouse's career, instead of re-starting every time they have to move. We heard from interviewees how constantly moving negatively impacted their careers. Consequences included the loss of their personal or professional support networks, cultural, and geographic isolation, and a delay, sometimes for years, in re-entry.

- **For fun.** A lucky few women were able to take a sabbatical to try something they want to do. Some chose to do something completely different and expansive, such as traveling, writing a book, changing careers, or upgrading their skills. Brand Manager Samantha, thirty-five, negotiated a two-year leave of absence in which she did an MBA. Jodi took a four-month sabbatical and traveled as she transitioned from a job abroad to grad school. Kelly took a six-month sabbatical early in her career to travel through Europe and move to the U.S.

Staying Strong During a Sabbatical

During a sabbatical, several problems can arise that can have long-term career implications:

- **Negative financial impact.** There is a financial penalty for not working over an extended period of time. If women are on sabbatical due to illness or layoff, the financial implications loom large as they try to figure out what to do next. Some women prepare for this, others rely on their spouse's income, but many underestimate the cost and ultimate impact of the decision on their life-time earnings. Important considerations like how the family will manage the reduction in family income and how health insurance and retirement are funded often are ignored. Some underestimate the long-term impact on their 401k savings or their ability to fund further education.

- **Negative emotional impact.** For some, the sabbatical experience is fulfilling, while for others, it can lead to feelings of self-sacrifice, powerlessness, loss of identity, and eventual resentment linked to their and others' belief that their career is secondary or not important. For those who took an education or travel sabbatical, there may be external pressure to "get a life" or "do something more industrious." If women are on sabbatical because they were laid off or because of illness, the emotions can be even more overwhelming. As with any change, there is an initial reaction where they feel sad and distraught. Gradually over time, they may get angry and then start to accept the reality. But dealing with those feelings can be challenging and others may not be that open to helping you. You may feel pressure from those whose lives have also been impacted by your decision. Finally, an unwelcome side affect of being away from work for an extended period of time is the risk of depression. Sometimes, the relaxed pace and lack of daily structure can actually be stressful. It can be easy to ignore symptoms like elevated anxiety, apathy, too much sleep or too little, and severe procrastination, instead of seeking professional intervention early.

After opting-out to stay home with her young family, Kelly said that she was in a grocery store with her kids and a woman in a business suit with a cell phone in hand pushed past her in line. The woman looked right through her like she didn't even matter. Kelly felt terrible and wanted to scream that she used to be a player. After all, she was once a VP and had lots of responsibility. Now, she felt she didn't even deserve the courtesy of a quick grocery checkout.

Depending upon how the sabbatical is going, women may decide to prolong it, cut it short, or let it run its course. They may also decide to renegotiate the terms of the sabbatical with their family.

Regardless of what decisions you make, how you use your Orange Line Sabbatical matters. You need to learn the fundamental skills to ensure you are making the most of your sabbatical and that you will be ready to return to work when you are ready.

Skills for Living The Orange Line

1. Recognize when the Feminine Filter is at work

Even when you decide to take a break from your career on a sabbatical, the Feminine Filter can be working its magic to tell you how you "should" live. As when in the other stages, you must be continually vigilant for how it is impacting your choices. One way to uncover its core assumptions **is to listen for and recognize Filter language**.

The chart that follows illustrates the common language we heard from interviewees on sabbatical. It helps to take it apart and debunk it to reveal the messages you receive and perpetuate with this language. We then reframe the language so you can respond in a way that is true for you.

SABBATICAL ASSUMPTIONS	DEBUNKING THE ASSUMPTION: WHAT'S REALLY GOING ON	REFRAME
I feel guilty about not working. I really shouldn't be taking a sabbatical. **Feminine Filter underlying assumption:** I am never good enough.	When you internalize others' judgment about your decision, you devalue your own input. You suggest to yourself and to others that they know what's best for you. Allowing your guilt to decide hides the best course of action because it's externally decided.	*I chose to take an Orange Line Sabbatical for a reason. As long as this reason is still valid, then what I chose is important.*
Because I am not working, I should be helping out everyone else and taking on other responsibilities. Others expect this. **Feminine Filter underlying assumption:** I need to be perfect in behavior and appearance at all times.	When you need to prove to others that even though you aren't working, you are important, you suggest that your decision was subpar. If you sacrifice your purpose in taking a sabbatical by filling it with items that others value more than you do, you prioritize their values over yours.	*I have chosen not to work for an important reason. I will say yes to those responsibilities that make sense within that context, but I am also okay with doing "well enough" at things that are not important.*

SABBATICAL ASSUMPTIONS	DEBUNKING THE ASSUMPTION: WHAT'S REALLY GOING ON	REFRAME
I can't ask my spouse to help around the house because I am the one at home. **Feminine Filter underlying assumption:** Women are primarily responsible for home and family and taking care of everyone.	Over-protecting others by not asking or expecting them to contribute, limits their broader development so they never learn how to take care of these aspects of their lives. It also reinforces the work norm that there will be someone to take care of their home needs while they focus on work. As a result, nothing changes.	*My spouse is also responsible for the home and children. Asking him to take responsibility for these aspects builds his skills and will enable me to return to work more easily when I decide to.*
I don't make money therefore I don't deserve to spend it. I am conscious others are supporting me financially. **Feminine Filter underlying assumption:** If I follow the rules, good things will happen.	Even a purchase that makes your home beautiful, and brings you joy, can be foregone because you question whether you deserve it. Investments in your sabbatical can feel extravagant. In reality, you imply that since others are making the money, they get to control how it's spent. This is not a healthy perspective.	*Even though I don't make money right now, I deserve to spend money on those things that are important for my health, growth and needs. I also am willing to invest in my eventual re-entry plan.*

You can impose this pressure internally and **become aware of guilt**. Statements from others like, "What does she do all day" or, "Honey, where's dinner?" suggest that you are not contributing as "expected." You may feel like a failure; thus, guilt surfaces, leading to bad habits such as submerging your interests and working harder, not smarter, as you buy-in to the assumptions.

It can be telling when you **observe your behavioral response**. When you turn a hobby like quilting into a full-time obsession, you may be reacting to an assumption that you must do it all, rather than using your sabbatical for what was intended—being with the children, resting, getting well, traveling, and so on. Or when you become a helicopter mom, you overcompensate for stepping out of your career to show you can be type-A perfect at something else. Each of these is a behavioral response to the underlying assumptions you've internalized. That is, all you've done was change the external representation of that assumption. You did it all at work and now you must do it all at home. Observing this and noticing the connections, for example, that you seem to choose to do it all regularly, helps you stop and step back. You can then ask yourself why you are doing this. Once you uncover the core assumption, you can then let it go. For example, if a woman realizes she is overcompensating with parenting because at her core she believes her children must be perfect or it's a reflection on her, she can start to realize that, in fact, she can choose not to pressure her children like that.

In our interviews and research, we saw women behave in ways that enacted the Filter's assumptions. Here we highlight these, describe what happens when women enact these behaviors, and highlight how you might reframe the underlying assumption to help you change the behavior.

SABBATICAL BEHAVIOR	CONSEQUENCES	FEMININE FILTER ASSUMPTION
Failing to invest in their long term financial future or career such as investing in a retirement account or savings during the time off, maintaining a professional network, or building a personal credit history. **Bad habit:** Acquiescence and self-sacrifice.	Failing to maintain work credentials may mean you re-enter behind where you exited in terms of responsibility and salary level. When you consider the lost time from the sabbatical as well, this can make a significant impact on your long-term earning potential.	Women are primarily responsible for home and family and taking care of everyone. **Reframe:** *I will ensure my future financial security is maintained throughout my sabbatical. This is my responsibility.*
Absorbing all of the household management tasks because they are not working. Women become the owner of taking care of anything house-related regardless of why they are on sabbatical. The reasons for taking time off become secondary to feeling a sense of control in accomplishing these tasks. **Bad habit:** Acquiescence and self-sacrifice.	You may like to control the household tasks, but this may waste time and energy on things that are not helping you reach your goals or pursuing your *métier*. This may also cause resentment and internal conflict about why you are on sabbatical.	Women are primarily responsible for home and family and taking care of everyone **Reframe:** *I will protect the integrity of my sabbatical and re-entry plan by sharing household tasks and getting sufficient support.*

SABBATICAL BEHAVIOR	CONSEQUENCES	FEMININE FILTER ASSUMPTION
Getting caught up in the minutiae. Some-times, without dead-lines and expectations to scaffold their day, women can let time slip away or allow themselves to spend inordinate time and energy on items of little consequence. **Bad habit:** Working harder, not smarter.	You may signal to others that you can't actually manage your time well or that you've lost your ability to prioritize. Interests that you had such as world events, exercise, or movies get submerged in your micro focus on your other responsibili-ties.	Commitment to some-thing is measured by how much time you devote to it. **Reframe:** *I will keep perspective and priori-tize my time on actions that are important.*
Obsessing about checking every box or becoming obsessed with perfection. **Bad habit:** Risk avoid-ance and over-compen-sation.	You can waste time obsessing over unim-portant things. Further, you are setting yourself up for failure instead of allowing yourself to be fulfilled. Your obsession reduces your confi-dence, making it harder to complete everyday tasks.	I need to be perfect in behavior and appear-ance at all times. **Reframe:** *I am ok with being an imperfect per-son. I can stay focused on what is important.*

SABBATICAL BEHAVIOR	CONSEQUENCES	FEMININE FILTER ASSUMPTION
Evangelizing about not working. Women may over-validate their decision with emphatic statements such as, "I don't need to go back to that crappy job, bad boss, salary. I'm not cut out for corporate America." They may also judge other women negatively who have made a different choice. **Bad habit:** Seeking external validation.	Using language like this limits your flexibility to make changes later on, should circumstances shift. Further, loudly expressing your opinions tends to alienate others, people who could actually be friends or employers and support you later on.	I am never good enough. **Reframe:** *My choices are mine and are working for me right now. I am also open to change in the future.*

As you become aware of the language, guilt, and behaviors that mask Feminine Filter rules, you can start to **challenge your assumptions and be more conscious in your choices.** You can reframe the sabbatical as something you are entitled to take because you are responsible for yourself. You've chosen the sabbatical for legitimate reasons; therefore, it is important you honor that.

2. Bring yourself into the equation

When on sabbatical, remember that regardless of the reason for your choice, like caring for a family member or returning to school, you are important as well. As you figure out what being on Orange Line Sabbatical means, you need to ask yourself: If I am equally important in this decision, what does that look like in practice?

It starts with **setting boundaries and expectations**. When you are not working, there is a temptation to absorb other people's needs, tasks, and priorities. If you took a sabbatical to get some rest, then you need to make sure you are resting. If you are homeschooling children, nursing a sick relative, or writing a book, then you should not be spending all your time cleaning your house or absorbing all of the family chores. It helps to keep articulating, out loud, why you are taking the sabbatical and what your goals are during this period. This helps keep other people and their creeping requests in check. Rather than immediately filling your time with new activities, volunteering, or household chores, you should negotiate what you are willing to do, set expectations, and create boundaries early on, saying "No" to activities that drain your energy.

Setting clear expectations about what you are willing to do in this stage is critical; too often there is the assumption that because you are not working, you can take on everyone else's "to do" list. Try looking at is as if you were being paid; if you hired someone for this role, you would set clear boundaries and expectations of the job. You can do the same with others. **Ask for what you need.** You might say that one night a week you are going out with friends or that your spouse can drop the children off at school most mornings. Differentiating between what you are willing to do and what you "should" be doing is important.

A ROOM OF MY OWN

"After breaking my leg, I realized the importance of being still and taking time for myself. Once I was up and running again, I made sure I crafted a good hour each day to read, pray, and center myself. I've come to realize the benefits of planning and looking at how you are investing your time, so you can live more purposefully.

"I talked briefly with a life coach over a year ago; I was trying to simplify my life, de-clutter. I wanted a plan before my kids went back to school. This coach asked me questions: 'Tell me about your home, your family.' She asked, 'What is the first thing you see when you enter your home?' I told her there was a large music room to the right, with all kinds of electric guitars, basses, drums, a piano, soundboard, and microphones. Our kids and my husband are all musicians. By the end of our ten-minute conversation, she asked me what I liked to do with my time. I shared with her that painting was my passion. She then asked me where I like to paint. I told her I usually paint in the kitchen after everyone is in bed and I get my supplies down from the rack in the garage. The coach then asked, 'Why is your passion hidden away while your family's passion is right out in the open?' Our conversation made me realize that I had to feed my soul. We moved our home around and created an art room for me, and now I feel such liberation. There's a new flow of energy and creativity in our family life. Adding this art room has given me a sanctuary in the home. I wish I had figured that out ten years ago."

— *Eleanor, Business Owner, forty-five*

Another element to bringing yourself into the equation is **self-promotion**. Even when you're taking a break from work, you can be leading the discussion about your long-term career path and sharing your developmental experiences with your professional network. Too often women let time pass without kindling professional relationships, keeping their résumé updated, or taking advantage of strategic opportunities to showcase their work abilities. This can make re-entry extremely difficult and be detrimental to their lifetime earnings.

You can take time annually to attend a course or a conference to keep credentials up to date. If you know, you can inform former colleagues how long you plan to be out of work. If you are getting a degree, keeping key contacts in the loop with your intentions can help you find a job more readily. You can keep up on reading in your area of expertise and plan regular conversations related to these topics to share ideas and show others that you are still knowledgeable.

Finally, you need to ensure your **self-care** needs are being addressed. This may mean you need to carve out time to go for a run, exercise, or meditate. Sometimes, you might need child- or eldercare support so you can attend a doctor's appointment or a lunch date for yourself. Even when you are physically present with your family, it is acceptable for them to respect your quiet time to read or rest.

As you practice bringing yourself into the equation as a key skill for living on The Orange Line, you show others and yourself you have accepted the principle: I am important, too.

3. Develop self-awareness

Taking a sabbatical provides a unique opportunity to foster self-awareness. You can successfully use the extra time and space to build your professional expertise as well as the essential life skills that will keep you living The Orange Line.

The first step in this process is to **solicit feedback.** You may want to tap your spouse or close friends to get an honest assessment of you. Particularly, if you took a sabbatical to regroup after a bad work experience or burnout, you can use feedback to discover how others think you contributed to the problem. Do they see patterns in your behavior or responses to situations? What did they notice about what happened and how you reacted? You might also want to connect with former work colleagues for this. If you have nothing to lose, i.e., if you don't think there will be any future career repercussions for sharing your observations, they may provide extremely valuable insights.

Depending on why you are on sabbatical, there may be clear mechanisms to help you get feedback, such as a graduate school program or understanding how your lifestyle may have contributed to your illness. Some feedback may be hard to hear and you may not be ready for it. One way to deal with this is to write down the feedback as you get it and wait to process it. That is, wait to respond; analyze the feedback for several days after receiving it to enable you to calm down. This will give space to understand it more objectively.

It's also helpful to conduct a **self-assessment**. Self-assessment at this stage can take the form of questioning yourself: Which aspects of your work, personal, and family life do you enjoy? Which do you dislike? What are you really good at? What lies are you telling yourself? How can you learn more? Depending on why you are on sabbatical, there can be tools to help, such as a continuing education course or a transition firm that provides guidance during a layoff.

Another way to self-assess is to tune into your body sense. How your body reacts can act as a barometer, indicating when you feel strong and powerful versus stressed and uncomfortable. Especially because there is often so little external support when you are on sabbatical, your body can be a useful indicator. For example, if you are energized by volunteering or being around other people, this could be a sign you need stimulation and collaboration. If you feel anxious whenever you leave the house, you may have become risk-averse or lost confidence.

Armed with this perspective, **reflect and analyze** the information you gathered. Ask yourself some important questions. For example, are you taking a sabbatical to recover from burnout and finding yourself consistently overwhelmed? What is driving you to continue taking on too much in every aspect of your life? What does this tell you about your ability to self-manage? The answers to these questions help you learn more about yourself at a deeper, more authentic level.

As with the other stages, after gathering and analyzing it, you can then turn this information into your own unique **self-development plan**.

If you have always been busy, you can explore doing less. If you have always worked, you may want to try volunteerism. The self-awareness part is doing something that is unique to you. One woman volunteered for years at the library during her sabbatical and realized through this process that this was her calling. She went back to school in library science.

Good self-awareness habits are never too late to build and can benefit you during your sabbatical and beyond.

4. Build a support system

Whatever the reason you are out on sabbatical, you still need to practice building a support system around you. Being on sabbatical does not mean you do not need help. You can often feel as if you are isolated and financially incapable of getting help. But this does not diminish the need.

Acknowledging that you need help respects your current reality and identifies the core problem so you can solve it. A graduate school workload could take most of the day. Illness could drain you of energy. Small children could ensure you get very little done. Just because you are not working does not mean you should fire the housekeeper, cancel daycare, and stop grocery delivery. It also does not mean other family members get to dump all of their responsibilities on you. Again, think of this period as a job: Getting well, going to school, or looking after small children will put the need for help into better perspective.

Figure out what help you need and to whom you can delegate. When you are not working, your first line of support is usually friends and family. Other parents can share in carpools. If you are in school, other students might share team tasks. If you are dealing will illness, friends can help with meals or driving to doctor's appointments. These relationships can be reciprocal.

It's during sabbatical that women seem to have the most trouble paying for help from anyone, so reframe this. You may feel that since you are not generating an income, suddenly your time is not valued and that you can pick up all of the menial tasks. Once on this slippery slope, it gets harder and harder to get help. Family members may act like it is suddenly a burden to contribute to household chores or to pay for outsourcing them. But by staying focused, leveraging free help whenever possible, and using paid help to keep you focused on your long-term goals, you set yourself up for a stronger re-entry. It is still an investment in both of your careers to get the help you need.

Finally, you won't get the support you need unless you effectively **manage the work**. Just because you are home now or leveraging unpaid help doesn't mean your standards for support are lower. You are still in charge of your support system and how it meets your needs. Clear communication of expectations up front helps to ensure everyone involved is on the same page about what those needs are. Demonstrating how you want things done can help train people to do things the way you prefer.

5. Get comfortable operating in imperfection

Just like there are no perfect jobs, there is no perfect sabbatical. You may have some initial vision of how things will be: Mom home, serenely baking cookies for the kids and hosting fun, creative play-dates; the world traveler, out to conquer Kilimanjaro; the author, leisurely researching her next book. But in reality, things won't always go perfectly. One woman whose husband was a lawyer with a good salary decided to stay home with her two small children. She got involved in the community, volunteered, and enjoyed her time with the kids. When she was pregnant with her third, her husband left her for another woman. Her sabbatical came to an abrupt end as she spent her third child's infant days working part time and going back to school to upgrade her credentials so she could resume her career.

The first step in living with imperfection is **accepting it**. This can help remove any feelings of self-doubt or failure women might otherwise have when things inevitably get messy. Sometimes, you have to accept what life has thrown you. Maybe you've been forced into a sabbatical because your spouse is ill. Maybe you are too sick to do anything else. Or a layoff completely surprises you. Initially, when life puts you in these positions you would never choose, you resist and may even be angry. After she was laid off, one of our interviewees said that she spent a year or so lying on the couch, trying to figure out what to do next. Accepting imperfection means that while you may hate the position you've been put in for a while, like all transitions, you will get through it eventually.

Once you've accepted imperfection, it is possible to **embrace it**. It can be such a relief to realize that you don't have to be perfect. As you come to expect and live with imperfection, you can even **plan for it**. You may find you don't like being on sabbatical and want to re-enter quickly. You may cut your sabbatical short, or you may decide to prolong it. Planning can help remove panic when things get messy or don't work out the way you had hoped. The best way to plan for imperfection is to have money saved in advance and continue to contribute to this saving during the sabbatical, if possible. Of course, you cannot plan for everything, but knowing the big things are covered can certainly make things go more smoothly.

Because so much of your life has been dictated by the constraints of a career, you may be less comfortable with the flexibility, freedom, or different constraints that a sabbatical may bring. Like anything else in life, nothing is perfect. Sometimes, you will love being away from work and other times you will long to be back. Living with imperfection can teach flexibility and help you relax a bit. With acceptance and a plan, you can even have a little fun with life's messiness during your time away.

6. Expand your universe.

When you are on sabbatical, you need to keep yourself open to myriad possibilities. This skill is important across all the career stages, but is essential for The Orange Line Sabbatical because it is so easy to make your world smaller when you temporarily leave a career to focus on other pursuits.

You can expand your universe during sabbatical in many ways. First, you can **seek out people who challenge you** and push you forward. It helps if they are a diverse group who think differently from you so you don't get stagnant or subject to groupthink. One way to do this on sabbatical is to maintain your network of work contacts while you are gone. If at all possible, by being available when they call, even if you only do a small project, you can maintain the connection. You can also stay connected by having lunch occasionally or emailing an interesting article to former colleagues. Recruiter Zoe, forty, advises women "to never leave the workforce completely, if possible. Even a few hours of work a week can keep your network, skills, and talents up-to-date. In addition, a feeling of self-worth can be hard to find when adult interaction is sparse day after day. By working a few hours a week, a woman can get a break from the 'mommy mushy brain' that I suffered from and was pleased to relinquish on my work days."

You can also make new friends that will help challenge your thinking and push you to grow. One woman joined a group for just that purpose. She was on sabbatical because her husband's job required that they move frequently. As a result of the group, she learned to develop her interests to the point where she started several businesses and negotiated with her husband to move less often.

You can also grow by simply **thinking bigger**. Whatever your comfort zone, you can push yourself to stretch a little further. Non-profit

Coordinator Vivian, forty-seven, took a sabbatical to care for a special-needs child. She didn't just become an expert in her daughter's syndrome, she collaborated with doctors, patients, and caregivers to write a book that is now the primary resource for that syndrome.

Maybe your company will pay for your sabbatical. Rally Software states that, "After completing seven years of full-time service, every employee is eligible for six weeks of fully paid leave. The adventure does not have to be work-related, and we encourage our employees to do something grand—to pursue a passion, to think big, to go deep." Jodi's company offered sabbaticals, enabling her and her husband to travel for four months. Maybe your company offers something you don't know about. Or maybe find a company that does.

Sabbatical is potentially a time to try new things. You might learn to row or travel to a new city. One woman took her three children to a remote village in Mexico for a month. Another had her family do a volunteer project both in the U.S. and abroad with their church. It may be a good time to go back to school or take some courses. Even if you are off work to heal from illness, you might be able to do some web-based education. Several interviewees went to grad school during their sabbaticals.

Another way to expand your universe is to **take a big risk** toward personal growth that helps you face your fears. In a sabbatical, it may mean using the time off to prepare for a change in careers or to launch a business. It may not even be something others would find risky, but to you, it's scary. One interviewee faced the lifelong effects of her father's alcoholism by going for therapy, and so shedding demons from her past.

By using sabbatical time wisely, through expansive people, opportunities, and risk-taking, women can expand their universe of possibilities.

In this way they can prime themselves for a successful re-entry and long-term career.

Conclusion

By practicing the skills outlined in this chapter, you can maximize your Orange Line Sabbatical. Because your intention is to return to work, your break needs to include progression both personally and professionally. Re-entry will be less daunting for you and your family if you put good behaviors in place. By making conscious choices for yourself and minimizing the impact of the Feminine Filter, you can make the right choice about the next phase of a long-term career. Further, by enlisting sufficient support, avoiding the pitfalls of perfectionism, and focusing on your goals, you can ensure a positive break experience.

CHAPTER EIGHT:
Re-entry

I TOOK CARE OF EVERYTHING

"In college I was an art major with the goal of becoming a graphic designer. My first full-time job, I worked on two magazines and a website. It was a great job, but there was not a whole lot of room for growth, so I started looking for other opportunities. Around the same time, I started dating someone and, when I got pregnant, we got married.

"It was a bad decision. I only married him because I was pregnant. He didn't treat me well, but I didn't know if I could do it on my own. My husband wanted me to stay home with the baby. He was raised by a single mother. Because he didn't understand the dynamics of how a man and woman should treat one another and raise a family, he had an unrealistic view of what life would be. He had no idea of the work involved in taking care of a baby, nor did he know how to treat a wife. Because he was working, he felt that I had to take care of everything else. I know a lot of women would have been grateful for the opportunity to stay home, but it was hard for me. I loved being a designer. All of my college friends were unmarried and childless. I didn't know anyone nearby I could relate to.

"After I had been home ten months with my son, my sister forwarded a job opening and I applied. I was given an offer and I accepted. I was excited to be returning to work. It made me feel I had a purpose besides being a mom. It was hard work balancing it all and then I became pregnant again and had bad morning sickness. My husband was in graduate school and gave me no help at all. I was dropping off and picking up—my husband's only duty was going to work and school. In one argument we had, he mentioned breaking up. I spoke up and said, 'At least I'd have every other weekend off!' After almost five years of marriage, my husband met another woman and moved out. Although it was difficult, it was a blessing in disguise. My husband was faced with paying a lot more child support if he didn't keep the boys more, so he stepped it up. It was then I started to achieve some balance in my life. I had some badly needed alone time. I had a flexible schedule and telecommuted three days a week.

"I've dealt with guilt sometimes. For example, if the kids have a field trip and I have an obligation at work, I have to choose. Sometimes I have to put work first, because this is how I support my family. I've become much better about letting go of the guilt. I realized that taking care of me is the best thing for my sons—being happy makes me a better mom. After the divorce, I recognized how much I'd neglected myself and allowed others to do the same. Not only am I happier than I've ever been, I feel that I have a bright future ahead of me."
— *Georgina, Web Designer, thirty-six*

For several of our interviewees, it was time for re-entry. The sabbatical was over and it was time to return to work. They found it exciting and stressful at the same time. They got to embrace their careers again and follow their passions. They looked forward to the rewards, recognition, social relationships, and opportunity to learn new things again.

There are many common reasons we found for career re-entry:

- **Break time is up.** Women may have negotiated a set amount of time for their sabbatical and that period has ended. In this case, they likely will return to the same employer they left. They may even return to the same role. Even so, they likely feel changed from the time spent away and thus will experience an adjustment as they re-engage. This may cause them some initial consternation as they struggle to re-adjust.

- **The children are older.** The age at which a mother considers her children old enough for her to return to work may vary: some will think preschool or kindergarten is a good time. Others need to ensure their young adults are safely off to college before they consider focusing on work again. The business career of former Technology Manager Natalie, fifty-two, stopped dead in its tracks when she took on her new job of raising a baby with equal vigor and intensity. He's now ten years-old, and even though she's had a long list of volunteer assignments and part-time jobs, she knows it is now time for re-entry.

- **Life circumstances change.** Whether women were laid off and need to get back in the saddle or have realized their progressively dwindling financial condition is untenable, sometimes financial pressure sends them looking for work. Women may even be forced to take a job that falls below their expectations, just to earn a paycheck. This might lead them to question their career path or even lead them to opt-out again as they search for work that makes them happy.

THE SYSTEM FAILED

"We had decided I would stay home and take care of the children, but when our marriage broke down, I couldn't financially sustain that lifestyle anymore. At first, I thought I would be okay because

he would be forced to pay me child support. But the separation phase was long and I was racking up a lot of debt because he wasn't paying for anything. Then I found out he lied about his earnings to lower his amount of child support. I had believed in the system, but I learned in time that the system is flawed. I realized that even if I won in court, he was going to find loopholes and ways to get out of paying. It would be a lifelong battle to support my children. I couldn't rely on that so I finally decided to go back to work."
— *Brenda, Senior Account Executive, forty*

- **Resolution of illness.** Women may have stepped out for a while to heal from illness, grieve the loss of someone close, or care for a sick parent. Though the whirlwind of that process may be over now and the timing is right to go back to work, they may have mixed feelings about focusing their attention on work or simply picking up the pace again. While some organizations can be very accommodating and sensitive to the situation, others may expect business as usual from day one.

- **External pressure from friends or a spouse.** Sometimes, women feel pressure to return to work because they have internalized others' perceptions of their worth. They may feel that their spouses or former colleagues no longer seek out their opinions or value their ideas since they've been out. Or they may feel they can no longer justify staying at home. They may feel judgment that they are not adding value since they are not working. This puts a tremendous amount of pressure to invest in a job search, rather than the career change desired.

- **Dissatisfaction with not working.** Women may start to feel that something is missing, even though they have taken a sabbatical from their careers. While they've enjoyed the time away, using it to rejuvenate, heal, or be with their children, they may now notice an internal conflict or tension. In our interviews, we also discovered, especially among older women, a desire to contribute and continue with their passion.

TRIAL BY FIRE

"When I re-entered, I started as a VP with a large company after relocating and the first few months were a blur! Everything was different: the telephone system, procurement process, legal requirements, financial system, and budgeting. The Blackberry started buzzing at 6:30 a.m. on my way to the gym and didn't stop until 9 p.m. every night. Four days out of five I had back-to-back meetings with individual team leaders. There were processes to streamline and the daily deadlines and expectations kept rolling in. The clients and their requirements were totally new. This intensity continued for the first ten weeks until I got up to speed. Then I curbed the meetings. It was stressful until I became familiar with the structure and grasped how it all worked." — *Alison, VP of Marketing, fifty-seven*

Re-entry Challenges You May Face

Because it is a change, women will face challenges during this re-entry phase that can affect their long-term careers:

- **The gap on their résumés.** Sometimes, employers may perceive the chronological gap on their résumés negatively. Certain types of organizations may resist "out of the box" candidates and this can make using their résumés as a marketing tool more difficult. Some leave the gap and don't discuss or they refer to it only in the cover letter. Some put in something like "full-time mom" or "sabbatical." Some highlight volunteer work they did during that time. Others shift or eliminate dates on their résumé. According to Cohen and Rabin in *Back on the Career Track: A Guide for Stay-at-Home Moms Who Want to Return to Work*, there are many ways to overcome the gap by re-framing it positively.

- **Bad timing.** If women wait too long, or engage in lengthy experimentation as they search for an ideal role, they can limit their options. Similarly, if they re-enter following a burnout without changing the underlying behaviors that led to the burnout, they could simply restart the process again.

  Re-entry during a recession can be especially problematic because there are a plethora of qualified candidates competing for fewer opportunities. Alternatively, women could capitalize on the bad economic environment by working with a start-up or taking temporary positions.

- **Lack of clarity in their career goal.** Another challenge women face with re-entry after children is lack of clarity about their career goal. Women may have competing and contradictory motives for re-entering. Cohen and Rabin identify motivating factors women should identify, such as needing external validation, leveling the marriage playing field, career ambition, becoming a role model, and avoiding the empty nest syndrome.

LAST IN, FIRST OUT

"I was in advertising, but my husband moved around a lot. My career was second, so it was easier to quit when my daughter was born. I thought I was doing what everyone wanted—being the at-home mom. That was, until my divorce when I had to reinvent. I moved back to be near my parents. I went back to school to become a nurse, thinking it would give me more flexible hours. I married again and became a stepmom. We moved across the country. I got a few years of nursing experience, but then got laid off with budget cuts. It was last in, first out—very bad timing for career restart. I did contract nursing roles: I never knew when work would call. I decided to have another baby with my new husband. I took on a part-time sales specialist role, but between that and contracting, I had no real consistent income. Plus daycare was a significant challenge. There was no part-time daycare for infants. And the cost of full-time daycare eclipsed my part-time earnings." — *Lois, unemployed former Nurse, thirty-five*

- **Pushback from the family**. If women re-enter after time at home with the family, they may experience pushback from their family and friends. Because they are not physically available when the children arrive from school or they are not able to make dinner every night, their family may object to their career resumption.

- **An increase in guilty feelings**. After their decision to return to work, women may experience external voices that elicit guilt. Women might hear, "I can't believe you're going to leave the children with a stranger," or "But who will take care of the house?" Their children may express fear about not having them around. "How will I get to soccer practice?" or "Who will help me with my homework?" Even friends may share their own uncomfortable feelings including their fear of being left behind, or of being judged about their own life choices.

Knowing what you want, feeling grounded and confident with your decision despite some apprehension, helps. As fifty-six-year-old, non profit Senior Executive Maya, whose family members kept offering their opinion, remarked, "I was okay with the advice. I'd say, 'Thank you for your comments.' You learn that you can't become confused between people's opinion [based on the Feminine Filter] and what you know you should be doing."

The re-entry process is a transition period. Here are the skills you will need to live on The Orange Line and adjust to the workplace.

Skills for Living The Orange Line

1. Recognize when the Feminine Filter is at work

To recognize rules-based decision-making in action, you first need to **listen for and recognize Filter language** when it shows up. In re-entry, because you are prioritizing your career again, you may get pushback, as others have to adapt to this change. The pushback usually comes in the form of language designed to move you back in alignment with Feminine Filter behavior.

When you start noticing Feminine Filter language from others, you can then decide whether or not you agree and avoid becoming part of someone else's belief system. Remember that you can't change anyone else: You only need to live your own truth.

The following chart illustrates the common language we heard from our interviewees when they discussed the re-entry process. We use it to highlight the Feminine Filter assumptions at play. We then take it apart and debunk it to reveal the messages women receive and perpetuate with this language. By reframing the language and recognizing The Orange Line Principles, you can open up new possibilities.

RE-ENTRY ASSUMPTIONS	DEBUNKING THE ASSUMPTION: WHAT'S REALLY GOING ON	REFRAME
I can't re-enter. My skills are out-of-date. I will never be able to get a job. **Feminine Filter underlying assumption:** I need to be perfect in behavior and appearance at all times.	There is a job out there somewhere; it just may take a while and a different marketing strategy to uncover it. Stressing about the outcome as a means of avoiding the messy work of searching is counterproductive.	*I can find a job. I am willing to take a step forward and start to work.*
There are too many options. I can't decide what I want to do. I need to find the perfect job. **Feminine Filter underlying assumption:** I need to be perfect in behavior and appearance at all times.	Paralysis by analysis drains energy. Not deciding is also a decision. There is no perfect choice. Every role offers potential learning opportunities. That's not to say you shouldn't be discerning. But waiting for the perfect role to appear is just an excuse not to start looking.	*I am willing to find a "good enough" job at first to start the process.*
I'm too old to re-enter. Nobody will hire me. **Feminine Filter underlying assumption:** I am never good enough.	This assumes that just because you chose to leave work, you stopped learning. This is untrue. People work well into their 70s; some start a second or third career after traditional retirement.	*I can start to work regardless of my age. I am capable and will do my best.*

RE-ENTRY ASSUMPTIONS	DEBUNKING THE ASSUMPTION: WHAT'S REALLY GOING ON	REFRAME
I've been working very hard applying for everything out there, but it's just not working. **Feminine Filter underlying assumption:** Commitment to something is measured by how much time you devote to it.	People rarely get jobs on Monster.com or by applying to postings, especially later in their careers. By wasting your time spending hours on your résumé or blindly applying for positions, you avoid doing the riskier tasks required like meeting people and talking with them about job opportunities.	*I will determine what's required to get a job and focus my efforts there. I will take a risk and put myself out there, even though it feels scary.*
If I work for free or agree to get paid less than I'm worth, it's okay if I don't do a good enough job. Then I can make mistakes and learn. **Feminine Filter underlying assumption:** Tangible, material rewards are not supposed to be important.	When you get paid less than what you're worth or you regularly volunteer rather than getting paid, you convey a message that you are not good enough. You put yourself in a smaller pond so you can be a bigger fish. In the short run you may find success, but long term, you diminish your opportunities.	*I am capable of doing the job required and getting paid fairly for that work.*

RE-ENTRY ASSUMPTIONS	DEBUNKING THE ASSUMPTION: WHAT'S REALLY GOING ON	REFRAME
I can't ask my family to help now. It's my responsibility to take care of everyone. **Feminine Filter underlying assumption:** Women are primarily responsible for home and family and taking care of everyone.	Just because you made dinner every day for five years does not mean that is your responsibility forever. Are you afraid of losing control because you like to be the one who ensures tasks get done? Situations change all the time. Routines that were made can be remade; nothing is set in stone. It takes a team to make a home run smoothly.	*Both parents are responsible for home, family, and taking care of themselves. A combination of spouse, children, friends, and paid help can work together to make it all flow.*

Be aware of guilt. Guilt is internal pressure to buy into Feminine Filter assumptions. You feel guilty when you want to do something that is counter to the Feminine Filter rules.

No one likes to feel guilt. As a result, you often succumb to what's being asked of you in order get rid of the short-term pain. But taking the easier path here will only prevent your career from flourishing.

Another way the Filter shows up is in your **behavioral response**. For example, when a woman chooses to limit her search to jobs that can be done during school hours, is she doing this because she feels guilty about looking for a better role that might require more time away from home? At this level, she may not want to be honest with herself. She may feel, "Of course I want to be near my kids!" An honest examination is required.

In our interviews, we saw women behave in ways that enacted the Filter's assumptions. Here we identify these, describe what happens when you enact these behaviors, and highlight how you might reframe the underlying assumption.

RE-ENTRY BEHAVIOR	CONSEQUENCES	FEMININE FILTER ASSUMPTION
Enabling others so they don't need to take responsibility for themselves. Because of fear and ambivalence about relinquishing control, women choose to own the entire burden of managing the household, rather than ask others to step up. . **Bad habit:** Acquiescence and self-sacrifice.	If you don't share the responsibilities of everyday life, you increase your over-burdened life and enable others' lack of accountability. The same thing may happen when you get back to work, where you might tend to take on far too many responsibilities, having become used to "running the show" at home.	Women are primarily responsible for home and family and taking care of everyone. **Reframe:** *Together we can determine what needs to be done and who can do it.*

RE-ENTRY BEHAVIOR	CONSEQUENCES	FEMININE FILTER ASSUMPTION
Keeping busy with lots of activities to keep from having time to focus on the re-entry process. Re-entry is a job requiring focus and persistence; beware of justifying trivial distractions. Or focusing only on tasks that are easy, like searching for jobs on the Internet, rather than networking or conducting informational interviews. **Bad habit:** Working harder, not smarter.	You waste time and justify it because you are busy. As a result, you do not find jobs that are useful, you don't go to interviews, and you don't take risks to move forward. You tell yourself you are doing well but lack results.	Commitment to something is measured by how much time you devote to it. **Reframe:** *I will set tangible goals and measure results during the re-entry process. If certain activities are not yielding results, I will stop doing them and try something else.*
Considering unrealistic plans. Sometimes, this period of vulnerability can cause women to clutch at unrealistic ideas. They may grasp at schemes that seem easy, flexible, and viable, but are really long shots. Examples include: selling cosmetics or any "direct marketing" scheme, building websites, or flipping houses. **Bad habit:** Risk avoidance and over-compensation.	Fun hobbies aside, these things are not considered by many to be "real jobs." You may waste precious time on these things and others may assume you are not serious about your career.	I need to be perfect in behavior and appearance at all times. **Reframe:** *I am capable of finding a "real job" that maybe isn't perfect and/or I'm not perfect at it, but it pays well enough and builds my résumé for the future.*

RE-ENTRY BEHAVIOR	CONSEQUENCES	FEMININE FILTER ASSUMPTION
Too many false starts. Employers like to see proof of performance and the ability to live with decisions you have made. This usually comes from staying somewhere long enough to have some solid performance reviews and a progressive salary history. While experimentation is important, there is something to be said for simply accumulating experience. **Bad habit:** Creating a diversion.	There is a financial and emotional cost to constantly switching jobs and professions. It is harder to accumulate wealth, institutional power, and confidence.	I am never good enough. **Reframe:** *I can create space to try new things without feeling the pressure of perfection. I can also find creative ways to experiment within existing and adjacent work environments so I maintain some continuity during the process.*
Reacting defensively to pressure to re-enter. Women can become attached to the way things are and the fear of re-entering overwhelms them. They defend against taking a risk by doing nothing or looking for safe choices. **Bad habit:** Risk avoidance and over-compensation.	You may disengage from the process and limit looking for creative ideas. You may discourage friends from helping because you don't want to hear their ideas. Defensiveness is an indicator that you are afraid and diverts you from dealing with the fear directly.	I need to be perfect in behavior and appearance at all times. **Reframe:** *I can learn to recognize my own defensiveness and find ways to deal with my fears.*

RE-ENTRY BEHAVIOR	CONSEQUENCES	FEMININE FILTER ASSUMPTION
Short changing themselves and believing a negative self-narrative. Women may under-invest in what they need to get a job. Instead of a new suit, they wear an old one. Instead of taking people out for coffee, they talk on the phone with them. Instead of hiring a babysitter for the children, they only make appointments when the children are in school. **Bad habit:** Creating a diversion.	You fail to get a job, which can reinforce your negative self-narrative and excuses for avoiding the investment. It perpetuates the diversion. Further, it prolongs the re-entry process.	I am never good enough. **Reframe:** *I am a good person, and I am worth investing in.*
Seeking approval. Sometimes, women seek everyone else's approval before taking the next step. **Bad habit:** Seeking external validation.	To avoid conflict with others, you follow their advice and neglect your own instincts about your goals. You gather so much information that you lose sight of what you really want.	I am never good enough. **Reframe:** *I am capable of finding my own way.*

RE-ENTRY BEHAVIOR	CONSEQUENCES	FEMININE FILTER ASSUMPTION
Setting their sights too low. Women may try to re-enter the workplace at a level too low. They only look for jobs that can be done part time or flexibly, instead of finding the right career, then job, and figuring out the logistics later. **Bad habit:** Lower career and reward expectations.	You could end up in a low-end career that does not provide you sufficient financial stability or retirement funds. You may also miss out on exciting roles by narrowing your focus too much.	Tangible, material rewards are not supposed to be important. **Reframe:** *I can earn what I am worth.*
Failure to negotiate. Women may be so grateful for the job they don't ask for an appropriate salary, future promotions, flexibility, or support at home. **Bad habit:** Avoid asking for what you need or challenging the *status quo.*	You end up not getting paid what you are worth, existing in a dead-end job, or working in ways you didn't want such as too many hours. You don't get the support you need at home and struggle to manage your home-life and career.	If I follow the rules, good things will happen. **Reframe:** *I will take responsibility for myself and ask for what I need.*

With these methods of recognizing the Feminine Filter, you can now start to **challenge these assumptions**. A woman who decides, for instance, she wants her brother to help more with their ailing mother, can free up more time to focus on her career. There are other ways to challenge these assumptions. You could say, "I am not responsible for dinner tonight." Once you change your language internally, you can start to say it out loud. You could tell your spouse, "I am willing to be responsible for four dinners. I need you to own the rest. Let's figure out what this could look like."

Owning responsibility for these assumptions makes everyone aware of how they are operating in your life. As a result, you can **be conscious in your choices**. Being conscious helps you decide whether you accept or reject these messages and how you choose to respond. It also opens up many more creative possibilities. Our interviewees made lots of creative things work; re-entry is possible. When you decide you are good at your craft and deserve a chance to explore it, you can come up with many ideas for how to make it work. One interviewee, who had convinced herself that a job with travel was impossible with children, is now traveling two days a week in a job she loves. You could speak to an expert on Alzheimer's and realize your mother will actually get better care in a facility. Or you could talk to your child's teacher and learn that the school has a wonderful after-school program. Removing the limitations of the Feminine Filter allows you to see many new options.

Women usually are happiest and at their best when they are conscious in their choices, not when they are letting external noise limit their options and determine their direction for them.

2. Bring yourself into the equation

Setting **boundaries and expectations** enables you to bring yourself into the equation so you can create space to re-enter. After being out of work, you have probably developed certain routines, filled your time with activities, and taken on many household and volunteer duties. You will now need to stop many of these activities because you will want to devote your time and energy to work again. Mothers or caregivers may find it hard to renegotiate tasks because others in the household are used to your doing most of the household duties. But to protect your re-entry decision and free up time and energy for work, a re-negotiation is necessary.

Setting expectations up front can be very helpful. While family members might have been excited about the re-entry decision, or at least supportive, they may not have fully appreciated how their world could change once re-entry begins. By having direct conversations about your intentions and expected changes, you can get the support you need. Speaking directly will help lay out your boundaries. For example, saying, "I will no longer be able to make breakfast or lunch and I no longer want to do laundry. How do we fill the gap?" If you get resistance, you can state, "I understand that this transition is difficult. Because I am working again, everyone has to step up. Change is hard. Once we settle into a routine, it will get easier. Thanks for your help." If you anticipate the resistance, you can have these conversations before the emotions heat up. You can negotiate the transition while everyone is calm.

Setting expectations, especially when you anticipate a rocky road, can help create comfort. For example, when Jodi ramped up to full time, she told her children that there would be new expectations since she had to work more, and that they would be enrolled in an after-school program. She said it would be different and they talked about the pros and cons. When one of her sons complained, Jodi could point back to the initial expectations and explain that everyone had to help.

I KNOW WHEN TO TURN IT OFF

"I don't feel guilty about turning it off at 5 p.m. I get up early, and I'm very responsive. I've trained my employer and customers to know I will have their answer before they get to the office tomorrow. They trust me. I set up the boundary that I will deliver, just on my terms. My message: 'When I'm on the clock, I'm on, but you have to give me my space when I'm off.'" — *Neeta, Technology Sales Specialist, forty-one*

It helps to verbalize what is going on in a non-emotional way so you can bring the underlying assumptions to the forefront and help clarify the potential misinterpretations of all parties. Notice Neeta didn't say she wasn't available for a work crisis needing attention after hours. But she also has made clear that when there is a personal crisis during work hours, she expects that nobody will push back when she leaves to attend it. Otherwise, she could say, "I worked Saturday to get the product launch done, but I need to take time on Wednesday morning to get my car fixed. Doesn't that seem fair?"

Watkins, in *Your Next Move: The Leader's Guide to Navigating Major Career Transitions*, discusses three conversations you should have with your boss to manage expectations of your role:

- **Style**: How can you fit in with the team; what are the communication preferences, and how are decisions made?
- **Expectations**: What are you expected to achieve and in what time frame; what are possible early wins; what outcomes do you need to avoid?
- **Resources**: What resources are available; what scope do you have to make changes; what's the process for requesting resources?

You can also bring yourself into the equation by **asking for what you need**. At home, this could mean outsourcing some of the household tasks you previously had time for. Or, it could mean giving yourself space to explore several job opportunities or projects to see what will stick. At work, it could mean asking for flexibility or negotiating a compensation package that swaps benefits you don't need, like medical insurance or a golf club membership, for the ones you do, such as extra time off for appointments or an extra week of vacation.

Sometimes, by negotiating, you can cut your own deal—something customized to your specific situation and outside the usual company policy. Often times the most effective time to do this is on the way in, when the company is still trying to woo you, rather than once you're there and subject to the company culture. Janie, fifty, wanted a corner office, status, and a big car. When she wasn't offered one as the VP of HR, the CEO gave her reasons why. She looked at the responsibility of the position compared to other executives and the only difference was that she was a woman. So she gathered the facts and made a business case. She got what she wanted. You can't expect to magically get what you want if you don't feel confident enough to articulate what that is.

NO MORE STRICT SCHEDULES

"I temporarily moved my kids away from my husband so I could start a new business. Now I'm here full time. My husband comes down on weekends. The kids are with me—my parents do the childcare. The nice thing about it is I can pretty much set my own hours, so if my parents have an errand, I can flex it so I'm there for the kids. I adjust time to my needs. I never thought I could have done this. I started with a strict schedule at my first job to a more relaxed one at my second, to my own schedule. It took me a long time to get there. I have a support system available. It's not just for them: I'm equivalently creating my own world." — *Heidi, Insurance Specialist, thirty-nine*

An important element continues to be **self-promotion** at this stage. You need to round up all of the experiences and relationships you have developed during the sabbatical and package them to tell a strong story about your career development. You need to show employers how much value you can add to your organization and how you are uniquely positioned to do so. It is also important to reconnect with any former professional colleagues with whom you may have lost touch.

YOUR PERSONAL JOB-MARKETING PLAN:
MORE THAN JUST A RÉSUMÉ.

Think of your re-entry as a new product launch. Consider your target audience: If it's "anyone who will hire me," get more specific. What are the likely ways to engage with these target organizations? You may need to do some research to figure out who, specifically, makes the hiring decisions for the positions you are seeking. You can then figure out ways to connect with these people—perhaps a meeting at an industry event or professional association meeting such as a product launch, and you will need marketing materials. Consider if it is a résumé or professional bio you will need. What about your Linked-In profile? Do you need to produce a portfolio of your work? Will it require a professional photo? Finally, you will need to construct a sales follow-up plan to track whom you have contacted and what results you have achieved.

Finally, you need to continue to ensure you are getting sufficient **self-care**, and that you have prioritized yourself equally with your family and friends. If you left due to illness or burnout, you may need to build a wellness regimen into your life and ensure your re-entry plans include time and space for these activities. You can fuel your energy levels with healthy living, but with increased pressure and fewer hours in the day you may tend to forget to protect and refresh your body for the challenge. Often when you feel good, you decide to skip the practices that helped you achieve your good health. To accomplish this, some interviewees found that scheduling workouts or healthy lunches just as they did a meeting made them harder to skip. You can find a workout location close to work or home. Taking holidays and using sick time also helps ensure you maintain energy and fitness levels to sustain yourself.

Adapting any self-care habits you had while on sabbatical will be more sustainable than stopping and having to restart. Maybe working out six days a week is untenable, but four is realistic. Maybe you change lunch with friends to a dinner monthly. Or have the children make their own breakfast so you can take time to pray or meditate. Rethinking how you can do self-care will make it easier to maintain.

Because you are adding something large to your life, it can feel easy to just drop "you" in the process. Instead, your re-entry will be most successful if you can ensure you remain in the conversation about your own life.

3. Develop self-awareness

Self-awareness is a critical skill during the re-entry phase to help you eliminate issues of the past, clear the slate, and position yourself for long-term success. Because it can be an emotional transition, you have many opportunities to get to know yourself more deeply.

As with other phases, we find the first step in this process is to **solicit external feedback.** This can be especially challenging in this phase because your friends and family generally want to support you and may resist sharing their honest feedback to preserve the relationship. Former co-workers may be a better place to start. Though their feedback might be outdated and you may have grown a great deal since you last worked with them, they may be willing to tell you now what they wouldn't have told you then. Colleagues at a volunteer position are also useful places to seek out feedback as they have seen you in work-related tasks. Recruiters or hiring managers are also a helpful place to gain feedback, particularly if you interviewed and were not selected for a job. Although it can be painful, this is a unique opportunity many people hesitate to leverage for fear of embarrassment. But with little to lose because the job is already gone, you can possibly get the best, most honest feedback available.

When IT Manager Madison, forty-two, interviewed for her first job, she didn't get called back. After getting advice from a mentor, she got up the courage to call the interviewer and ask what she could have done differently. As a result, she was called back to the firm and subsequently hired.

If you miss out on a job, don't personalize the rejection: Business is business. Instead, try to understand what external feedback you can gain from the rejection: Was it your résumé, the interview, or a skill mismatch? It might not even be something you can change. Did you share the organization's values? You might not have wanted to work there if you didn't. Was the hiring manager ineffective at hiring or managing people? If so, that might have made for a difficult employment. Once you've determined the reason and whether it is something you can or want to fix, you can move forward and consider the experience good practice.

The next step is to **conduct your own self-assessment**. What is realistic for you to do once you re-enter? Can you get your old job back? Do you have the skills you need to transition to something else? Do you need to upgrade skills or get some additional training? Have you lost touch with important connections you will need? There are a number of strength-finder assessments that might help with this, as well as coaching services to help guide you along the journey.

Perhaps you didn't enjoy your pre-sabbatical career or you had difficulties that forced you to leave it. To have a smooth transition and "onboard" experience this time, it may be helpful to review the past. You might want to consider your past roles, competencies, skills, talents, successes, passions, and values. You may also want to consider how you spent your sabbatical—what types of activities were you involved with? How did you use your time? By determining what worked, what didn't, what energizes you, what drained your energy, and where you were weak, will help you choose differently this time.

Armed with information, you can create time and space for **reflection and analysis**. As you move forward in this process, you can take time to reflect on what you are experiencing and analyze the underlying message. For example, one woman took a course to revamp her law skills in mediation and realized that she didn't enjoy it. Testing and evaluating your feelings can indicate what you really want. What is merely resistance and what is a true indicator of your interests? Say you take a course and feel anxious and have low confidence for the first semester—this may not indicate that you are on the "wrong" path, but rather that you are simply doing something new.

We've said this before, but it applies at this stage as well: A technique many of our interviewees said helped improve their self-knowledge and grounding was incorporating a spiritual ritual into their day. Some found they gained perspective from nature. Others found it through faith or religion and others in solitude—deep breathing, yoga, prayer, and meditation. Many find that journaling each day helps them block out the noise and go deeper to discover their joy, harmony, and sense of oneness. For example, Consultant Briana, thirty-seven, takes time daily: It "might be a walk, going to the beach, taking thirty minutes to sit and breathe, being present in the moment—it always works. I get myself grounded again." By incorporating a spiritual practice, you may be able to slow your thoughts down and bypass the outer clutter and external expectations.

You can use this feedback and insight to **create your own unique self-development plan**. At this stage, it can incorporate the re-entry process itself or even become a full career plan. It can help you determine which jobs to consider upon re-entry and give you better ways of dealing with stressful situations. You may consciously develop more interpersonal effectiveness or get a better grasp of the financial side of your business. When you get feedback about a possible weakness, you need to discriminate between a weakness that is unlikely to change, such as,

"I'm not a detail person," and a capability that can be developed, such as delegation.

Executive Coach Marshall Goldsmith describes in his book, *What Got You Here Won't Get You There,* how to "turn off" certain over-played behaviors that have become so extreme as to be self-limiting. He highlights the most common ones he has seen in his many years of coaching, such as "winning too much" and "needing to add value." It may not be the case that you need to do more of something; to develop, you may actually need to do less of something.

Bringing self into consciousness is an evolutionary process; there are no short cuts. If you don't do the work, it is easy to repeat past patterns and even give up because you avoid these old feelings. You may blame your past employer or the profession you once loved instead of making changes within you to make things work. Sometimes, you might blame your spouse or workload when it is your inability to draw boundaries that is the real problem. By understanding more about yourself before embarking upon the re-entry process, you can overcome past mistakes and set yourself up for an Orange Line career.

4. Build a support system

Building yourself a support system means creating the net that supports you in the re-entry process. You need to figure out what you need and how to get it, including résumé help, coaching, domestic support, schooling, and whatever else you need for your transition.

First, acknowledge **you need help**. The transition back to work is going to be taxing, even for the most well-prepared people. The first ninety days will be about proving yourself, making relationships, and getting inducted into a new organizational culture. It will also be about learning new routines. It is unlikely at first that you will be able to delegate much at work since you haven't yet built relationships or don't yet understand others' skill sets. Learning these things during your on-boarding process requires time and creative energy.

That's why you'll need to figure out where you can get help on the home front. If you went back after taking time out for family or health reasons, those reasons may still be there and still demand attention. Fifty-one-year-old VP of Operations Shawna is a good example. When her second child was born, she found a nanny who could live with her. Every raise she got was spent on the nanny. She scraped by on what she was making, but having help with childcare was essential. Having the nanny allowed her to travel when she needed to. Now her children are older so she doesn't need as much childcare and her career has flour-ished because of the investment she made in support.

Since you can't be successful long term if you try to do this alone, you can start by **figuring out exactly what help you need and delegating**. When hunting for a job, you initially may want to hire pre-employ-ment support to help update your résumé and create a marketing plan. You might hire an outplacement specialist or coach to do some assess-ments to help find appropriate roles, or you may contact recruiters to secure introductions. These resources are plentiful, valuable, and often priced reasonably. You might also research what services your *alma mater* offer for alumni to re-establish themselves in that network.

When you are back to work, you can consider seeking out a colleague to sponsor you for a project, be your mentor, or introduce you to an or-ganizational affinity group. This can help you through the on-boarding process. Senior Account Executive Brenda, forty, signed up for every single training course her company offered so she could hit the ground running. It also signaled to them that she was serious about being back.

It may be helpful to expand the network in other ways as well such as joining industry trade associations and attending conferences. You can also join groups of other job-seekers to hear their stories and share experiences. Often this helps provide feedback and checks to see if you are on target. At the very least, it is good practice to make your self-marketing pitch over and over again, honing it along the way.

I GOT BOGGED DOWN

"I found it very easy to get bogged down. And when I first started, it was overwhelming. I was being pulled in many different directions and it was difficult to know what would be the most fruitful direction. The Chamber of Commerce and the Small Business Association are great resources, but I had to learn which ones are worth spending time on. No matter what, you need to develop relationships. You can't just send an email and expect to be able to get the most out of these resources." — *Terri, HR Manager, thirty-four*

Finally, you need to **manage the work**. This means getting comfortable with letting others do things for you and also managing them to complete the work. You can ensure higher quality if you set expectations up front, train them how to do the tasks, monitor results, and communicate feedback. At first, managing others to do jobs you're used to controlling can feel awkward. The key is to recognize that they may not do the work the way you do and that it is okay. For example, whenever you hire a new sitter, there is a learning curve in terms of the tasks: where to pick up the children and how to prepare different meals. So what does it matter if the spoons are put in the wrong drawer at first? By telling the sitter once, the next time it is likely they will be in their proper place. Things may not be perfect, and this may require some time and energy to manage, but eventually it will allow you to free up your creative energy to focus on getting a job you love.

5. Get comfortable operating in imperfection

Just as there was no perfect job or career path early in your career, there is no perfect job or re-entry transition. But as Rhonda, fifty-three, a professional Career Coach, counsels, "You will, eventually, get a job."

Because re-entering is a transition process, accepting and embracing imperfection will make the change easier. You can give yourself permission to make mistakes or have sub-optimal days, remembering that the job and the integration of work and life is new.

Watkins says to expect you will initially act in ways incongruous with organizational norms. You can embrace imperfection by showing your ability to learn as you gradually understand the organizational culture. Or adapt to the changes at home: Kelly accepted that she and her husband were not going to be able to make it across town to pick up their children from daycare by 6 p.m. perfectly every day. They made arrangements together and did their best, but when they were late, they chalked the late fee up to a cost of doing business, not a personal failure.

When you expect things will be messy, plan for imperfection. If you know you have a gap on the résumé, for example, you need to address it. You may even need to find a different way, other than through a résumé, to market yourself to an organization, such as through referrals from existing employees or meeting hiring managers at industry events. If the hiring manager is worried about risk, you can introduce information that could help the manager justify his or her decision to hire you—information that is important and can make it easier to hire you. You could even offer to mitigate the hiring risk by suggesting a temp-to-hire situation, consulting, or another creative idea.

At home, things are not going to be perfect, either. Tasks you previously did well because you had ample time may get done sub-optimally.

It's okay to plan to do certain tasks less well. This allows you to plan to do the important things better. For example, you may miss some of your child's key milestones while at work. If this is important to you, consider asking the childcare center to take photos or connect with the nanny on Skype. Let the nursing home staff know in advance what they are authorized to do for your parents when problems arise. Schedule less at work during months you know will be busy at home, such as September when the children return to school and through the holidays. Conversely, if it is expected to be a busy time at work, quarterly reports, taxes, or end-of-year close, consider relaxing the holiday plans a little and setting expectations early for someone else to host the family get-together.

You may need to tolerate disorder temporarily as things ramp up, and to some degree, permanently, as life can be generally messy. When you get comfortable with this and plan to do all "well enough," you can live a fuller and more fun life.

6. Expand your universe

In this stage, you have spent time away from your career. By leveraging what you have learned during that time off, you can decide how to expand your universe of options before, during, and after the transition, and be even more creative in the future.

As we have said before, it continues to be important to expand your universe by **seeking out people who challenge you and push you forward.** It is important you have the right circle of colleagues. You want those around you to be reinforcing your decision to re-enter and bringing challenging, expansive opportunities your way, not challenging your resolve to go back. You can also proactively drop relationships you aren't comfortable with.

This is time to expand beyond the safe inner circle of support. Research suggests it is not your close circle of friends who get you jobs, but rather leads from contacts you saw only "occasionally" or "rarely." You may be able to surface opportunities when you spread out and connect with people who exist on the periphery of your existing relationships. Jodi has had students find jobs by talking to people when bartending, meeting someone they talked with at a networking event, or by informational interviewing with a total stranger connected via another total stranger. The world works in a web with surprising ties beyond your close connections and by tapping into it, you can open doors for yourself.

Learning how to **think bigger** opens opportunities. Thinking bigger could be thinking completely out of the box, such as starting your own business or changing your career. Or it could be simply broadening your perspective. Instead of starting just one retail store, start in several locations. Instead of re-entering a law firm as a mid-tier lawyer, consider becoming in-house counsel for a mid-sized company. Thinking one step bigger than your existing comfort zone will help stretch you. These roles will take just as much effort and time, but yield a better result in the long term.

One woman, whose husband's company offered to relocate him to another country, convinced the company that she would agree to it only if they created a role for her there, too. The company made it happen. By leveraging the experience she gained in the role, she eventually got promoted and now actually outranks her husband in the company. What could have been a prolonged sabbatical or stunted re-entry became a glorious opportunity.

Sometimes, women limit their re-entry career choices too early and too narrowly by the logistics of their family or personal needs. Instead, try to first figure out what kind of work you like, then what company or job you want to do, and then how the logistics will work. Often, it's not having good role models as examples, making it more difficult to imagine what roles are possible. Among our interviewees there was a wide variety of roles women were filling including those traditionally considered "non-flexible" ones.

Think bigger by talking to people with different ideas, solicit advice, do research, and conduct informational interviews. Your vision of what your career could be will likely expand.

Another way is to **expose yourself to something new**. When you re-enter, you might feel less self-confident. One way to build your confidence is to try something challenging. It can also connect you with others who are doing the same. When Kelly was getting her MBA, she was surrounded by smart people with great credentials. The professors and her fellow students challenged her and expanded her view of business. It was a competitive environment, but also very supportive. Her respect for her classmates motivated her to work really hard to keep up. Her confidence got a huge infusion and it opened her eyes to a world of career possibilities. Many of our interviewees spoke about how their MBA or other post-graduate degree gave them the confidence and credentials to re-enter or change their jobs.

Once you have started to take on small changes, you may be ready to **take a big risk** and face your fears. Some of our interviewees decided to launch a business or become a consultant. Some were successful and others were not. Regardless, they all said they learned a great deal and gained from the experience.

Conclusion

Re-entry after a sabbatical is something many of you will do. It can be an exciting and scary time. You are likely to experience some push-pull from various sources like family and friends, making you think twice about getting back in the marathon. To transition effectively, you have to expect and respect the noise from others and know what you want. By reassuring them and pushing back on their own fear of change, it provides you with an opportunity to ask them for their help. You also need to accept that the first year after re-entering is likely to involve considerable skill development and negotiation at work and home. Expand your universe so the barriers and noise of others are less likely to derail you. By practicing The Orange Line Skills, you have an opportunity to resume an exciting career and pursue new frontiers.

CHAPTER NINE:
The Mid-Career Transition

"I started in an office working for one of the baby Bell phone companies. People would call with questions about their telephone bills and I would help them. I thought that would be my whole career. During that time, the women's movement was encouraging us to try other jobs. So management came through and tested everyone in the office for their propensity toward other things—I took the test and blew away the electrical aptitude part. They sent me to school to become an installer. I was a pole climber and all that! Then I did electrical engineering, product marketing on a product my group developed, and database management. When I was in high school, women could become teachers or nurses. Who knew I would end up as an electrical engineer? But it was fun.

"I spent thirty-two years at this. After I got transferred from Illinois to Texas, I went to school on work's dime. They taught me about business. But I also always had side businesses and was doing entrepreneurial ventures. I even worked with the military for a bit.

"Then I retired for the first time. I'm now an entrepreneur. My main business is a Western and English tack and clothing store focused on people who show horses. I've ridden for a long time, so after I

retired this was a good choice because I've always enjoyed horses. I got tired of going into a hardware-style store to buy riding clothing and accessories so our store is an upscale boutique, and most of our customers are women. Recently I also decided to go back to school and get a real estate license. I never knew realtors worked this hard!"
— *Kimberly, Business Owner, sixty-one*

Some call it the mid-life crisis. Others call it career derailment. It sounds so cliché. Yet many women told us that they reached a point where they suddenly felt the need to switch career direction midstream. In some cases, they sacrificed leadership roles to start over at the bottom of a different ladder. Others quit to pursue something they thought would be better, only to find the grass wasn't greener or that they bumped around so much, they couldn't re-gain the traction they once had. Some found a previously undiscovered passion; others ended up ultimately back on their original track.

Still others used "retirement" as an opportunity to pursue something completely different, finding an "Encore Career," as Marc Freedman calls it in his book, *Encore: Finding Work that Matters in the Second Half of Life.* As people live longer, healthy lives, and as traditional pension plans disappear, experts predict baby boomers will work longer than their parents for financial necessity as well as for a sense of purpose.

Whether a milestone birthday prompts a disappointing realization that you haven't done things the way you wanted to, or an inner voice is telling you that you're not fulfilled, it's never too late to break free of stale routines.

Daniel Levinson, in *Seasons of a Woman's Life,* calls this stage the "Midlife Transition" where we question, "Who am I," "What is the purpose of my life," and "What am I meant to contribute." In his model, the Middle Adult years follow a phase during which people chose their work and focused on "making it." Women have now become their own person and pursue their own values. They have rebalanced work, family, and play and are ready to march to their own drummers. Later on, in this stage, they may begin to concentrate less on building their own wealth and more on making a contribution to the company and community. Their energies may focus on developing others, broadening their perspectives, and leaving a legacy.

From our interviews and research, there seem to be two distinct age ranges in which this phenomenon occurs for women: Either in their mid-thirties, when the crush of life, family, and work responsibilities begin to weigh them down and they struggle to regain their Green Start career traction, or in their late forties to mid-fifties. This is often when women's kids are launching their own lives, and women look ahead to a limited number of remaining working years and wonder how best to maximize them.

This stage is not about early career experimentation in which women explore what they really want to do. Early on, women likely figured out what they enjoy about their jobs and where they'd like to develop their skills. In contrast, in the mid-career phase, women might feel they have become derailed and are being prevented from reaching their career goals. It's time to hit the reset button and figure out how to "do their purpose" and get paid for it.

Feelings of discomfort, pressure, or lack of certainty may manifest externally. The stereotypical mid-life crisis for men is when they buy the bright red sports car and adorn it with a twenty-something blonde girlfriend. For women, the symptoms may be less obvious and could include:

- Alcohol or drug abuse
- Personal physical changes aimed at making them feel younger:

Tattoos, braces, face lifts, dramatic weight loss
- Expensive showy purchases: cars, clothing, jewelry, houses
- Less-than-healthy focus on helping their children excel: over-involvement in college prep, sports, dance, and so on
- Sudden interest in younger men

An unfortunate consequence of feelings and associated behavior such as these is for many the breakdown of their marriage. It's so much simpler to let the little annoyances become big, marriage-ending problems when women feel uneasy about themselves and that something is personally amiss. The temptation is to place blame externally rather than take personal responsibility or to seek validation about being out of sync with what had been their passions. If attention comes in the form of flattery from an admirer, they may be vulnerable to the outside interest. Once a spiral of self-destructive behaviors has begun, it's often hard to stop.

Similarly, women heading toward a mid-career crisis may show signs of sudden dissatisfaction with their job. They may have conflicts with former allies or lower the standards for the quality of their work. Further, they may be enticed by headhunters and begin switching around the industry, hoping for the job panacea that will make them feel satisfied again.

It is unknown how much menopause contributes to this problem for women. Anecdotally, some interviewees talked about being filled with anxiety and that they knew this affected their decision-making. One woman described the frustration she experienced about her fluctuating levels of energy: One minute she was soaring, the next minute she wished she could stay in bed. Another woman described it as, "several years of just not feeling right." The realization that their child-bearing years are behind them and their temporary loss of control over physical and emotional body states most certainly plays a role in women's attitudes toward work and life.

Regardless of how it manifests, there may be several reasons women may end up in this stage mid-career: Perhaps they never did much early experimentation or career planning, or they've exhausted the career track they were on. Maybe they've become bored with their chosen profession. Forty-nine-year-old former Banker Gerry said when she graduated, her passions were politics and clothing. She ended up working in technology and then finance, where she was on a successful upward trajectory. However, when she got overwhelmed or hit a career roadblock in banking, she took time off and consulted for a clothing line. Then she would resume finance again until the next big roadblock. When her husband was diagnosed with a terminal illness, she opted out again from work to care for him. Eventually she resumed freelance work in clothing and is now trying to decide what she wants to do next. "I need to love something that requires me to put in so much time and effort," she says.

Career coach Jennifer Gresham believes career women today are expected to be "high-achieving," but do not get the guidance required early in their career. As a result, women tend to use the Feminine Filter rules as guidance. Gresham continues that women wake up mid-career and "realize they've been living up to someone else's definition of success. They look successful, but they don't feel like it. And if they find the courage to switch, many of them start over in new careers, which makes it look like there's a career advancement problem. "

No One Said It Was Going To Be Easy

Underneath the exciting opportunities and self-discovery of this period may be some problems that can affect your long-term career and personal life.

- **It can be hard to figure out what you really want to do.** As you search for a job that matches your passion, you might also be looking for one where you are paid fairly and that works for your family situation. It can be difficult to separate a bad work environment, ineffective manager, limited local job options, or bad feedback from a truly bad career fit.

- **Getting a job in a new field can be difficult.** You may lack specific industry knowledge or a particular ability. Or you may hesitate to experiment with a new role.

- **You may have to start at the bottom.** Starting over in a field may mean starting at the bottom of the pay grade and scale, which may not be practical. Worse, some companies won't even consider hiring someone older for an entry-level role due to factors like long hours, bad pay, grunt work, and travel involved. In addition, an employer may assume that a mature-aged worker will be unwilling to work in a high intensity environment or be less willing to learn.

- **Emotional pressure.** This phase may last for a significant amount of time, which can eat at self-confidence. If you're in the mid-career crisis phase and you've already left your former job, this period is similar to an expensive and protracted job search. It can lead to feelings of vulnerability and unworthiness.

The choices you make in this often difficult and uncertain stage, such as quitting, starting a business, or deciding which career to work in, require focus and discernment. Orange Line Skills provide the tools to enable you to be successful on your new career trajectory. Here we have provided examples of how to apply these skills to this stage.

Skills for Living The Orange Line

1. Recognize when the Feminine Filter is at work

When you begin to pause and realize that something needs to change in your career, whether due to a critical event or an overall creeping feeling of unease, you need to be able to figure out whether and how the Filter is influencing your thinking.

As we've said in previous phases, first you need to **listen for and recognize Feminine Filter language** behind widely used and accepted statements so you can start to break down what people are really saying to you. For example, if someone says, "Changing careers mid-stream is impossible," you may internalize a vision of career *perfection* that doesn't include deviations from a single, linear, Green Line path. Or if you hear, "I don't want to work for a big company anymore. It's all about profit and it is too political," you may feel the external pressure to adopt the assumption that *tangible, material rewards are not supposed to be important*. Listening for Filter language allows you to ask, "Is that true for me?" For example, it may be that you have only ten years left of working before retirement and actually need to increase your retirement savings. Or you may want to pursue your *métier* until the end of your life.

The following chart highlights the common language we heard in our interviewees and through research. We use it to highlight the Feminine Filter assumptions at play. We then take it apart and debunk it to reveal the messages women receive and perpetuate with this language. We then reframe the language, identifying Orange Line Principles so you can become more receptive to possibilities.

MID-CAREER TRANSITION ASSUMPTIONS	DEBUNKING THE ASSUMPTION: WHAT'S REALLY GOING ON	REFRAME
I absolutely cannot continue with my life or my career as it has been in the past. There is no way to make this work. **Feminine Filter underlying assumption:** I need to be perfect in behavior and appearance at all times.	This assumption implies you are too inflexible or lack the creativity to figure out how to make it work. Plenty of people make work work and you can, too.	*I can be good enough at my job and my family/life. I can figure out how to make it work.*
Everyone says I should be doing what I'm passionate about. This is more important than making money. **Feminine Filter underlying assumption:** Tangible rewards are not supposed to be important.	Sometimes the pressure to mold a career around your passions limits your options. Enjoying painting doesn't mean you have to paint for a living: It may mean you will be successful in roles that require visual talent, such as a window designer for retail stores or point-of-sale display manufacturer.	*Getting paid what I'm worth is important. I can be creative in figuring out how to use my passions.*

MID-CAREER TRANSITION ASSUMPTIONS	DEBUNKING THE ASSUMPTION: WHAT'S REALLY GOING ON	REFRAME
The grass is always greener somewhere else. If I move, change jobs, follow my passion [insert wish here] I could achieve my dreams. **Feminine Filter underlying assumption:** I need to be perfect in behavior and appearance at all times.	Here you are externalizing your angst, looking outwards for the "answer." Your own internal problems with managing time, drawing boundaries, and inserting yourself into the equation will not be solved simply by changing the environment or the venue.	*I can determine what is really making me fearful. I can figure out how to solve it. Doing my best and "good enough" are perfectly acceptable.*
If I take time out, I can think and discover and do the thing I'm passionate about. I can't do that at work. **Feminine Filter underlying assumption:** I need to be perfect in behavior and appearance at all times.	This assumption implies you can't discover your passion and create a space while working, yet many women find a way to do this and maintain their income at the same time. If you plan to leave anyway, why are you still working at the top of your game?	*I can lower the intensity level of my work or take a vacation to plan my next steps.*

MID-CAREER TRANSITION ASSUMPTIONS	DEBUNKING THE ASSUMPTION: WHAT'S REALLY GOING ON	REFRAME
I need to give back, and I can't do that working at a for-profit company. I need to switch to nonprofit, but I won't make much money there. **Feminine Filter underlying assumption:** Tangible, material rewards are not supposed to be important.	For-profit companies often have more resources, which, used well, can do enormous good. If a nonprofit is the right fit, many people ask for and receive competitive salaries from nonprofit roles.	*It is possible to make a contribution and leave a legacy anywhere. I value my contribution and can expect to be fairly compensated for it.*
I'm not sure I can make the change. I'm not really cut out for a new career, but I don't have the energy to continue in this situation for another decade or more. **Feminine Filter underlying assumption:** I am never good enough.	Uncertainty is a natural part of this transition process. Allowing your doubts to take over derails your opportunity.	*Change can feel scary and overwhelming, but I'm capable of working through it.*

MID-CAREER TRANSITION ASSUMPTIONS	DEBUNKING THE ASSUMPTION: WHAT'S REALLY GOING ON	REFRAME
Actually, I don't really like working. I enjoy doing more "arty," "creative" pursuits, but I need to work to pay the bills. **Feminine Filter underlying assumption:** Tangible, material rewards are not supposed to be important.	This may be code for not enjoying some aspect of your current job. It also may be hiding an assumption that you feel money is not valuable. Often translating a hobby into a job yields lower pay and less satisfaction than just keeping it as a hobby. Or it may show an unwillingness to do the messy work of turning art into revenue.	*I can find a career that utilizes and rewards my creativity, abilities, and experience.*

Next, you need to **be aware of guilt**. Hopefully, by this stage you've learned to recognize guilt as the internal pressure you put on yourself to act based upon assumptions. You feel guilty when you show ambition because you believe, "I can't set my sights too high. I don't deserve great roles. I should have gotten my masters." Or when you start to explore new career options, guilt appears and you may think, "I shouldn't change careers now. I've invested too much in the path I am on." Whenever guilt like this appears, you can recognize it for what it is: A sign that an assumption has been made. Ask yourself why you feel guilty. What are you afraid of? As you ask these questions, you get to the heart of the assumption and then can work with it.

The next step is to **observe your behavioral response**. What did you do? Did you buy-in to the underlying assumption or just react out of habit? How do you feel? For example, you might be feeling anxious about how much you hate your job and how you can't possibly stay at your company a minute longer. You might be sending out résumés and telling everyone you know that you need to make a change. Or you might freeze, content to stagnate in your current job because you are worried that challenging the *status quo* will cost you what you have built to date. In both cases, you are reacting to the assumption that you must be perfect in everything you do. This assumption causes you to over- or under-react. When you observe your response, you can again step back and look at it objectively, discovering the reasons for your behaviors.

In our interviews and research, we saw mid-career women behave in ways that enacted the Feminine Filter assumptions. Here we highlight these, describe what happens when you succumb to these behaviors, and highlight how you might reframe the underlying assumption to help change the behavior.

MID-CAREER TRANSI-TION BEHAVIOR	CONSEQUENCES	FEMININE FILTER ASSUMPTION
Throwing the baby out with the bathwater. The feelings of mid-career crisis might cause women to make drastic changes in their personal lives—changes that may not resolve the problem. Examples include having an affair, quitting a job abruptly without a plan, or having cosmetic surgery. **Bad habit:** Catastrophizing.	Changing jobs, partners, or your appearance is not going to soothe your internal feelings of discontent. Further, these things can be self-destructive.	I am never good enough. **Reframe:** *I am a good person, and I am working on my own development. I can take the time I need to work through this period without making drastic and destructive decisions.*

MID-CAREER TRANSITION BEHAVIOR	CONSEQUENCES	FEMININE FILTER ASSUMPTION
Confusing a career crisis with just feeling bored. Sometimes, women fabricate excuses to leave jobs when they're really just bored. Often they are waiting for someone else to solve it. They may look externally for the reason, rather than internally at what stagnation is telling them. **Bad habit:** Creating a diversion.	A major consequence of boredom is a tendency to stop investing in your career. You might resist innovation or lose interest in networking. This can send a signal to others that you are not interested in career advancement and that you have become less valuable. You may get fewer opportunities.	I am never good enough. **Reframe:** *I am capable of recognizing when I need a new challenge and finding ways to create opportunities that will pay off for my career.*
Under-investing in the process. Sometimes, women embark upon a period of discovery without the resources to help them through. Perhaps they feel they cannot spend money when their careers are in upheaval. Or they start a business on a shoestring and from scratch instead of asking for funding. **Bad habit:** Creating a diversion.	Sometimes a toe-in-the-water approach to work can be counterproductive. Waiting to have "enough money" to hire a career coach or get a personal assistant could cause you to waste time tinkering. Starting a business from scratch, for example, can take years of selling and building your operation without reliable revenue.	I am never good enough. **Reframe:** *I am committed to this change and I will invest what it realistically takes to make it work.*

MID-CAREER TRANSITION BEHAVIOR	CONSEQUENCES	FEMININE FILTER ASSUMPTION
Undervaluing time, credibility, and accomplishments. While considering alternative career options, some women get wrapped up in working with nonprofits, volunteering, providing pro-bono work, or exploring creativity at jobs below their current earning level. **Bad habit:** Lower career and reward expectations.	It signals to others that you don't value your time and this makes it difficult to later convince an employer otherwise. Further, you can get caught up in a "brain drain" environment where you are not surrounded by inventive, creative forward-thinkers, causing you to stagnate.	Tangible, material rewards are not supposed to be important. **Reframe:** *I can find strategic ways to maximize my time and energy to build my career.*

Once you understand the pressures and reasons for your behavior, you start to feel more powerful. You can now begin to **challenge your assumptions**. Ask yourself, "Is the current situation really that inhospitable or am I just making excuses for myself?" "Is the career change I'm contemplating really about work or is it something at home driving this?" Or "Is it true that I am unable to try new things, contemplate new directions without jeopardizing everything?" This awareness can help you make better, more informed decisions.

Finally, you can **be more conscious in your choices** and realize that you have an infinite number of options available. Instead of seeking perfection in the job at all times and over-reacting when things get messy, you can open yourself up to imperfection and learn to work within it. When you are ready to take a first step in changing your career, you can do so without the weight of the Feminine Filter attached.

2. Bring yourself into the equation

By the time you get to the mid-point in your career, hopefully you have realized that your career will be more successful with you in the driver's seat.

To do this, you need the ability **to set boundaries and expectations**. There may be a lot of pressure right now to do what other people think is best for you: your boss, your friends, your family. You may feel pressured to change jobs or to "find and follow your passion," before you even know what that means for you. It's important to become comfortable pushing back and saying "No" to this external pressure. If you were laid off or are experiencing a crisis event, such as a death in the family, it's especially important to give yourself space and time to adjust to the crisis and get your bearings before making a drastic career change. To make a transition effective often calls for additional time, space, and ample resources to get through the period of change.

It is also important to **ask for what you need** at this stage. If it's time and space, then ask for it. It can be such a relief for all parties to know where everyone stands, out in the open, during this time. Your family can brace for the impact of transition, potential employers can plan, and members of your professional network can help with referrals. Because you are entering a more reflective period in your life, it may be helpful to create space for reflection. That may involve negotiating a sabbatical from work or stepping away from a hobby. Or it may simply mean leaving work at a reasonable hour and resisting the urge to work weekends for a few months.

As with re-entry, you may need to ask others to take on more responsibilities. Family members can share more of the household chores; current co-workers can become more capable at aspects of your job so that they can free up your time for more urgent projects.

You must also ensure your career is on the right track by practicing **self-promotion and self-care**. Speaking on a panel at a women's conference, Robin Goldstein, Principal Program Manager, Windows Portable Devices at Microsoft, cautioned women not to "put the needs of everyone else in the organization ahead of your own." It's your responsibility to learn and understand the value that you bring to the table. Sometimes, people notice and sometimes they don't. Why should they have the responsibility to think about you as well? Rather than waiting to be discovered, own the responsibility for figuring out the next step.

THE IMPORTANCE OF SELF-CARE

"At this age, health is really important. I find that every January something comes up related to stress. So now, in the fall, I'm really careful to pay more attention to my body and health. I also try to anticipate what might crop up to cause January stress and if possible ward it off. Addressing the whole mind/body thing is really key: It's related to every aspect of life. When there are times I can't prevent stressful events, I just accept them and manage my time and self so that I can deal with them." — *Doreen, HR Specialist, fifty-one*

3. Develop self-awareness

It's likely that something in your awareness drew you to make this transition—understanding who you have become both personally and professionally in your life and career to date can help you make better decisions at this stage.

One method to develop this understanding is to **solicit feedback**. It may help to get this from a peer or friend, but you have to be open to accepting the feedback and build sufficient trust so the observer doesn't become the focus of your negative emotions or blame. If you are not truly open, don't ask. As you get older, it can be really hard to accept the judgment of others, especially if you have become set in your approach. You may want to hire professional help, such as a career coach or a therapist, to help you sort out what's really going on.

Be sure to make your requests for feedback in such a way that you can get real insight from what you hear. Ask specific, open-ended questions. For example, "How would you describe my strengths? Challenges? What's your experience of how I handle frustration? Success? How would you describe my ability to be open-minded and creative?" Focused, strategic questions such as these will provide feedback that will clarify what you may be able to offer in a new career.

Next, you can **conduct a self-assessment**. Before making rash long-term career decisions or doing anything dramatic, it's important that you recognize the symptoms of a mid-career crisis. If you are suddenly overly focused on your appearance, or your work performance is missing the mark, be honest with yourself that something is going on. Instead of panicking, self-assess and ask yourself whether you really love what you are doing or are you ready for a change.

It is really crucial to be familiar with your true likes, dislikes, strengths, and weaknesses. Journaling can help you become more conscious of these; try taking a one-to-two-week period to focus on and write about what you observe about yourself during this time. This effort may lead you to find that essential intersection of what you love to do and what you are really good at.

During the weeks you concentrate on understanding your likes/dislikes, watch to see which activities at your job bring joy and contrast them with those that cause you stress, drain energy, or leave you feeling negative. The list may contain comments such as: "I like to resolve conflicts between diverse groups of people," or "I do not enjoy organizing logistical moving parts to prepare for an event." Of course, keep in mind that all jobs have elements you don't enjoy; the key is to have these elements be a *small* part of the job. Creating these lists may open up an enormous set of possible occupations and roles within organizations.

DO YOUR PERSONAL WORK

"Personal work means to go inward on a journey to find out what limiting beliefs you have and how can you manage them. First, figure out a process that will work for you. It might be a retreat, but there are many modalities for working through these things, including psychotherapy, meditation, and yoga. The second thing is to be sure the process truly helped you become clearer about what your vision is. Many people hear about an opportunity, think it's for them, and jump into it without getting the details. Spend time and do your research so you know what is actually going on. The third thing is to evaluate whether you really have a passion and a love for the change you are contemplating. Dollar signs alone are not enough if you don't really love the work or your values aren't aligned with the company or opportunity. However, if all of those things are in place, it indicates that you have a good chance for success. Doors will open. People you need will show up. All will fall into place."
— *Marcie, Business Owner, forty-three*

Nancy Anderson, author of *Work with Passion in Midlife and Beyond*, suggests comparing the following to decide what you could do:

"PASSION CLUES"	SIGNALS YOU COULD BE OFF TRACK
• You would do the work even if you didn't get paid • Mastery is your goal • You are transformed as you do the work • You are not aware that time is going by • You are paid to be who you are	• Money is your priority • You worry about what others think • You focus on the end result not the process • You take shortcuts to achieve your objectives • You take on more than you can handle

Once you have external and internal feedback, it is time to apply **reflection and analysis**. What have you learned? How far off was it from what you thought you knew about yourself? How much of what you know about yourself do other people also know? Can you reconcile this?

This reflection process is a pause in which you take the time to step back and consider the positive and negative implications of making a change. Consider the impact it would have on you and others and how taking on a new role might make you feel. You could even "try on" the new role, using your exploration and research to imagine what the changed career might be like. Businesses often create this kind of scenario as part of planning their new strategies. It is effective for individuals as well because it offers the opportunity to play out what a change looks and feels like. One interviewee explored dropping her current career to return to her former high-powered role. As she "tried on" this role, using discussions, self-assessment, and feedback as input, she realized that the thought of regular travel and high-stress assignments made her feel tired and worn out. Realizing this now enabled her to look down different paths for other ways to change her career.

Armed with more awareness, you are ready to create your **own unique self-development plan**. You may find you don't need to change fields completely, just figure out a different stepping-stone that will get you to the same place. Architect Charmaine, thirty-seven, after losing her job when the housing market crashed, said, "I just started a real estate investment company. Homes are cheap in my area and the banks aren't loaning, but there's private financing. Hopefully that will give me a base salary, and I'll continue to do architecture on a project-by-project basis. I think this will help me in the long term. It's been a good way for me to keep going forward because the end goal is still the same—developing my own projects. It's just that the pathway there has changed."

As part of your transition and development plan, you may need to upgrade your education. A well-timed MBA, for example, could provide the necessary education and contacts to launch a new or amended career, not to mention enormous confidence. It expands the universe of people and possibilities. However, watch out—there are many businesses out there designed to take the money of experimenters—for example, travel agency companies that "teach" people to be travel agents, giving you a single tour, and then are never heard of again. Community colleges and non-degreed Executive Education Programs thrive on this time of confusion: how to negotiate or invest in real estate, how to become a personal trainer, or how to day-trade. One interviewee was considering a $4,000 investment in a course to upgrade her expertise in hopes of getting on corporate boards, an unlikely career-change option.

As you determine your career transition plan, you need to be aware that plans do change, especially as you become more aware of what you want. Keep your plan flexible: a living plan that moves with you as you learn what you like or dislike.

During a mid-career transition, you have the opportunity to launch yourself in a completely new direction or derail yourself. Understanding yourself and working on your own self-awareness skills can positively influence your outcomes.

4. Build a support system

When you embark upon a major career shift mid-stream, you will surely need support to get you through the process. Building a support system in anticipation will give you that necessary space.

First **acknowledge you need help.** A career transition is a big deal. In addition to the logistical problem of finding work that matches your interests and background, there may be new emotions at play that can further drain your energy levels. Or you may be experiencing a marital crisis or family upheaval along with feeling the loss associated with being laid off, or fears you won't be able to be re-hired.

At this stage, it's time to reconsider your attitudes toward securing the help that transitions most often require. Although you may believe you can handle it alone, it is crucial to acknowledge that that is not the case. Business Coach Alicia, thirty, had to recognize that to get herself motivated required getting help. It took her time, she said, to "come to grips with the fact I need to be around other people to be creative."

Once you accept you need help, **figure out exactly what help you need**. Think of this transition phase as a job. As such, you need to reserve your time and creative energy for the job, rather than spending it on non-productive tasks. Whether it is emotional, career-related, or even psychological, don't be afraid to bring in the experts. This may be hard, particularly if you are out of work or money is tight, but qualified help will minimize transition time.

You can also derive support from sharing ideas or challenges with members of a group or organization. School Counselor Sarah, sixty-one, "connected with a great group of women who are so supportive and have helped me through doubts and fear and the transition to having my own business. Previously I found women in corporations backstabbing, but in this group we don't need to be competitive because we are all supportive."

Next, you must **figure out to whom you can delegate**. At home, if income is tight in this period, ask friends for help in the interim or tradeoff childcare so you can focus on this process. Renegotiate household responsibilities so you can pay attention fully to your transition. No one will take you seriously, including your family or prospective employers and clients, if you are treating your search for work like a hobby.

Often there are opportunities to tap your network to find people who can vouch for you to potential clients or employers. At first glance, it might look like your network is small, but whether it's someone you worked for previously, a friend of a friend, or colleagues of your spouse, you likely have many connections you haven't explored. By informational interviewing and exploring your network, gathering details about your prospective jobs, you can start to build a picture of what you want.

These relationships help you as you change jobs, either within your current company or externally. Fifty-six-year-old Marketing VP Elizabeth said, "I have a group of friends at work I can talk to and trust. Knowing people in high places who think a lot of you and who advocate for you is essential. Mentorship implies it's just one person. One person isn't going to do it for you. You need a half-dozen, strategically placed advocates."

Finally, you must **manage the work**. People can't be expected to do a good job unless you have told them what you expect. If your career coach doesn't seem to understand what it is like to work in your world, you may need a new career coach. Complaining to your friends won't make it better. By giving the people who work for you clear feedback, you can ensure the quality of support.

Figuring out that you need help, the specific support you require, who will support you, and how to manage this is critical to finding success across your career. In this way, you can ensure a successful mid-career transition to bigger and better things.

5. Get comfortable operating in imperfection

Perfection expectations can lead to disappointment in yourself and how your life has worked out so far. Mid-career, you might even start to panic about it. Figuring out how to operate in imperfection can help you regroup, focus on what you really want to do, and be happy with your choices.

The first step is **acceptance**. Life isn't perfect and there wasn't some perfect path you were supposed to have followed. Even if you're unhappy in your career right now, or if you were laid off, you have not failed. You know, from looking back at your life, that when things didn't go smoothly, you learned from it, or found a new direction. You gained something from each experience; knowledge of relationships, business skills, and wisdom. So, instead of indulging in feelings of failure or measuring yourself against some external standard of perfection, start to accept that you are good enough and move on.

When you lose the idea that things have to be perfect, you open yourself up to more creative options. You can **embrace imperfection** as an opportunity to try new things with the expectation that trying your best is the goal, not perfect results. You can even have fun with it. Caroline Dowd Higgins, in her book, *This is NOT the Career I Ordered— Empowering Strategies from Women who Recharged, Reignited, and Reinvented Their Careers,* illustrates how women can let go of perfection with her own story. She was an opera singer, but found she couldn't make enough money to sustain herself with it. So she "realized that singing opera was something I did, but it did not entirely define who

I was as a person." She figured out how to still perform, but now she doesn't have the "stress of earning my living as a singer." She makes her living as a career coach, and continues singing opera on the side, using it to raise money for charities. By letting go of the pressure to be perfect or to do what people expected, she was able to completely redefine her career.

Many people want to throw the baby out with the bathwater: If they can't do it perfectly, they won't do it at all. Forty-two-year-old former Marketing Manager, Dominique, feels she "can't" do her old marketing career perfectly because the job requires late hours and travel, something she is not willing to do with small children at home. But does that mean she doesn't have something valuable to offer a company looking for marketing experience and wisdom? By embracing imperfection, perhaps she could come up with creative options for how to use her abilities on *her* schedule.

I CREATED A WHOLE NEW NICHE

"I had a knack for technology, but I didn't have the formal training and I wasn't sure how far this was going to take me. Exploring marketing was the chance to take my technology understanding, stay involved in the technology wave, and build a business. It gave me the chance to branch out on my own." — *Alexandria, Business Owner, sixty-two*

Embracing imperfection at this stage requires that at some point, you do have to take a leap. For example, IT Manager Madison, forty-two, is in the middle of shifting her work to a new focus. She is struggling to let go of the work she's confident in. But if she doesn't make space for the new work, she can't experiment and test it out. The old work is blocking her from transitioning faster.

Finally, by **planning for imperfection**, you can remove the panic that occurs whenever things don't go smoothly and help yourself navigate the uncertainty. Changing careers mid-stream could take you a while, for example, so it is important to have sufficient savings available or to maintain an income during the process. That may mean you need to remain in your current role or accept a similar position at another company to get you through the transition. You may even need to keep the door open to return to your old role if your new career path doesn't work out. Additionally, you may need to consciously let go of less important things, like keeping your house perfectly clean, while you devote energy for exploration and experimentation.

Experimentation through trial and error will allow you to learn from your mistakes and begin to recognize nuances that will enable you to decide your next move. Marketing VP Elizabeth, fifty-six, was in publishing when she got laid off. "I then did consulting, and I tried writing a book since I always wanted to be an author. But my IRA was not getting built up, my career path was in stasis, and I needed to get health benefits." She decided the right move for her was to go back into her previous career. Operations Manager Caitlin, thirty-five, was "not sure I wanted to stay with my company. For me, its corporate locations didn't work and I don't like the culture of a manufacturing company. I thought, *Maybe I should just take this for a while and then figure out where I want to live. I've been moving for years, I'm tired of moving around.* I took the job for a time to figure out where I want to live." For both women, planning for imperfection helped them determine their best next step for their careers and their lives.

By getting comfortable with your imperfect self and the imperfect world, you are more likely to take risks and explore during your mid-career transition.

6. Expand your universe

It's easy to get into a groove that makes you comfortable with the scope of your life. Then when you decide you want or need a change, being in a groove limits your understanding of possible options. Therefore, at this stage, when you are trying to figure out how to remake your career, you must look at your change from fresh vantage points. By consciously expanding your universe of possibilities, you will open up to the world in a way that you may not have been aware of before.

Keep sight of the fact that to expand your universe, you need to seek **out people who challenge and push you forward**. It may be helpful to associate with other people going through the same thing because you can empathize and work together to get out of it. This is why job support groups and coaching circles can be so effective. Instead of being surrounded by questioning faces wondering what's going on with you, you will have the support of people who understand your experience. For example, one group of wannabe entrepreneurs attended a weekend retreat to power through building a business plan. Their contract: They couldn't leave without building their business plan. This kind of challenge group can force you to act, while supporting your efforts. Even so, be careful in a group to avoid those who are overly absorbed with self-pity, anger, or negative emotions. Instead find those who have a supportive *and* critical eye that will genuinely help you look at yourself and the challenges of the group. Role models also help. Women seem to feel less risk averse when someone they know has already tried something new. One woman changed fields and went into aerospace late in her career. Several friends thought, *There's no way you can get in at this late stage—everyone in aerospace has been there for their entire career.* Once she was in, she was so successful and having such fun, she recruited several of her friends to join her. Surrounding yourself with people of varied experiences and backgrounds ensures a wider universe of experiences and opportunities to model.

If you struggle to find this in your social circles, try going online. There are numerous groups set up to help people find others with similar interests. You can look at www.meetup.com groups focused on specific aspects. Role models abound outside an inner peer group. Brainstorm what aspects you would like to work on to facilitate your career change goal. Do you need to improve your speaking ability? Join a speaking club. Do you need to improve your ability to confront others and be assertive? Find groups focused on this or take a class. The support and role models you seek are already available somewhere if you make the effort to look.

Another element to practice is **thinking bigger**. Thinking bigger starts with thinking widely—even in areas you may feel are completely un-related. You see inspiration from a variety of sources. Maybe you need to enlist a friend who is strong in idea generation, or even post your question online to creative groups like many companies are now doing in the process called crowd sourcing. Maybe you can do something completely unrelated, like take a weekend in the mountains or go to a modern art museum to foster creative thinking. You start with an open slate and avoid weeding out possibilities at first.

THINKING BIGGER

"When I was nearing the end of my maternity leave with my second child, I knew I needed to decide how to approach returning to work. I put a proposal together and set up a meeting with my boss. I created a new job within the company for myself along with a proposed significant increase. This was a big step up for me in terms of salary. Part of the reason I felt justified in the proposal was the fact that I had finished my MBA. I had the experience and now I had the degree, so I felt the new position was a better fit for me going forward. I was very nervous about the response I would receive but was very pleased when the position was quickly approved. I've learned that if you work hard and are committed to doing a good job, managers want to keep you and will be creative in approving options that keep you on board and contributing to the team." — *Donna, VP Business Development, forty-one*

If an immediate change is necessary for some reason, being open and getting creative will allow you to investigate expanded opportunities within your existing company first. There are all kinds of creative ways to change a role without giving up the security, salary, benefits, seniority, respect, and network that exists in your current organization.

Perhaps you would like to consider a portfolio career where you focus on more than one role simultaneously. According to Margaret Lobenstine in *Renaissance Soul,* some individuals get more career satisfaction when they hold multiple roles under one over-arching theme. One woman runs a small angel investment firm, is an executive coach, consults for an educational nonprofit, and has an active volunteer life as well. She has cobbled together a variety of mini-careers to keep herself whole.

As you figure out what your new career might look like, it may be possible to experiment on someone else's dime. Consider Business Owner Sheila, thirty-five, who worked for two years in the travel industry before going out on her own. She got to know many people in the industry, understand common pitfalls, and learn the financial model of the business, before she opened her own place. "I wanted to make sure the business was going to work before investing in a license of my own," she told us. Her employer was happy to mentor her and she earned money at the same time. Following this as a guideline might also offer the option of buying out your employer, when the time is right. Maude, fifty-one, decided to stretch by starting a school. She researched a model and submitted a proposal to the local school district. The proposal was accepted and funding granted. Maude has been employed as the Dean for the past two years. Now in its second year, the school has over five hundred students. There are many approaches to accomplishing this including observing and discovering industry best practices. For example, consider working at Starbucks before opening a coffee shop. You will get to know common processes, techniques for staffing, demand, and customer service policies.

Another variation of this is do strategic volunteerism. Sometimes, to build expertise in a new field, pro bono projects allow you the space to learn. Professional Facilitator Shirley, thirty-five, established an entire career on volunteering. It built her network and illustrated what she was really good at doing. She volunteered with a local business association while working full time and then got a job with them. Later, she volunteered with a national group and transitioned from business planning to full-time professional facilitating.

The only caveat to volunteering is to ensure it remains strategic. One woman spent many years volunteering at a nursing home because she dreamed of opening her own someday. However, often the roles she got assigned were menial and didn't expose her to the real operations of the business. If you volunteer, you need to make sure it is at a senior level and that the organization knows what you are donating, like a tax receipt for your donated time. As a volunteer, you often have more bargaining power than a full-time employee to determine the roles that would best suit you. Also, you must ensure your position is something that can be documented on a résumé to build the résumé story, with clear goals and measurements. For example: "I automated a process and saved $40,000," or, "I increased donations by 250 percent." You can put this on your résumé just like any other job. This applies to non-profit volunteering and pro-bono consulting equally.

Once you start to think bigger, you can **expose yourself to something new**. Exposing yourself to something new doesn't mean you have to do it; just take a small step toward it. You can decide later whether you want to work the longer hours. By taking that first step, you can learn more about the job and discover whether your assumption is true and if there are other aspects of the job you would love.

MUSIC KEPT PULLING MY SLEEVE

"I found that there was a point in my career where some things shift-ed, and I had this moment of clarity when I started thinking what was ahead. I was at a mid-manager level position at a technology company, and I started looking at the executives above me on the corporate ladder. I was putting in sixty hours a week and I was seeing these executives working eighty-plus hours a week. They had terrible relationships with their families, and they didn't look healthy because they never went outside; they weren't the kind of people I wanted to become. When I realized what was ahead of me, more hours and more money, but less of a life, I started to look at my career differ-ently. After praying about my direction, I felt impressed to quit my job and go on tour with my music. When I explained this to my family they freaked out, but it was a pivotal point in trusting myself. The day I was going to turn in my notice was the same day I was going to be laid off, ironically. That was a huge confirmation for me—it was like the universe was also supporting my career shift. I ended up going back to school to study music. I believe we all have a specific purpose in life, and for me music was the thing that kept pulling at my sleeve. It's not easy to pursue your passion, but nothing 'worth it' ever is."
— *Diana, Professional Song-writer, thirty-five*

Exposure helps prepare you for taking bigger risks. Most people don't go out and travel the world without any previous experience. Most don't run the marathon without any training.

Finally, you can expand by **taking a big risk** indicating you are confident and ready to make the move. You are taking a concrete decision to implement your career change to move forward. You could even consider risking a lateral or backward move.

According to an article by William J. White, *How to Get Ahead by Going Backward*, most people seek promotions to grow their career and experience. But sometimes, stepping back or sideways can help build skills, make new connections, or change perspective. White notes that this needs to be done strategically—not as a default, but as a means to achieving your career goals. In addition, these executives "were pursuing a goal they felt passionate about. They weren't running away from problems or dissatisfaction at a current job. Their back-tracks were also grounded in success in one venture, which provided confidence and often a financial cushion to pursue an interest elsewhere. Finally, with a secure cushion, they were confident enough to take a backward step at any stage of their career—even on the cusp of retirement." White warns not to use this type of strategy to run away from problems or a bad work environment, but rather to be exposed to new experiences and follow a passion. Used effectively, taking a side- or back-track can actually *build* a career.

One woman used this strategy to find more meaningful work in the same company plus give herself a little more free time to be with her children. She felt she had maximized her current role and looking down the road, realized a promotion would mean a lot more of the same work, but no new learning. With young children, she felt more work was not a good option. She took a different role in the company, one that could be done part time and with fewer responsibilities, but one that offered her new opportunities. At first, she was a little worried the role was too junior, and it took her a while to be able to frame it correctly with enquiring peers, but within six months of the transition, she had been promoted in the role, received a huge bonus, and was feeling completely revitalized. Plus, she had carved out the space she needed for her personal goals, so she had shed an enormous amount of pressure.

One way to take an expansive risk is to become a consultant. Independent consulting can be a way of experimenting in different fields. It's not without its pitfalls, but consulting can give you freedom to choose the type of work you do, the types of customers you deal with, and the level of service you can provide. Often, one gig begets additional work and soon you have a reputation and a solid pipeline of work. It can start with using your existing expertise as a launching pad, and then branching toward something different. For example, thirty-four-year-old HR Manager Terri parlayed her connections from her previous firm into gigs to get her consulting business started. As she experimented, she discovered her talent at getting business, enabling her to build the company.

To be successful at consulting, like any other service business, requires an upfront investment in sales and marketing to attract clients, proposal and agreement materials to establish client engagement, time and space to meet clients face-to-face, and billing/collections support to ensure payment. Since the consultant is the product, revenue is limited by the number of hours available to work on client projects. Deciding when to delegate sales or administrative tasks can be challenging. Consultant Molly, forty, said when she started consulting, "My market niche was anyone who'd write me a check." Even when a new technology she'd built took off with one client, "I was still hesitant to specialize. I would still do almost anything." A year or two later, when she got a second similar client, she didn't initially trust herself to convince someone else to quit his job to work for her but she took the plunge and an even bigger risk by becoming more specialized. The company is now five years old and has fourteen employees.

Finally, taking a big risk can mean that you try something completely out of your comfort zone. Brand Manager Samantha, thirty-five, built her career of marketing and finance across multiple firms. But on an unrelated business trip out of the country, she "was inspired to change career course and combine my passion for human rights with my business experience." She created her own business, linking foreign small businesses with Western markets.

Expanding your universe is sometimes about taking risks and stepping outside of your comfort zone. Especially in mid-life, this can be extremely difficult to do. You get comfortable and you build up a list of "I could nevers," or "yeah buts," that get really hard to overcome. Aisha, VP Corporate Counsel, fifty-eight, said, "Take a little risk first and notice how you feel about it and learn from any failure. The more risks you take, the more comfortable you become."

Once you get past your fears and perceived limitations, expanding your universe can open you to possibilities you never thought available. You can even start to have fun doing it and make it part of your daily life.

Conclusion

Successfully navigating the transitions of mid-life offers endless possibilities. Nonetheless, there are considerations, including being strategic about the process, exploring alternatives, flexibility, adaptability, and mitigating the risk before you jump. Plus, mid-life career change has become a bigger area of focus now that the Baby Boomers have reached this stage *en masse*. For this reason, there is a lot more research on the topic and attention given to it by organizations than ever before. Discussions about how different generations in the workplace interact with one another and how to tap the experience of older workers abound. By practicing Orange Line Skills, you can either avoid unnecessary disruption or experience an enriching journey through this mid-life transition.

CHAPTER TEN:
Living The Orange Line

"You were born with wings, why prefer to crawl through life?" —*Rumi*

Across our interviews and research, we heard women consistently say they want to live an integrated, well-paced life. Women want to live on The Orange Line. Throughout this book, we've offered skills to help you find your own Orange Line path, so you can do the work you love.

What Can The Orange Line Look Like?

As we've shown, across all the stages of your career, by reframing your core assumptions to:

- We are all responsible for home and family and taking care of ourselves
- Outcomes and personal fulfillment are what matter
- Doing my best and good enough is perfectly acceptable
- I am a good person and I am working on my own development
- I am paid what I am worth
- I take responsibility for myself and ask for what I need, then,

You can implement the three core principles of Orange Line living:

Three Core Principles

What do these three principles look like in action? Sales Manager Cecilia, forty, has four children and shares her story of how she embraced these principles:

Do what's required: Doing what's required, no more or no less, means that you focus on tasks that add value to the organization, your family, or yourself:

"I'm good at delegating at work and home. My husband and I are 50/50—he does the morning shift and I do the evening shift. (Actually it's 33/33/33 if you include the help from my parents who are retired.) He can do all of the kids' stuff, such as diapers, baths, packing lunches, etc. If one kid gets sick, he can grab all four and truck them off to the doctor's office. If I feel overwhelmed with housework, I can always ask him to pitch in more. Sometimes, if I have to take a conference call from home, I will put a bowl of snacks on the coffee table, throw in a video for the kids, and then lock myself in my office. When I had my fourth baby last summer, I asked for flex hours and got them."

Do what's right: Doing what's right means you figure out what's right for you, physically, emotionally, and spiritually, while honoring and respecting others.

"For longer-term projects that stress me out, I do a sanity check-in with my boss to make sure I'm meeting his expectations. If needed, I realign my workload and priorities to his, just to be sure I am constantly focused on what matters most.

"I don't want to take on too much at work, but that doesn't mean I'm out. If I were to take on more than forty-five to fifty hours per week, I would quickly lose my work-life balance I've fought hard to achieve. I'm doing my best right now and that seems to be enough. However, I feel they have granted me the privilege of flexible hours, so I do try to give them more. After I get the kids off to hockey or religion class, or after we get homework out of the way, I get back online and keep working."

Be authentic: Being authentic means you are aligned with your values and are not easily persuaded to behave in a way that feels contrary, is taxing, or unrewarding.

"In my previous job, I hated the work environment, despite being given favorable performance reviews and pay raises. My bosses were not supportive of the work-life balance concept, so having two little kids, and with a third on the way, I made the decision to leave. My friends went to a company in another industry, and they were enjoying it a lot; so they recruited me over. It was a lateral move, but it was more money and a healthier work environment. I was promoted within my first year. It's lower stress, lots of fun, and I can work at my own pace.

"I really enjoy working. I need my own career and my own money. When my third son was born, I considered stepping off, but then I read *The Feminine Mistake* and decided to keep going. I am so glad I did. I think if I had left the workforce, I would have had a harder time getting back in, if at all. If I'm ever overwhelmed at work or home, I take a mental health day. I am a firm believer in mental health days, as they are just as important as other sick time."

Cecilia has an optimistic outlook. Right now, with her newest and fourth child, she is still figuring out how to find time to exercise. Sometimes, she takes two kids in the jogging stroller, while the other two ride their bikes just so she can go for a run. Getting to the gym continues to be a struggle, so she's considering workout tapes in the short term. She has had the opportunity to attend a few business trips, which actually have turned out to be quite relaxing—a chance to get a bit of a break from the routine.

Cecilia integrates all three aspects of her life: work, family life, and self. By knowing what she wants and asking others to do their part, she's able to stay true to herself. It's a rich, full, and often messy life. She is not perfect at implementing The Orange Line skills, but she is practicing them conscientiously.

Underlying each of these aspects is an essential vision of women valuing themselves. Fundamentally, you begin to believe wholeheartedly that you are equally as important as others. As a result of living on The Orange Line, you can take responsibility for yourself and have more energy for your passions. When you do what you enjoy, following your own view of your life, and integrate this across all aspects of your life, you have more energy for all of it.

When you find these points and listen to yourself, you may realize where you want to go, but struggle with how to get there. It's tempting to succumb to the Feminine Filter rules: It seems easier, especially when you are under pressure or feeling confusion about what to do about a particular problem. Instead, on The Orange Line, you can learn to figure out the "how" for yourself. Early in Jodi's career, she kept asking her managers, "What book can I read to tell me how to do my job?" They kept answering "There is no book." Jodi learned to figure it out. Looking back now, she says, " I figured it out myself, and the way I did it was natural to me. Whenever I followed someone else's 'how,' I wasn't as happy with the result. When I figured it out for myself, I liked the outcome. I loved that I found a way that was my own."

You might find The Orange Line often does not yield external success as fast as the Green Line, but if you have patience, the results will come. When she had children, Sales Engineer Lela, forty-four, took a job that didn't require much responsibility. Then her children got older and she was ready to make a move. "There was an opportunity in my large software company with more visibility, responsibility, and all the things that come with it. My husband looked at me and said, 'Now that the kids are older, it's time for you to do the career lady move.' So I did. It's worked out. Sometimes, it infringes on weekends and evenings, but my kids understand."

You also might find you love the Green Line and struggle to stay on The Orange Line. If so, ask yourself what you love. Is it the work? Is it the potential rewards? Is it the shared energy? Or perhaps the rush from checking the Smart Phone constantly? If you are on the Green Line and are willing to consider Orange Line principles, then your responsibility is to ensure you aren't working at that pace at the expense of someone else. Are you hiding from an insecurity about yourself? Are you afraid to feel loss, sorrow, disappointment, or even love? A Green Liner may work a lot, but if you only work, and that's all you do, is it your best work?

Living The Orange Line is being strategic about life. It's not about winning; it's about living a whole life. It's about implementing the Galloway Running Method in your life, alternating "running and walking, from the beginning of a run" so that you extend your endurance. Extending endurance means you can expand your energy. But to do that, you have to train. Just like when you train for a marathon, you have to build up your skill set.

How Do You Practice Orange Line Skills?

In this book, we focus on skills and not rules. Rules are something people "have" to do to achieve some outcome. You have heard a thousand times, "You have to network" and what has happened? You force yourself to go to a networking event and introduce yourself to three people. Then nothing happens and you don't attempt it again until someone else says, "You should network." Rules are "either/or": Either you follow them and succeed or you don't and fail. Following them takes a lot of energy as you check with yourself: Are you following the rules? What do the rules say? Do you feel guilty when you don't follow them? At first glance, rules look easier because you can just do what the rules say. Jodi's undergraduate students ask, "Professor, how many pages should the executive summary be?" But what does this suggest? It suggests that what's most important is the rule—here the number of pages—rather than the content. Jodi's answer? "If it's ten pages and every page counts, then ten is the right number of pages. If it's one page and you've included everything, then one is long enough." This answer forces the students to figure out the best answer for what they want to achieve. They choose, not their professor.

When you focus on skills, you look at them more as goals. You practice them and understand it takes time to achieve mastery. When children are learning to walk, they fall hundreds of times. They make mistakes, such as falling, to learn how to walk. They don't run until they have mastered walking. Skills are like that. You try them out, starting small; you make mistakes and you learn.

Sometimes, you will get what you ask for, other times not. But over time, you will get better at it and will have shown others that you believe you are important enough to be considered. For example, you can set expectations about what time you will be home from a meeting, working with your partner to figure out childcare arrangements and the family dinner. You can schedule your exercise as if it were a meeting, so it can't be postponed. You can learn how to say "No" to absorbing extra work when you are already swamped. Living The Orange Line means that you are implementing the six core Orange Line Skills daily, practicing them a little at a time and being conscious of your own development.

Let's take the first Orange Line skill: **Recognize when the Feminine Filter is at work**. This is not a muscle many women have used. Most women have operated under assumptions and just react to them. It's unlikely that on your first try, you are going to recognize and dismantle each of the Feminine Filter's assumptions. So you start small. First you notice when you feel a "should." Perhaps you see a mother leaving at 4 p.m. every day and you think, *She shouldn't be leaving*. Notice that. Ask the questions we raised when we debunked the previous chapters' assumptions. Start simply at the notice stage.

Then, as you become an expert, you can recognize it elsewhere. You can start to experiment with pushing back or dropping the assumptions. You can play with it and see what happens. But you start small. Then as you get better, you work up to the other dimensions of that skill, such as reframing. As you become expert, the Feminine Filter ceases to work on you. You begin to make decisions from a place of freedom. You see the Filter in action and shrug it off, not letting it impact you emotionally. This is a powerful place in which to live; it feels "light" as you eliminate the heaviness of others' judgments. Freed from the assumptions, you get better at learning what you actually want and need in any given situation.

You can also practice the second Orange Line skill, **bring yourself into the equation**, this way. When Anne-Marie Slaughter talked about having to quit her high-pressured job at the State Department, she made the decision after more than two years of enduring the long hours and pressure. If she had started small and set boundaries at the point she first recognized the demands as an issue, she may have found it easier to renegotiate the work at a more fundamental level. But Slaughter felt she couldn't do this at the point where she was ready to quit. Further, the employer didn't get a chance to make a change either. Bringing yourself to the table early and often makes it fairer for all parties and gives everyone the chance to contribute to solutions.

You must decide consciously to include "you" in your decisions. You assertively use Direct Speak to do this. As you get more practiced in this approach, you start to adapt it to your own personal style.

DIRECT SPEAK

Being direct with others in conversations allows both parties to take what is said at face value and vice versa. You can clarify if there was an assumption made instead of turning it into a drama. You can avoid taking things personally.

For example, Lawyer Elaine, 35, uses this approach. "Now I can say 'The purpose of the call is for you to overrule me' and be direct even with customers—e.g. the other day I said: I understand your view, you understand mine; now, how are we going to solve it."

This approach is useful at work, business, or with friends. There are three steps:

- Describe what you are observing in others' behavior ("I notice you are sitting on the couch while I cook").

- State the impact of this behavior on you ("I feel frustrated because I feel like I am working hard to serve you at a time when I also feel tired and hungry").

- Explain what you'd like done differently
  ("I would like you to help by chopping the
  vegetables and taking over three meals a week").

This is not typically an approach women excel at but it will change your ability to deal with conflict. It's about being direct and clear about what you are really experiencing in a way that respects everyone.

Once you are adept at bringing yourself into the equation, your life can start to change fundamentally. Now everyone is equally important and your views and ideas become part of what you "do" in life.

The third Orange Line skill, **develop self-awareness**, is also a life-long journey. You can start small by just listening to feedback from others and reflecting on it. At first, you might get defensive and reject the information, but over time, you may be able to listen more openly. At that point, you can start to integrate external feedback into your own experiences and self-assessment. As you become more self-aware, you gain a deeper understanding of who you are and your needs. It becomes a self-reinforcing cycle that enriches your life. Self awareness feeds and supports all the other skills. As you deepen your self-understanding, you act from a place of wholeness from which it is no longer possible to give yourself up for a "should." From this place, you share yourself out of choice and love. You take risks whereas before you might not have put yourself "out there." When you are comfortable with yourself and your decisions, you become more powerful.

You can practice the fourth Orange Line skill, **build yourself a support system,** incrementally as well. To start small, you may just practice making a list of everything that you would prefer to have someone else do. Even if you don't act upon it, just listing the ideas can help you learn how to prioritize later. Many interviewees described delegation and outsourcing as being addictive; once they started, it grew and they soon found themselves so much more productive and energized that there were few low-value tasks they didn't delegate.

You support yourself because you now recognize everyone is interdependent and that your support enables you to give to others. You realize that your previous approach of one-way giving left others unable to give back to you. You see the inherent unfairness in this and now accept help because you understand the gift that it is.

The fifth Orange Line skill, **get comfortable operating in imperfection**, is easier to practice because opportunities show up every day. You can start by just laughing at yourself when something goes wrong. Seeing the humor can take the pressure off and remind you that "stuff happens." Over time, you can practice looking for opportunities and planning better in anticipation of imperfection.

As you learn how to do this well, you start to see the beauty in the imperfection. You see how imperfection allows you to find a different way of doing things. Whether it's the kids' messy room that fosters their creativity or the project you joined that failed spectacularly, you embrace the imperfection of a full life because it makes you feel more alive.

Stretching yourself to **expand your universe**, the sixth Orange Line skill, is harder to practice because you may not like to disrupt your comfort zone. A good place to start small is in your friendships. You can usually find room for one new friendship so you can get to know someone different from your usual crowd. One woman does a fabulous job of this. She doesn't hesitate to introduce herself and strike up a conversation with new people. Further, her circles of friends are extremely diverse, from politicians and activists regardless of political party, to musicians, bridge partners, work colleagues, academics, and students.

With the other skills as support, your world grows bigger. Your heart really sings as you explore and expand what you're capable of. It is here that you can start to use your power and awareness to change the world.

What Are the Barriers to Change?

And there's also reality. It is not possible for anyone to wake up one day and be an expert at these skills. Women have been subject to the Feminine Filter for a very long time. As a result, many women have developed some bad habits, such as catastrophizing and avoiding risk to keep up an appearance of perfection. It has become entrenched in their psyche. These bad habits can make attempts at living on The Orange Line feel heavy, overwhelming, and impossible. Women have reinforced these bad habits with themselves and others. As a result, they have trained others to expect this behavior. When women attempt to change and practice these skills, people who have been expecting this habitual response will react negatively because it's new and it usually requires them to change their behavior, too.

To change your habits, you first need to be clear why you're on this path. Maybe you are feeling un-centered or generally just out of whack. Maybe you are ready for more in your life. By understanding your "why," you are able to get through the difficult parts of change. One woman decided to go back to school, knowing that it would be an extremely challenging two-year process. Her sense of urgency was a desire to change her career and also have a job in which she could have more stability. Her sense of the goal's importance helped her manage through the late-night studying, the stress of the projects, and the difficulty navigating this with her husband and children.

Expect the inevitable resistance to any change you try. Sandy, thirty-five and a doctor, has colleagues who think she is "nuts" trying to be a full-time physician and a parent of young children. These colleagues think that it's too daunting for her and her husband to manage this together. She thinks, "Everyone who feels this way had moms who stayed home. They feel that it 'should' be this way. I don't have these hang-ups because of how I was raised. These are their own expectations of a woman's role, not mine." She has figured out how to avoid taking others' comments personally so she can feel comfortable with her choices.

Expecting internal and external pushback enables you to move forward anyway and practice taking responsibility for your decisions. You take responsibility for your actions *regardless of the outcome*. Here's the reality of the change process: It is a risky choice. We may think, "If I try this, I need to accept the responsibility that I might fail. If I don't try, I won't fail. I can just blame others—legislators, the cultural environment, the organizational structure, at-home moms, working moms, and men in general."

Maybe your vision is unclear. Maybe you are not yet confident in your decision to take up more space, so any resistance increases your doubts. After a certain number of challenges, there is always the risk that you will now decide to give up. Conversely, by making small, incremental changes, measuring progress, and getting comfortable with yourself again before you press on, you can make lasting change.

We all go through the change curve when we embark on change. At first, you may have the certainty that you want to change, but immediately doubts start to show up. By making incremental changes, you can get comfortable with these fears and move on to hope and building confidence. As you do this gradually, you develop your ability to manage change, and then you can take on bigger challenges.

Change Curve

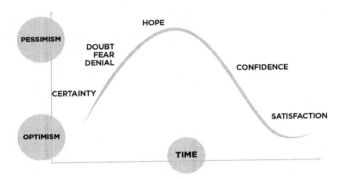

When IT Manager Madison, forty-two, started to become more assertive, she ran into tremendous resistance as people wanted her to continue to passively agree with their approach. In essence, she was saying to everyone else, "No, I am not going to just acquiesce to what you want, I want a voice, too." She started small, saying "No" to easier things, such as always being the one to leave work early to pick up children or asserting her desires by picking a place to go out to dinner with friends. After months of this approach, she experimented with being assertive in a much more challenging situation where someone was talking disparagingly about her. Once she experimented with that, she started using it more often at work, even confronting others when emotions got heated. After many years of practicing, she says, "I've gotten to the point where I now really enjoy confrontation and have to ask myself whether it is really necessary! That first real confrontation was scary. I was nervous, literally shaking during the conversation. But I knew I needed to do it. Then I congratulated myself for days on my courage so I would try it again." The success was in the trying, not the outcome.

Tiny decisions, in aggregate, can make big, long-term changes. Consider a small, maybe somewhat uncomfortable salary negotiation early in a career that makes a massive difference to a lifetime of earnings. Or sitting at the table for a major meeting, instead of on the sidelines, thus enabling key decision-makers to hear your ideas and raise your visibility. Little things can gain momentum and turn into big things; consciously leveraging this for your own benefit can be powerful. By breaking your bad habits, you can start to develop twenty-first century leadership abilities that can make a difference in your life.

Your new habits and skills enable an Orange Line life. By doing so, you start to operate on new principles. You realize that you cannot control other people or "the system." You can control only yourself and your response. You learn it is only by changing yourself that you can eliminate the Feminine Filter's effects and change your destiny. You operate under new principles and reframed assumptions. You replace the bad habits and rules of the Feminine Filter with this new belief system:

I AM
important.

I AM allowed to
achieve my métier.

If you implement this one belief, just this
one, you will change everything.

When most women look at the world's problems, they feel over-whelmed. If each woman finds her métier, if each puts her needs as equal in her conversations with friends, family, and work, women's voices will begin to be heard in numbers not seen before. Change will occur, not by pushing and shoving the world's decision-making systems to change, but by women simply asking for and expecting their needs to be met. You are the change you seek.

By doing this collectively, we believe women can finally break through to more powerful roles and change the system around them. And most importantly, they can live a full, integrated life.

NOTES

Prologue

Page 5. http://www.thirdpath.org.

Chapter One: Introducing The Orange Line

Page 10. Men and work/family balance. Seven out of ten dads report that they struggle to figure out how to integrate family with work. See Bakst, D. I. et. al. *Beyond The Breadwinner: Professional Dads Speak Out on Work and Family*. 2011:8. Web. http://www.abetterbalance.org/web/images/stories/Documents/valuecarework/Reports/ABB_Rep_BeyondBreadwinner.pdf. However, the language and practice evident in the cultural mainstream consider this to be almost exclusively a women's issue.

Page 11. Hammonds, K. E. "Balance is Bunk!" *Fast Company*. 2004; (87); 11. Web. http://www.miu4.org/textfiles/curriculum/2010sharedvision/Balance.doc.

Page13. Penalties of opting out: Hewlett, S. A. *Off-ramps and On-ramps: Keeping Talented Women on the Road to Success*. Boston: Harvard Business School Publishing, 2007. Print.

Page15. Note that men could choose to live this approach as well. We wrote this book from a female perspective to address the many challenges women have across their careers. Men have other issues restrict-ing their lives.

Page 15. Throttling up and down is introduced in Deloitte's Mass Ca-reer Customization Model at http://www.deloitte.com/view/en_US/us/Insights/Browse-by-Content-Type/deloitte-review/35912ee3fad33210VgnVCM100000ba42f00aRCRD.htm.

Page 16. Galloway, J. E. *Marathon.* California: Phidippides Publication, 2000. Print.

Chapter Two: The Feminine Filter

Page 18. Filter definition: "Filter." In *Webster's New World Dictionary.* Web. http://websters.yourdictionary.com/filter.

Page 19. See Chris Argyris and Peter Senge's work on mental models and the ladder of inference for more detail on the use of mental mod-els, assumptions, and biases.

Page 19. Amy Duncan is the mom from The Walt Disney Company's *Good Luck Charlie* (played by actress Leigh-Allyn Baker).

Page 20. Oneto, K. A. et. al. "Today's Women: Newfound Power, Per-sistent Expectations." *Anthem Worldwide,* 2011; 19. Web. http://www.schawk.com/knowledge-center/documents/white-paper/today% E2% 80% 99s-women-newfound-power-persistent-expectations.

Page 20. Roth, Susan. *Women's Initiative.* Report. Durham, NC: Duke University, 2003. Print.

Page 20. ---. *Report of Steering Committee on Undergraduate Women's Leadership at Princeton University.* Princeton, NJ: Princeton Univer-sity, 2011. Print.

Page 22. Research on Women and Housework: Wade, L. I. "Of House-work and Husbands." *Sociological Images.* 2009. Web. http://thesocietypages.org/socimages/2009/07/11/of-housework-and-husbands/. See also Couprie, H. "Time Allocation within the Family: Welfare Implications of Life in a Couple." *Economic Journal*, Jan. 2007; 117(516): 287-305. See also Kolb, Deborah, et. al. *Her Place at the Table: A Woman's Guide to Negotiating Five Key Challenges to Leadership Success.* New York, NY: Jossey-Bass, 2010. See also Barsh, J. O., and L. A. Yee. "Changing companies' minds about women." McKinsey Quarterly, Sept. 2011. Web. http://www.mckinseyquarterly.com/Changing_companies_minds_about_women_2858.

Page 26. We are not saying it is wrong to work in non-profit or that service to others is wrong. We are simply highlighting how often women use these assumptions to hold themselves back from pursuing their true passions.

Page 26. The pay disparity: Porter, E. "Motherhood Still a Cause of Pay Inequality." *The New York Times*, 12 Jun. 2012. Web. http://www.nytimes.com/2012/06/13/business/economy/motherhood-still-a-cause-of-pay-inequality.html.

Page 26. Funding your own business: Nelson, T. E. et. al. "Women Entrepreneurs and Venture Capital: Managing the Shadow Negotiation." *International Journal of Gender and Entrepreneurship.* 2009: 57-76. Web. http://www.simmons.edu/som/docs/Women_Entrepreneurs_and_Venture_Capital.pdf.

Page 26. Kingston, A. N. "Medicine's deadly gender gap." *Macleans.ca.* 30 Apr., 2012. Web. http://www2.macleans.ca/2012/04/30/medicines-deadly-gender-gap-2/.

Chapter Three: The Feminine Filter Problem

Page 28. Hewlett, S. A., and C. A. Luce. "Extreme Jobs: The Dangerous Allure of the 70-Hour Workweek." *Harvard Business Review,* 1 Dec. 2006: 49-59. Web. http://hbr.org/product/extreme-jobs-the-dangerous-allure-of-the-70-hour-w/an/R0612B-PDF-ENG.

Page 28. Women's labor force statistics: "Statistical Overview of Women in the Workplace. Catalyst." Updated 19 Jun.2012. Web. Updated 19 Jun.2012 http://www.catalyst.org/publication/219/statistical-overview-of-women-in-the-workplace.

Page 28. Mothers in the workplace: Lublin, J., and L. Kwoh. "For Yahoo CEO, Two New Roles." *Wall Street Journal*, 18 Jul. 2012. Print.

Page 29. TV and impact on children's assumptions, see: http://news.bbc.co.uk/2/hi/business/6382429.stm.

Page 30. Chudacoff, Joy: http://smartwomensolutions.com/.

Chapter Four: The Green Start

Page 39. Young women's decisions on family-flexible jobs: Barrett, K. "Gen Y Women in the Workplace." Focus Group Summary Report. 2011. Report. Web. http://www.bpwfoundation.org/documents/uploads/YC_SummaryReport_Final.pdf.

Page 39. The maternal wall is defined as a point where women will want to prioritize their families over their career. Women often hold themselves back career-wise in anticipation of the maternal wall.

Page 39. Sandberg, S. H. "Why We Have Too Few Women Leaders" TEDWomen. Dec. 2010. Online video.
http://www.ted.com/talks/sheryl_sandberg_why_we_have_too_few_women_leaders.html

Page 39. Liking work is important: Terjesen, S. I. et. al. "Attracting Generation Y graduates: Organisational attributes, likelihood to apply and sex differences." *International Journal of Career Management*, 1996: 504-522. doi: 10.1108/13620430710821994. Web.

Page 39. Money is less important: Ng, E. D. et. al. "New Generation, Great Expectations: A Field Study of the Millennial Generation." *Journal of Business & Psychology*, 2012: 25 (2): 281-92. Print.

Page 39. But career is important: Patten, E. I., and K. I. Parker. "A gender Reversal On Career Aspirations." *Pew Social & Demographic Trends*, 19 Apr. 2012. Web. http://www.pewsocialtrends.org/2012/04/19/a-gender-reversal-on-career-aspirations/?src=prc-headline.

Page 39. Rewarding different models of work: Henderson, J. "Shut Up Sheryl Sandberg: Millennial Women Reject Role Models, Mentors." *Forbes*, 2 Jul. 2012. Web. http://www.forbes.com/sites/jmaureen-henderson/2012/07/02/shut-up-sheryl-sandberg-millennial-women-reject-role-models-mentors/.

Page 42. Still proving their worth: Barrett, K. "Gen Y Women in the Workplace." Focus Group Summary Report. 2011. Report. Web. http://www.bpwfoundation.org/documents/uploads/YC_SummaryReport_Final.pdf.

Page 43. Weissmann, J. O. "53% of Recent College Grads Are Jobless or Underemployed—How?" *The Atlantic*, 23 Apr. 2012. Web. http://www.theatlantic.com/business/archive/2012/04/53-of-recent-college-grads-are-jobless-or-underemployed-how/256237/#.

Page 43. 70% of women rate their own performance as equivalent to that of their co-workers while 70% of men rate themselves higher than their peers: Borisova, D. A., and O. L. Sterkhova. "Women as a Valuable Asset." *McKinsey.* Apr. 2012. Print.

Page 60. Rewards at work. Hogue, M. et. al. "Gender Differences in Pay Expectations: The Roles of Job Intention and Self-View." *Psychology of Women Quarterly.* 2012; (34). Print.

Page 60. Self promotion, men v. women: Babcock, L. I., and S. A. Laschever. *Women Don't Ask: Negotiation and the Gender Divide.* Princeton, NJ: Princeton University, 2003: 6, 46, 95. Print.

Page 60. Work attributes and Gen Y: Terjesen, S. et. al. (2007): 504-522.

Page 62. A new App created via a challenge.gov competition called Aequitas: Equal Pay App, helps women find and compare wages so they can negotiate more effectively: http://www.fuzionapps.com/#/ae-quitas/4567448917.

Page 63. Effects of job control, workload, and supervisor and co-worker support on morbidity and a variety of health outcomes: Sparks, K. et. al. "The effects of hours of work on health: A meta-analytic review." *Journal of Occupational & Organizational Psychology,* December 1997; 70(4): 391-408. Serial online.

Page 63. Workplace support: Karline, W. A. et. al.. "Workplace Social Support and Ambulatory Cardiovascular Activity in New York City Traffic Agents." *Psychosomatic Medicine,* Mar.-Apr. 2003 65:167-176; doi:10.1097/01.PSY.0000033122.09203.A3. Web.

Page 64. Jay, M. E. *The Defining Decade: Why your twenties matter—and how to make the most of them now.* New York: Hachette Book, 2012: 11. Print.

Page 64. Self-assessment tools include Strengthsfinders, MYERS-BRIGGS, DiSC, Big 5 personality assessment, Enneagram, etc.

Page 66. Anxiety in their 20s: Jay, M. (2012): 6, 147, 149.

Page 71. Type A and Perfectionism: Beck, M. "Inside the minds of the perfectionists—researchers used to blame parenting, but studies suggest a genetic link; procrastination is a problem." *Wall Street Journal,* 30 Oct 2012: D.1. Print.

Page 73. Pfeffer, Jeffrey. *How Companies Get Smarter: Taking Chances and Making Mistakes.* Boston, MA: Harvard Business Press, 2007. Print.

Page 74. Jay, M. (2012): 42, 47.

Page 76. Deemer, C. A, and N. A. Fredericks. *Dancing on the Glass Ceiling.* New York: McGraw-Hill Books, 2003. Print.

Page 77. Be creative: IBM, Global CEO Study: "Creativity Selected as Most Crucial Factor for Future Success." *IBM CEO Survey* (2010). Web. http://www.03.ibm.com/press/us/en/pressrelease/31670.wss.

Chapter Five: Approaching Burnout

Page 83. Phases of burnout: "Three Stages of Burnout." Texas Medical Association. Web. http://smhp.psych.ucla.edu/qf/burnout_qt/3stages.pdf.

Page 87. Cortisol is a stress hormone.

Page 87. Research by Marianne Legato finds stress can overwhelm adrenal glands. It can damage healthy tissues if it remains too high for too long and women who are stressed may start experiencing symptoms such as weight gain, depression, insomnia, foggy brain, cravings for certain foods, mood swings, and fatigue: Pearce, C. I. "What Are the Effects of Cortisol in Women." eHow health. Web. http://www.ehow.com/about_5157195_effects-cortisol-women.html.

Page 91. The inverted stress U curve is called The Yerkes-Dodson Stress Performance Curve.

Page 103. Ideas for tools like journaling or keeping a log can be found at http://www.vocationvillage.com/job-burnout/.

Page 105. Allen, D. A. *Getting Things Done.* New York: Penguin Books; 2003. Print.

Chapter Six: Family Matters

Page 117. The phases of motherhood: http://www.motherhood-cafe.com/transition-to-parenthood/.

Page 118. Parents adjusting to school: Krelder, H. O. "Getting Parents Ready for Kindergarten: The Role of Early Childhood Education." Apr.

2002. Web. http://www.hfrp.org/publications-resources/browse-our-publications/getting-parents-ready-for-kindergarten-the-role-of-early-childhood-education.

Page 118. Bennetts, L. E. *The Feminine Mistake: Are We Giving Up Too Much?* New York: Hyperion, 2007. Print.

Page 119, Aging transitions: http://www.seniorsforliving.com/blog/2011/04/11/seniorsforliving-coms-transition-resource-guide/. See also AARP. Caregiving Resource Center. AARP. Web. http://www.aarp.org/home-family/caregiving/.

Page 120. Elder care statistics: Kim, K. I, and R. A. Antonopoulos. "Unpaid and Paid Care: The Effects of Childcare and Elder Care on the Standard of Living." *Working paper No. 541,* Levy Economics Institute of Bard College. 6 Oct. 2011. Print.

Page 121. Moms and work: Brown, Lorra M., "The relationship between motherhood and professional advancement: Perceptions versus reality." Employee Relations, Vol. 32 Iss: 5, pp.470-494 (2010). Print.

Page 121. Momism: Correll, S. J., S. Benard, and I. Paik. "Getting a job: Is there a motherhood penalty?" *American Journal of Sociology.* 2005; 112; 1297-1338. Print.

Page 122. Yen, H. O. "United States Divorce Rates: 2009 Census Report Reveals Startling Marriage Trends." *Huffington Post,* 25 Aug. 2011. Web. http://www.huffingtonpost.com/2011/08/25/united-states-divorce-rat_n_935938.html.

Page 122. Research on costs of opting out: Bennetts, Leslie. *The Feminine Mistake: Are We Giving Up Too Much?* New York, NY: Hyperion, 2007. p. 32. Print. See also Sylvia Ann Hewlett reports women lose 37% of their earning power when they spend three or more years out of the workplace. Of those who opt out, only 40% are able to return to full-time professional jobs. Hewlett, S, and C. Luce. "Off-Ramps and On-Ramps." *Harvard Business Review,* Mar. 2005; 83(3): 43-54. Serial online.

Page 125. Assumptions on motherhood and career advancement: Schumpeter. "The Mommy Track: The real reason more women don't rise to the top of companies." *The Economist*, 25 Aug. 2012. Web. http://www.economist.com/node/21560856.

Page 127. Studies find such a variety of outcomes from daycare that the main conclusion seems to be that daycare just needs to be of good quality. Otherwise, it's the home life that matters more. Belsky, J. "Early Day Care and Infant-mother Attachment Security." van Ijzendoorn, M, topic ed. In: Eds. Tremblay, R. E, M. Boivin, and R. De. V. Peters. *Encyclopedia on Early Childhood Development*. Montreal, Quebec: Centre of Excellence for Early Childhood Development and Strategic Knowledge Cluster on Early Child Development, 2009: 1-6. Web. See also Giles, L. et. al. "Maternal Depressive Symptoms and Childcare During Toddlerhood Relate to Child Behavior at Age 5 years." *Pediatrics*, 128(1), e78-e84. (2011). Print. See also "Are Child Developmental Outcomes Related to Before- and After-school Care Arrangements?" Results from the NICHD study of early childcare. *Child Development*, 75(1), 280-295. (2004). See also Vandell, D. et. al. "Do Effects of Early Childcare Extend to Age 15 years?" Results from the NICHD study of early childcare and youth development. *Child Development*, 81(3), 737-756. (2010). Print.

Page 129. Stone, P. A. *Opting out?: Why women really quit careers and head home*. Berkeley, CA and London: University of California Press, 2008. Print.

Page 133. The new competition for mothers: "Are You Mom Enough?" *Time Magazine*, May 2012. Web. http://www.time.com/time/covers/0,16641,20120521,00.html.

Page 135. Maschka, K. *This is Not How I Thought It Would Be: Remodeling Motherhood to Get The Lives We Want Today*. Berkeley, CA: Trade, 2009. Print.

Page 138. Moneypenny, M. *Sharpen Your Heels*. New York: Penguin, 2012. Print.

Page 140. The number of women who actually worked historically and projected: Toosi, M. I. A century of change: the U.S labor force, 1950-2050. Bureau of Labor Statistics. May 2002. Web. http://www.bls.gov/opub/mlr/2002/05/art2full.pdf.

Page 140. Negotiating home responsibilities: Miller, L. E, and J. E. Miller. *A Woman's Guide to Successful Negotiating: How to Convince, Collaborate & Create Your Way to Agreement.* New York: McGraw-Hill, 2002: 157. Print. Also see www.thirdpath.org.

Page 142. These same judgments do not stick to dads. A growing body of evidence suggests that employers reward men for being fathers and penalize women for being mothers: Kmec, J. "Are motherhood penalties and fatherhood bonuses warranted? Comparing pro-work behaviors and conditions of mothers, fathers, and non-parents." *Social Science Research,* Mar. 2011; 40(2): 444-459: 444. Serial online.

Page 148. Levey discusses a shared care parenting model in: Levey L. I. *The Libra Solution: Shedding Excess and Redefining Success at Work and at Home.* Massachusetts: Baudin Press, 2012. Print.

Page 150. Kanter, R. O. "The Imperfect Balance Between Work and Life." *Harvard Business Review,* 8 Aug. 2012. Web. http://blogs.hbr.org/kanter/2012/08/the-imperfect-balance-between.html.

Page156. Work/Life Spillovers: Crouter, quoted in Marcinkus, W., K. Whelan-Berry, & J. Gordon. "The Relationship of Social Support to the Work-family Balance and Work Outcomes of Midlife Women." *Women in Management Review,* (2007): *22* (2), 86-111. Print.

Chapter Seven: The Sabbatical

Page 160. Reasons for Opting Out: Elizabeth, Perle. "When Work Doesn't Work for Us." McKenner P 164. 1997. Print. See also, Stone, Pamela. (2008).

Page 162. Pressure of caring for children and parents: Kim, K. I, and R. A. Antonopoulos (2011): 7.

Page 163. Company moving support: http://www.prweb.com/releases/spousal/outplacement/prweb8315624.htm.

Page 164. Women's financial status in Retirement: ING Retirement Research Institute. "What About Women (and their retirement)." 2011. ING. Prudential. Financial Experience & Behaviors Among Women. Prudential. Web. http://www.prudential.com/media/managed/Womens_Study_Final.pdf. Published 2010. See also, Hewlett, S. A. (2007).

Page 180. Groupthink is a psychological phenomenon that occurs within groups of people. It is the mode of thinking that happens when the desire for harmony in a decision-making group overrides a realistic appraisal of alternatives: Janis, I. "Groupthink and Group Dynamics: A Social Psychological Analysis of Defective Policy Decisions." *Policy Studies Journal.* Sept. 1973; 2(1): 19-25. Serial online.

Page 181. Companies do offer sabbaticals: Miller, Tim. "Sabbaticals Are Nice For Employees, Sure—But They're Also Great for Your Business." *Fast Company. 29* Mar. 2012. Web. http://www.fastcompany.com/1826489/sabbaticals-are-nice-employees-sure-theyre-also-great-your-business.

Chapter Eight: Re-entry

Page 186. Cohen, C. A, and V. I. Rabin. *Back On The Career Track: A Guide for Stay-at-Home Moms Who Want to Return to Work.* New York: Warner Business Books, 2007. Print.

Page 188. Cohen, C. A, and V. I. Rabin (2007).

Page 198. Options limited if wait too long: Hewlett, S., and C. Luce. (2005).

Page 201. Watkins, M. I. *Your Next Move: The Leader's Guide to Navigating Major Career Transitions*. Massachusetts: Harvard Business School Publishing, 2009. Print.

Page 205. Career Advice Guide: Bolles, R. I. *What Color IS Your Parachute?* New York: Ten Speed Press, 2013. Print.

Page 207. Goldsmith, M. A, and M. A. Reiter. *What Got You Here Won't Get You There*. Mundelein, IL: Round Table Companies, 2011. Print.

Page 210. It takes time to learn the culture: Watkins, M. I. (2009).

Page 212. Who gets you a job: Jay, M. (2012), p. 20.

Page 213. Career Strategy ideas: http://www.mindtools.com/pages/article/developing-strategy.htm.

Page 212. Informational Interviewing: Alboher, M. A. "Mastering the Informational Interview." *New York Times*. 29 Jan. 2008. Print.

Chapter Nine: The Mid-Career Transition

Page 216. Freedman, Marc. *Encore: Finding Work that Matters in the Second Half of Life*. Public Affairs. 2008. Print.

Page 216. Research challenges our cultural assumptions of a middle-age crisis: http://www.washingtonpost.com/wp-srv/health/seniors/stories/midlife042099.htm, http://www.livescience.com/12930-midlife-crisis-total-myth.html.

Page 216. Impact of pensions disappearing on work choices: Twigg, Mark. *The Future of Retirement: Why Family Matters*. N. pag.: HSBC, 2010. Report.

Page 216. Levinson, D. A. *The Seasons of a Woman's Life*. New York: Random House; 1996. Print.

Page 217. Impact of mid-life on relationships: Consumer Intelligence Ltd. *The Way We Are Now: The Relate TalkTalk Relationship Report.* N. pag.: TalkTalk and Relate, 2010. Report.

Page 217. Mid Career Challenges: Squires, S. A. "Midlife Without a Crisis." *Washington Post*, 19 Apr. 1999. Web. http://www.washington-post.com/wp-srv/health/seniors/stories/midlife042099.htm.

Page 219. Women switching careers: Madell, R. O. "How to Thwart a Midlife Derailment." *The Glasshammer.* 12 Jan. 2012. Web. http://www.theglasshammer.com/news/2012/01/12/how-to-thwart-a-midlife-derailment/.

Page 230. "Mid Career Course Correction." 2008 Women in Computing Panel. San Francisco, CA. 2 Oct. 2008. Panel.

Page 231. For assessment ideas: Strength finders, MYERS-BRIGGS, What Color Is Your Parachute, and other guidebooks on career changes.

Page 232. Anderson, N. A. *Work with Passion in Midlife and Beyond.* Novato, California: New World Library, 2010. Print.

Page 237. Higgs, C. A. *This Is Not the Career I Ordered: Empowering Strategies from Women Who Recharged, Reignited, and Reinvented Their Careers.* Indiana: Reinvention Press, 2010. Print.

Page 241. Brabham, D. A. "Crowdsourcing as a Model for Problem Solving." *Convergence: The International Journal of Research into New Media Technologies.* (2008): 14(75). Web. http://www.clickadvisor.com/downloads/Brabham_Crowdsourcing_Problem_Solving.pdf.

Page 242. Lobenstine, M. A. *The Renaissance Soul: Life Design for People with Too Many Passions to Pick Just One.* New York: Harmony, 2006. Print.

Page 245. White, W. I. "How to Get Ahead By Going Backward." *Wall Street Journal.* 1 Dec. 2007. Web. http://online.wsj.com/article/SB119619863214505610.html.

Chapter Ten: Living The Orange Line

Page 252. Smartphone addiction: Perlow, L. E. "Overcome Your Work Addiction." *HBR Blog Network.* 2 May 2012. Web. http://blogs.hbr.org/hbsfaculty/2012/05/overcome-your-work-addiction.html.

Page 252. Stepping away from a problem or work enhances creativity: Förster, J., R. Friedman, and N. Liberman. "Temporal Construal Effects on Abstract and Concrete Thinking: Consequences for Insight and Creative Cognition." *Journal of Personality and Social Psychology.* August 2004: 87(2): 177-189. Serial online.

Page 252. Rethinking the benefits of being "on" 24/7: Perlow, L. E. "Breaking the Smartphone Addiction." *HBS Working Knowledge Research and Ideas.* 14 May 2012. Web. http://hbswk.hbs.edu/item/6877.html.

Page 252. Galloway, J. E. (2000).

Page 254. Slaughter, A. "Why Women Still Can't Have It All." *The Atlantic.* Jul.-Aug. 2012. Web. http://www.theatlantic.com/magazine/archive/2012/07/why-women-still-cant-have-it-all/309020/

Page 255. Direct Speak: for an overview of Assertive Communication: http://www.mindtools.com/pages/article/Assertiveness.htm.

Page 258. Schuler, Mike. http://mikeschulerconsulting.com/pages/facilitation.

Page 260. The change curve is used extensively in Change Management and is based on the Kubler-Ross model of bereavement. Kubler-Ross, E.L. *On Death and Dying.* New York: Touchstone, 1969. Print.

Barbie is a registered trademark of Mattel, Inc. Good Luck Charlie is the registered property of The Walt Disney Company.

INDEX

Aging parent, *See also* Eldercare, 24, 116, 120, 141, 145, 154, 157, 162, 186

Alumni, 208

Ambiguity, 34

Ambiguous, 108

Ambition, 23, 26, 40, 49, 225

Ambitious, 4, 39

Anderson, Nancy - *Work with Passion in Midlife and Beyond*, 232

Ask for what you need, 61, 80, 98, 138, 140, 173, 229

Assertive, 241, 261

Assertiveness, 20

Assumption, 7, 19-33, 45-52, 57, 64, 86-96, 111, 125-135, 140, 155-157, 166-169, 172-173, 190-194, 198-201, 221-228, 244, 248, 254-255, 262

Babcock, Linda and Laschever, Sara – *Women Don't Ask*, 60

Babysitter, *See also* Childcare, 3, 95, 197

Barbie™ - Mattel, 19

Be nice, 20, 31, 35

Behavior, 7, 19-24, 28-29, 39, 42, 45, 54-57, 67, 89-91, 94-95, 103, 111, 127-128, 132-134, 142, 167, 171-172, 175, 182, 188-191, 194-196, 207, 218, 222-223, 226, 255, 258

Behavioral response, 51-52, 92, 131, 169, 193, 225

Belief System, 7, 18, 31, 44, 190, 262

Bennetts, Leslie – *The Femine Mistake*, 118

Boundary, 4, 16, 29, 33, 35, 58-59, 66, 80, 82, 90, 96-97, 112, 136-137, 141, 172-173, 199-200, 207, 223, 229, 254

Burn-out, 3, 67, 83, 102, 111, 162

Career, 1-18, 22-25, 28-29, 32-33, 39-46, 49-50, 55-58, 62-67, 73-87, 94-95, 98-101, 115-131, 134-136, 139, 141, 143-146, 154-158, 161-166, 169-170, 175, 178-195, 198, 201-202, 205-208, 211-252, 258-261

Career path, 38, 44, 61, 71-72, 152, 174, 185, 210, 239

Career track, 3, 11-14, 17

Career trajectory, 10, 37, 220

Catastrophizing, 25, 113, 258

Challenge, 5-6, 17, 26, 34, 40, 44-46, 56-57, 64, 75, 80, 92, 95, 98, 111, 118-123, 134, 138, 144, 154-157, 161, 165, 172, 180, 187-189, 198, 203-204, 211-213, 226-228, 235, 240, 246, 258-261

Child, 10, 67, 76, 86, 115, 181, 184-186, 208, 211, 218, 241, 251

Childcare, 4, 41, 118-121, 127, 130, 135-136, 146, 153, 202, 208, 211, 236, 253

Children, 2-9, 13, 21-22, 24-25, 29, 39, 49-50, 85, 95, 103, 116-136, 140-157, 161-162, 168, 173-178, 188-189, 193, 197-200, 204, 209-210, 238, 245, 249, 252-253, 258-259, 261

Chores, See also Housework, 76, 102, 123, 148, 173, 178, 229

Chudacoff, Joy - Smart Women Sart Solutions, 30

Clean, 53, 68, 147, 152-153, 160, 239

Cleaner, 140

Cleaning, 58, 104-106, 145, 148, 173

Coach, 30, 58, 66, 73, 104-106, 121, 139, 156, 174, 207-210, 219, 227, 231, 235-238, 242, 258

Cohen, Carol Fishman and Rabin, Vivian Steir - Back on the Career Track, 188

College graduate, 3-4, 43, 67, 75, 79, 153, 175-177, 184, 213

Communicate, 70, 103, 107, 126

Communication, 71, 178

Confidence, 34-36, 40, 44, 54-55, 66, 72, 96, 117, 138-139, 142, 158, 162, 176, 196, 206, 213, 220, 234, 245, 260

Consultant, 2-3, 24, 41, 58, 63-65, 76, 79, 82, 97, 107, 139, 148, 206, 210, 213, 239, 243, 246, 259

Core, 31-32, 62, 103, 166, 169, 177, 248, 254

Courage, 102, 205, 219, 261

Creative, 15-17, 36-37, 41, 47, 50, 57, 68-69, 73, 96, 100, 105, 115, 135, 145-146, 178, 196, 199, 208-211, 231, 235-238, 241-242

Creativity, 1, 29-31, 34, 49, 81, 112, 120, 123, 174, 222, 225, 228, 257

Daycare, See also Childcare, 120-121, 135-136, 143, 149, 153, 177-189, 210

Deemer, Candy - Dancing on the Glass Ceiling, 76

Defensive, 21, 95, 101, 113, 256, 259

Defensiveness, 196

Delegate, 16, 24, 34, 51-53, 69-70, 90-92, 105, 112, 133, 146, 149, 177, 236, 246, 257

Delegating, 68, 79, 111, 208, 249

Delegation, 104-107, 147-148, 207, 256

Depression, 165

Detjen, Jodi, 3, 58, 74, 152, 155, 157, 164, 181, 200, 212, 251, 253

Development, 44, 58, 67, 77, 123-124, 152, 168, 176, 202, 206, 214, 226, 233-234, 242, 248, 254

Do it all, 4, 10, 20, 31, 35, 53, 71, 86, 90, 95, 105, 133, 169

Duke University, 20

Duncan, Amy - Good Luck Charlie™ - The Walt Disney Company, 19

Eldercare, 5, 119, 122, 175

Energy, 15-17, 20, 24, 29-31, 34-35, 44, 47-48, 51-53, 63, 66-68, 83-85, 91-95, 100, 104-108, 112, 117, 120-122, 126, 132-134, 137, 144-146, 152, 156, 163, 170-174, 177, 191, 199, 203, 205, 208-209, 224, 228, 231, 235, 239, 251-253

Enjoy, 13, 34-37, 66, 71, 74, 78, 106, 118, 127, 143-145, 160, 176, 205-206, 217, 222, 225, 231-232, 250-251, 261

Enjoyment, 120

Entrepreneur, 9, 215, 240

Exercise, 33, 63, 102, 171, 175, 251, 254

Exercising, 37, 100

Expert, 74, 108, 181, 199, 216, 235, 254, 258

Expertise, 174-175, 243, 246

Face time, 5, 84

Failure, 3, 6, 25, 55, 61, 80, 95, 109, 133-134, 155, 160, 168, 171, 179, 198, 210, 237, 247

Family, 1-17, 21-24, 28-29, 32, 34, 39, 42-44, 49, 53, 61, 78, 81-83, 92, 104-106, 116-147, 152-158, 162-165, 168, 170, 172-178, 181-184, 189, 193-194, 200, 204, 208, 211-214, 217, 220, 229, 235-236, 244, 248-249, 251, 254, 262

Family life, 3, 174-176, 251

Fear, 4-6, 13, 25, 37, 54, 66, 81, 85-86, 105, 113, 137, 148, 189, 194-196, 204, 214, 235

Feedback, 34, 44, 64, 70-71, 102-103, 142-143, 149, 155, 175-176, 204-206, 209, 220, 230-231, 233, 236, 256

Feminine Filter, 7, 18-20, 27-33, 43-52, 57, 60, 63-64, 71, 75, 80, 83, 88-93, 96, 98, 111, 116, 120, 124-132, 136, 140-141, 155, 158, 166-169, 172, 182, 190-193, 198-199, 219-226, 228, 251, 254, 258, 262

Flexibility, 2, 5, 21, 34, 37, 123, 138-140, 157-160, 172, 179, 184, 189, 195, 198, 201, 213, 234, 247, 250

Focus, 2, 5, 11-16, 31, 33-35, 38, 44, 48-50, 66-67, 111, 119-120, 124, 135, 140, 144, 155-156, 168, 171, 180, 192, 195, 198, 209, 217-220, 230-233, 236-238, 242, 247-249, 253

Follow the rules, 26, 32, 46-48, 56, 71-72, 90-91, 126, 130-131, 134, 168, 198

Freedman, Marc – *Encore, Finding Work that Matters in the Second Half of Life*, 216

Fulfilling, 32, 53, 138, 164

Fulfillment, 145, 248

Fun, 34-36, 39, 63, 85, 104, 118, 151-152, 155, 163, 178-179, 195, 211, 215, 237, 240, 247, 250

Galloway, Jeff - *Marathon*, 16

Goal, 23, 28-34, 51-59, 62, 65-67, 73, 80-82, 93, 96, 107-109, 122-123, 133-134, 142, 147, 153, 156, 170, 173, 178, 182-183, 188, 195-197, 217, 233-234, 237, 241-246, 253, 258-259

Goldsmith, Marshall – *What Got You Here Won't Get You There*, 207

Goldstein, Robin, 230

Graduate school, 3, 75, 79, 153, 175, 177

Green Line, 10-16, 28-29, 39, 221, 252, 259

Green Start, 17, 36-46, 66, 74, 78, 217

Gresham, Jennifer - Everyday Bright, 219

Growth, 26, 50, 73-75, 80, 88, 90, 123, 148-150, 155, 158, 168, 180-183, 245

Guilt, 3, 6, 29-33, 51, 68, 83, 92-93, 97-100, 131, 137-138, 157, 167-168, 172, 184, 189, 193, 200, 225, 253, 260

Habit, 8, 22-25, 52-56, 92-94, 132-134, 170-172, 177, 194-198, 203, 225-228, 262

bad habit, 27-29, 33, 44, 80, 95, 168, 227, 258, 261

Hammonds, Keith - Fast Company, 11

Happiness, 111, 117

Happy, 82, 116, 119, 137-138, 184-185, 237, 242, 252

Helicopter mom, 25

Housekeeper, 4, 70, 104, 149, 153-155, 177

Housework, 3, 22, 86, 145, 249

Human Resources, 6, 43, 58, 77, 110

Humor, 109, 151, 163, 257

Husband, 2-3, 10, 36-37, 57, 75-77, 86, 103-104, 116-118, 121-122, 131-137, 140, 143, 146-149, 153, 159-160, 174, 178-184, 188-189, 202, 210-212, 219, 249, 252, 258-259

I am never good enough, 50, 55, 130, 167, 172, 191, 196-197, 224-227

I need to be perfect, 24, 45, 51, 54, 72, 89-95, 127-128, 133, 167, 171, 191, 195-196, 222-223

Ideal mother, 125

Ideal woman, 18-20, 30, 85

Imperfect, 82, 150, 195, 237-239, 251

Imperfection, 34, 41, 54, 71-74, 79, 86, 107-111, 151-154, 178-179, 210, 228, 238, 257

embrace imperfection, 72-73, 108, 153, 179, 210, 237

Integration, 5-10, 14, 58, 150, 154, 210, 248, 251, 256, 262

Interview, 18, 24, 37, 49, 61, 72-73, 93, 122, 131, 137-139, 141, 155, 160-161, 169, 194-195, 212-213, 217, 226, 236, 248

Interviewee, 9, 14, 21, 26, 39, 45, 60, 68, 75-78, 83-84, 97, 103, 106-109, 116-119, 145-146, 153, 163, 166, 179-181, 184, 190, 199, 203-206, 218, 221, 233-234, 256

Jay, Dr. Meg - *The Defining Decade*, 64

Jobs, Steve - Apple, 11

Journaling, 103, 206, 231

Kanter, Rosabeth Moss - *The Imperfect Balance Between Work and Life*, 150

Karline, W. A. et. al. - *Workplace Social Support and Ambulatory Cardiovascular Activity*, 63

Knowledge, 68, 90, 144, 206, 220, 237

Language, 7, 21, 33, 45-46, 51-52, 57, 88, 94, 125, 166, 172, 190, 198, 221

Laschever, Sara and Babcock, Linda – *Women Don't Ask*

Negotiation and the Gender Divide, 60

Lead, 13, 16, 20, 44, 61, 67, 70, 73, 94, 103, 106-108, 142, 157, 164, 168, 174, 185-187, 201, 220, 231, 237

Leadership, 1, 11, 58, 65, 68, 90, 216, 261

Levinson, Daniel – *Seasons of a Woman's Life*, 216

Life, 3-19, 22, 28-34, 39, 44, 48-50, 61-67, 71-75, 80-86, 93, 103, 106-111, 118, 128, 135-136, 141, 144, 150-151, 163, 176, 179, 183-185, 194, 199, 203-204, 211, 216-217, 221-222, 229, 237, 240-244, 247-248, 251-252, 256-258, 261-262

career in my life, 1, 6, 14-15, 29, 58, 120, 123, 131, 156-158, 160, 198, 210, 218, 230

home life, 100-101, 123

personal life, 126, 219

Life choice, 14, 189

Life coach, 173

Life goals, 123

Life lesson, 148, 154

Life-long skill, 175

Lifetime decisions, 122

Lifetime earning potential, 60, 146, 164, 174, 261

Linked-In, 9, 203

Lobenstine, Margaret – *The Renaissance Soul*, 242

Look good, 20, 25, 31-32, 35, 42, 71, 139

Management, 5, 38, 41, 56, 71, 92, 95-96, 110, 120, 156, 215

Manager, 9, 25, 28, 42-, 52, 58-61, 65-66, 69-70, 75, 78-80, 99-109, 119, 142, 149-151, 159, 164, 185, 204-205, 209-210, 220, 230, 238-239, 242-246, 249-251, 261

Marriage, 4, 9-10, 22, 75, 103, 116, 122, 150, 159-161, 183-185, 188-189, 218

Maschka, Kristin - *This Is Not How I Thought It Would Be, Remodeling Motherhood to Get the Lives We Want Today,* 135

Maternity, 1, 84, 115, 121, 137, 241

Mayer, Marissa - Yahoo, 19

MBA, 2, 40, 78, 85, 164, 213, 234, 241

Meaningful, 4, 26, 37, 49, 53, 85, 116, 135, 245

Meditate, 102, 175, 204

Meditation, 206, 232

Men, 2, 5, 10-11, 20-22, 26, 39, 42-43, 48, 54, 60-62, 85-87, 122, 126-127, 139, 217-218, 260

Mentor, 75, 80, 156, 205, 208, 242

Métier, 18, 28-29, 80, 127, 142, 146, 158, 170, 221, 262

Mid-life crisis, 216-217

Mistake, 24, 54, 71-73, 87, 91, 118, 148, 192, 207, 210, 239, 250, 253

Momism, 121

Moneypenny, Mrs. - *Sharpen Your Heels,* 138

Motherhood, 1, 5, 21, 25, 28, 49, 69, 116-117, 121, 125-134, 141-143, 147, 151-155, 159-161, 183-185, 198, 199, 254, 259

perfecting motherhood, 2-3

Motivation, 56, 85

Navigate, 1, 72, 201, 239, 247, 258

Negotiate, 41, 48, 61, 126, 138, 153, 173, 198, 200, 234

Negotiaton, 59-60, 98, 199, 214, 261

Network, 106, 111, 160, 163, 170, 174, 180, 208, 229, 236, 242-243

Networking, 9-11, 76-77, 136, 195, 212, 253

Non-profit, 79, 180

On-boarding, 208

Oneto, Kathy - Anthem, 20

Opportunity, 4-6, 14, 34-38, 61, 73-78, 106-108, 158-160, 175, 183-184, 188, 191-192, 201, 204, 211-216, 219, 224, 227, 232-237, 240-242, 245, 251-252, 257

Optimism, 4, 251

Opt-out, 10, 13, 17, 122, 135, 141, 162, 185

Orange Line, 7-10, 14-18, 29, 32-33, 44-46, 64, 67, 79, 88, 101, 105, 114, 122-125, 136, 143-145, 149, 154-155, 158, 161, 165-167, 172, 175, 180-182, 190, 207, 214, 220-221, 247-248, 251-259

Orange Line life, 35, 80, 96, 113, 261

Outplacement, 208

Overwhelmed, 3, 68, 81, 86, 92, 97-102, 109-111, 137, 140, 143, 163-165, 176, 209, 219, 224, 249-250, 258

Overworked, 68, 84

Parent, 3, 13, 29, 75, 85, 100, 117-130, 133-135, 141-145, 150-152, 157, 177, 181, 188, 193, 202, 211, 216, 249, 259

Parenting, 22, 103, 156, 169

Patten – *Pew Social and Demographic Trends,* 39

Perfect, 19, 22, 24, 41, 45, 89-90, 96, 101, 130, 133, 144, 148, 150-152, 156, 162, 169, 191, 195, 223, 226, 237-239, 248

less than perfect, 48, 70-73, 110, 128, 149, 179, 209

Perfect job, 3, 71, 178, 210

Perfect role model, 19

Perfection, 4, 32, 50-51, 72-74, 108-110, 160, 171, 196, 221, 228, 258

Perfectionism, 25, 85, 134, 182

Performance, 5, 55, 61, 65-66, 83, 101, 121, 196, 231, 238, 250

Pfeffer, Jeffrey - *How Companies Get Smarter: Taking Chances and Making Mistakes,* 73

Princeton, 20

Purpose, 4-5, 17-18, 29, 122, 136, 167, 184, 217, 244, 255

Push back, 4, 42, 97, 109, 113, 137-138, 143, 148, 162, 189-201, 258-259

Pushing back, 35-37, 59, 157, 214, 229, 254

Recovery, 74, 100, 176

Recruiter, 116, 180

Red Line, 10, 13-14, 44

Re-entry, 13, 17, 124, 160, 163, 168-170, 174, 178-179, 182, 184-185, 187-191, 195-200, 203-207, 210-214, 229

Reframe, 31, 45-46, 52-57, 88, 93-96, 132-134, 166, 169-172, 178, 194-198, 221, 226-228

Reframing, 82, 125, 190, 248, 254

Research, 9, 16, 20, 26, 39-41, 45, 62, 66, 73-75, 83, 93, 127, 150, 169, 178, 203, 208, 213, 217, 221, 226, 232-233, 247-248

Resistance, 41, 44, 52, 64, 179, 187, 200, 204-206, 227-229, 258-261

Restore, 5, 122

Retirement, 2, 12, 40, 124, 163, 164, 170, 191, 198, 215-216, 221, 245, 249

Reward system, 5, 7

Risk, 1, 40, 54, 63, 73, 86, 94, 106, 111-113, 124, 130-134, 152, 159, 165, 171, 176, 181, 195-196, 210, 240, 260

Risk avoidance, 24, 258

Risk-taking, 13, 34, 49, 60, 72, 75, 79-80, 90, 157-158, 192, 213, 239, 244-247, 256

Role model, 5, 19, 129, 152-154, 188, 213, 240-241

Sabbatical, 17, 67, 123, 159-160, 164, 169-172, 177-181, 184-187, 202-205, 212-214, 229

forced sabbatical, 162-163, 179

Orange Line Sabbatical, 161, 165-167, 180-182

take a sabbatical, 122-124, 161-163, 167, 173-176, 181

Sabbatical assumptions, 167-168

Salary, 3, 38, 42, 48, 60, 80, 113, 135, 145-146, 170-172, 178, 196-198, 224, 234, 241-242, 261

Sandberg, Sheryl - Facebook, 39

Sandwich generation, 121

Seeking external validation, 55, 172, 197

Self-assess, 64, 101-102, 142, 176, 205, 231-233, 256

Self-awareness, 34, 64-66, 101, 105, 142-143, 175-177, 204, 230, 234, 256

Self-care, 63, 100, 141, 175, 203-204, 230

Self-destructive, 86, 218, 226

Selfish, 63, 96, 101, 141-142

Self-promotion, 61-62, 100, 202, 230

Sexism, 46

Skills, 6-8, 16-17, 34, 40, 45, 61, 67, 72, 78-80, 92, 96, 101, 106-108, 113, 121-127, 136, 141, 145, 150, 156, 164-168, 175, 180-182, 190-191, 204-208, 217, 221, 234, 237, 245, 248, 252-253, 256-258, 261

leadership skills, 11

Orange Line skills, 33, 44, 88, 114, 155, 214, 220, 247, 251, 254

Slaughter, Anne-Marie - Princeton, 254, 255

Sleep, 4, 21, 74, 82, 86, 107, 110, 117, 132, 141, 153, 165

Solution, 25, 94, 111, 129, 148, 155, 255

Sparks, K., et al. *The effects of hours of work on health*, 63

Spouse, *See also* Husband, 24-25, 28-29, 49, 57-58, 75, 85, 94, 122-124, 127-132, 138, 140, 148, 157, 163-164, 168, 173-175, 179, 186, 193, 198, 207, 236

Stay-at-home (mom or spouse), 2, 10, 28

Stereotype, 53, 134

Stewart, Martha, 19

Stone, Pamela - *Opt Out? Why Women Really Quit Careers and Head Home*, 129

Stop, 33, 50, 73, 89, 102, 113, 150, 161, 169, 177, 187, 195, 199, 218, 227

Stop investing in yourself, 123, 130, 191

Stop working, 50, 159

Stopping, 3, 82-86, 91, 204

Strategic, 20, 79, 147, 156, 174, 191, 228, 231-233, 237, 243-245, 252

Strength, 33-34, 64, 120, 137, 144, 205, 231

Stress, 1-3, 66, 74, 81-85, 88, 95, 99, 102, 105, 108-111, 122, 135-137, 230-233, 238, 250, 258

Succeed, 6, 36, 106, 253

Success, 11, 25, 33, 37, 40-41, 47-50, 56-58, 64, 67, 71-73, 76, 82, 93, 133-134, 147, 160, 192, 205, 231-232, 237, 245, 261

career success, 125, 158

long-term success, 204, 208

Successful, 1, 4, 16, 26, 77, 85, 96, 106, 110, 115-117, 125, 161, 182, 204, 208, 213, 219-222, 229, 240, 246

Suffolk University, 9

Support, 2, 13-15, 18, 25, 28, 48-50, 63, 69-71, 75, 81, 90, 111-112, 116, 141, 148-149, 163, 170-172, 175-176, 182-186, 204, 208, 212, 237, 241, 246, 256-258

getting support, 105, 178, 198-200

Support group, 154

Support system, 34, 67-68, 73, 105, 123, 145, 155, 177-178, 202, 207, 235

Supporting, 12, 77, 168, 240, 244

Supportive, 4, 99, 200, 213, 235-236, 240, 250

Team, 16, 24, 42, 51-52, 57, 65, 69-70, 109, 112-113, 116, 121, 140, 177, 187, 193, 201, 242

family team, 12

team player, 59, 160

Technology, 9, 42, 68, 77, 84, 119, 137, 185, 200, 219, 238, 244

Telecommute, *See also* Work from home, 2

Thinking, either/or, black and white, 14

ThirdPath, 5

Time management, 15, 110

Transition, 7, 87, 117-119, 153, 179, 190, 200-201, 204-207, 210-211, 214-216, 224, 229-230, 234-239, 245-247, 259

Transitioning, 238

Travel, 75, 78, 84, 122, 134-136, 146, 157, 161, 181, 208, 220, 233-234, 238, 242-244

Traveling, 2-3, 67, 72, 119, 164, 169, 199

Unfulfilling, 2, 13-14

Vacation, 77, 82, 88, 92, 118, 148, 201, 223

Venture Capital, 26, 79

Vocation, 12-14, 31

Volunteer, 24-25, 53, 143, 181, 185, 187, 192, 199, 204, 228, 242-243

Volunteering, 78, 144, 159, 173, 176, 243

Vulnerability, 90, 103, 195, 220

Vulnerable, 92, 95, 98-99, 124, 142, 218

Wall Street, 11, 65

Waters, Michelle A., 4, 144, 163

Watson, Kelly, 1-3, 42, 66, 72, 80, 140, 144, 147, 164-165, 210, 213

Welch, Jack, 11

Well-being, 33, 86, 131

White, William J. – *How to Get Ahead by Going Backward*, 245

Wisdom, 68, 106, 142, 237-238

Work from home, *See also* Telecommute, 4, 115-116

Working harder, not smarter, 53, 93, 133, 169-171, 195

Work-life, 10, 44, 84, 139, 250

Worrying, 44, 105, 137, 141, 151, 233

Yoga, 102, 113, 206, 232

ABOUT THE AUTHORS

Jodi Detjen is a Professor of Management at Suffolk University, Boston, and a principal partner of a boutique consulting firm, the InTrinsic Group. Jodi helps organizations develop leadership and internal strategies focused on outcome. Previously, she worked in London, England in international management with Global 1000 clients on large-scale organizational change. Her MA in International Development Policy is from Duke University and her B.Sc., from Virginia Tech in Management Science. Jodi lives in Boston, MA.

Michelle Waters is an experienced Senior Executive, consultant, integrated work/life/family facilitator and coach. She has held SVP roles in Business Development managing Fortune 100 accounts, HR Policy, Diversity and general management for the professional services, finance and university sectors. Michelle previously designed and implemented an award-winning Work Life Family Strategy for Australia's largest University. She holds a B.Sp.Ed. and M.Mgt. from Monash University, Australia, and a CWS from Australia's Institute of Social Welfare. Michelle now lives in Los Angeles, CA.

Kelly Watson is a former marketing executive and now provides consulting services to a range of companies. She has implemented large-scale operations projects including e-commerce, Point-of-Sale systems, inventory control, Paperless Practice Medical software, and ERP systems. She has filled executive-level roles for her clients and has launched new businesses on their behalf. Kelly also has taught a popular MBA Business Consulting class at Loyola Marymount University. She holds a BA in Political Science from the University of Western Ontario in London, Canada and an MBA from Loyola Marymount University, where she was recognized with high honors as a member of both Beta Gamma Sigma and Alpha Sigma Nu. Kelly lives in Los Angeles, CA. *Photo by Annette Buhl*

HOW TO ORDER THIS BOOK

To order additional copies of this book, go to:
E-mail: info@orangelinecareer.com
Or to: http://www.orangelinecareer.com
Bulk order discounts are available.

This book may also be ordered from 30,000
wholesalers, retailers, and booksellers in the US and
in Canada and over 100 countries globally.

To contact Jodi Detjen, Michelle Waters, or Kelly Watson
for an interview or a speaking engagement, go to:
E-mail: info@orangelinecareer.com
Or go to: http//www.orangelinecareer.com

Made in the USA
San Bernardino, CA
04 June 2017